Do What Works

Do What Works

HOW PROVEN PRACTICES

CAN IMPROVE

AMERICA'S PUBLIC SCHOOLS

Tom Luce
Lee Thompson

ASCENT EDUCATION PRESS

2005

Published by Ascent Education Press, Inc.
5950 Sherry Lane
Suite 550
Dallas, Texas 75225

Ascent Education Press books are available at special discounts for bulk purchases in the U.S. by corporations, institutions, and other organizations. For more information, please contact the Special Markets Department at Ascent Education Press, 5950 Sherry Lane, Suite 550, Dallas, Texas 75225, or call 512-232-0770.

All proceeds from the sale of this book are donated to the National Center for Educational Accountability. Single copies of the book can be purchased at www.nc4ea.org, www.communitiesjust4kids.org, or by calling Tapestry Press, the book's distributor, at 877-920-8856.

ISBN 0-9762192-0-4   Library of Congress Control Number: 2004098265

Book design by Mark McGarry, Texas Type & Book Works
Set in Minion

10 9 8 7 6 5 4 3 2 1

For Edith and Peter O'Donnell, Jr.,
both of whom have been role models, mentors, supporters,
and encouragers of everything I have ever worked on
in my efforts to improve public education.

T L

For my parents, Nancy Beth and Harry Roberts,
who instilled in me the invaluable gifts of an appreciation
for education and a love of learning.

L T

Do What Works shows how accountability systems all across America can become an effective tool to make sure that *no* child is left behind.

George W. Bush,
President of the United States
September, 2004

Contents

Illustrations

Introduction

IMPROVING our nation's public education system: the issue pervades American society today.[1] Calls for improvement have been at a heightened pitch for decades, particularly since the early 1980s. After investing billions of dollars and instituting scores of reforms, many are disheartened by what they perceive as disappointingly slight improvement in student performance in the nation as a whole. The picture is not entirely bleak: there are many schools that have attained excellence, and several states where students have achieved significant academic gains as a result of sustained, targeted efforts.[2] Yet people are looking for answers. How do we provide a high-quality education to every student? How do we make each school first-rate so that all students attain their full potential? This book aims to answer those questions and, in the process, equip educators, parents, policymakers, and the public with tools to provide an excellent education to every student. The tools presented here are research-based, proven, and replicable. They work. In light of the state of public education, the need for such measures is immediate.

For two decades, the call for improvement has been at the forefront of the public's agenda. The reform movement has gone through various stages. In the early eighties, the alarmingly weak state of our public schools became apparent as a result of various studies and publications.

Acceptance evolved into an ingrained belief among many that the education system was beyond saving. However, during the 1980s and 1990s, reformers rallied hard to convince others that schools could become viable—even excellent—if concerted, well-conceived reforms were put into place. These activists currently have won the day. State legislatures and the federal government have passed broad reform measures with optimism that they are facilitating real improvement. Indeed, President George W. Bush and Congress trumpet the cause and, in 2002, put into effect the most comprehensive revamping of federal law concerning elementary and secondary education in over three decades: the No Child Left Behind Act.[3]

Reforms have been numerous and varied, ranging from class size reductions to enhanced teacher credentials to increased spending per pupil. But the most effective reform regimes are comprehensive and incorporate three elements: standards, assessment, and accountability. First, educators have well-defined academic standards that clearly set forth what students should know at each point in their education. Second, regular student assessments reflect whether children are learning the content spelled out in those standards. Third, educators are given the freedom to determine how best to teach students and therefore reach their goals of student learning, but they are also held accountable for student performance and are rewarded or penalized accordingly.[4] Many states have instituted this promising framework, and federal legislation promotes this approach.[5]

In 1995, building on years of experience in the reform movement, co-author Tom Luce presented his vision for how to improve Texas public schools in his book *Now or Never: How We Can Save Our Public Schools*.[6] At the core of this vision were the building blocks spelled out above—deciding what results we want, giving authority to educators to attain these results, measuring results, and rewarding educators according to student outcomes. Texas has adopted this approach and stuck with it. Consequently, the state has attained among the largest gains in student achievement in the country during recent years—an achievement confirmed by performance on national tests.[7] Yet, there are still many schools—both in Texas and in the nation as a whole—that are not delivering excellent education, and thus there are many students who are not able to optimize their potential because they are being shortchanged in the classroom.

Why are schools not able to deliver education of the highest quality, even in states and districts that are using the accountability approach to its best advantage? Various circumstances influence school performance, but two aspects in particular hamper many educators: educators have not been given the tools to educate students most effectively and, when educators do have the tools, they have often not taken advantage of them. As Michael Cohen, president of Achieve, Inc. (a nonprofit organization that promotes accountability), notes, the accountability movement "assumed that our schools were populated with school leaders and teachers who were filled with the knowledge, skills, and great ideas to go take off and do outstanding things if we only unshackled them from state regulations." As a result, "what we missed, or underestimated at the time, was just how big a job we needed to do to build a capacity of people in our schools." Marc Tucker, president of the National Center on Education and the Economy, likewise points to capacity as the "biggest challenge we face as a country," particularly the "capacity to live up to the aims of the [new federal legislation] and everything that stands behind it."[8]

The aim of this book is to help us build the capacity to accomplish the laudable national goal set out in the No Child Left Behind Act of 2001: for all students to be academically proficient. States have twelve years from the effective date of the law—or by the end of the 2013–2014 school year—to attain this end. No other society has committed to this goal. To many (particularly educators), this objective seems overwhelming and frightening. The status quo is no longer acceptable in light of the great academic gains that students must achieve. This bold and valuable goal of 100 percent proficiency is thus akin to the aspiration for the United States to send a man safely to the moon and back to Earth by the end of the 1960s set boldly by President Kennedy in 1961. Many thought such an objective daunting and unattainable. But, with the goal clearly in sight, Americans worked steadily and vigorously to attain it. Commitment to the aim of a man walking on the moon forced a restructuring of how scientists, policymakers, and the public approached accomplishing the end goal. In 1969, when Neil Armstrong left his footprints on the moon's surface, the United States achieved what many in 1961 could not even imagine. Americans find themselves in the same position today with respect to the challenging aim of ensuring that all students are academically proficient. But, as with advances in the space program in the 1960s, focused and sustained efforts combined with a willingness to adopt proven approaches that may differ from long-standing methods along with accountability for results can enable Americans to attain this significant goal.

The tools presented in this book are vital keys to spurring such academic proficiency by all students, for they build the capacity of educators, policymakers, parents, and citizens to provide our students with a first-rate education. The tools are proven and replicable; they have resulted in outstanding performance in ages ranging from preschoolers to high schoolers.

Key to each of these practices are one or more of three central elements:

- Using student achievement data to see how a school is performing;
- Employing that data to locate high-performing schools that face comparable challenges to show the lower-performing school what level of performance is possible; and
- Determining what the high-performing school is doing to attain excellent performance from its students, and then replicating those practices on the campus that needs improvement.

These steps enable schools—regardless of how challenging their circumstances are—to provide a high-quality education to students. After years of work gathering data and best practice information, these elements form the centerpieces of reform efforts at the nonprofit National Center for Educational Accountability, operating under its trade name, Just for the Kids.

The aim of this book, however, is not just to benefit others by informing them of knowledge gained through National Center efforts. It is also, more broadly, to encourage others to adopt this approach and build on it—to recognize the power of the resource of comprehensive and well-used data, of determining what effective schools are doing to attain results, and of adopting those same practices in schools that need improvement. Thus, it is this focus on data and best practices that forms the crux of each chapter. The first chapter makes clear why there is a pressing and significant need for this book by tracing the history and present status of education reform. The next five chapters describe specific and proven tools to spur higher student achievement in our schools. Some chapters deal with National Center efforts and findings, while other chapters concern how others—such as high-performing urban districts recognized by The Broad Prize for Urban Education, high-quality preschool programs that use a language-rich curriculum, and high schools that expose students to demanding coursework through Advanced Placement Incentive Programs—are using proven tools to provide students with a first-rate education. All provide evidence that educational excellence in every school and for every student is an obtainable goal.

Do What Works

1

From *A Nation at Risk* to *No Child Left Behind:* Public Education Reform, 1983–2004

———

If it seems no US politician ever makes a speech today without insisting that education is his or her top priority, a quick glance back exactly 20 years may explain why that is.

MARJORIE COEYMAN, *CHRISTIAN SCIENCE MONITOR*

Early results indicate that accountability, combining high-stakes standards, integrated testing and assessment, and flexibility, produces better schools.

HANNA SKANDERA AND RICHARD SOUSA,
SCHOOL FIGURES: THE DATA BEHIND THE DEBATE

ON APRIL 26, 1983, a clarion call sounded. The National Commission on Excellence in Education released its report entitled *A Nation at Risk: The Imperative for Educational Reform.* U.S. Secretary of Education Terrel H. Bell had assembled the group of educators, business leaders, and public officials to address "the widespread public perception that something is seriously remiss in our education system." The alarming message of the report confirmed that the public's perception was correct. In forthright, clear language, the commission warned that "the educational foundations of our society are presently being eroded by a rising tide of mediocrity that threatens our very future as a Nation and a people." "If an unfriendly power had attempted to impose on America the mediocre educational performance that exists today, we might have viewed it as an act of war," the members asserted. "As it stands, we have allowed this to happen to ourselves." As a result, "We have, in effect, been committing an act of unthinking, unilateral educational disarmament."[1]

The indicators of risk that the Commission noted indeed were disturbing. On nineteen international academic assessments, United States students were last in seven, and, in the others, were never first or second. American high school students' performance on standardized tests was lower in 1983 than it was twenty-six years earlier at the launching of Sputnik. There had been an almost unbroken decline in students' SAT scores between 1963 and 1980, and the number and percentage of students performing at a superior level on the SAT had declined considerably. Seventeen-year-olds' scores on national science achievement tests in 1969, 1973, and 1977 had consistently dropped, while only 20 percent of seventeen-year-olds could compose an effective persuasive essay and only one third could solve a multi-step mathematical problem. Remedial math courses (courses covering matter that students should have learned in high school) at public four-year colleges increased by 72 percent between 1975 and 1980 and constituted a quarter of the math classes taught at those colleges.[2]

A Nation at Risk propelled education reform into the national spotlight. Reform efforts had taken place before the 1980s, but the subject had not captured the attention of the American public as it did in the spring of 1983. Various factors contributed to the report's influence: the fact that the authors spoke as members of a federally appointed commission, the stature of various members, and the absence of technical jargon from the report's uncluttered, compelling prose. Only ten months after the commission released *A Nation at Risk*, the U.S. Department of Education had issued 150,000 copies, the Government Printing Office had sold an additional 70,000 copies, and estimated millions more copies and excerpts were circulating as reprints.[3]

Other national panels and scholars issued similar dismal appraisals of public education shortly after the April 1983 release of *A Nation at Risk,* only further reinforcing the influence of the National Commission's find-ings. Among those reports was *Action for Excellence,* issued by a task force of the Education Commission of the States, an interstate education asso-ciation. The task force included thirteen chief executives of large corpora-tions and eleven governors among its forty-one members. *Action for Excellence* concluded that the nation's public education system was not producing graduates who could competently contribute to the workforce and thus was damaging the United States' economic condition. *A Nation at Risk* had also made a similar conclusion regarding how the weakness of public education was detracting from the nation's economic viability.[4]

Such economic arguments hit central nerves among Americans in the early 1980s. The nation was in the midst of an intense recession. As factory closures fed high rates of unemployment, Americans increas-ingly realized the imperative need to boost the country's productivity in order to effectively compete in the aggressive global economy of the late-twentieth century. No longer could the United States be assured of its post-World War II productivity gains and associated healthy economic conditions. Many viewed improving the abilities of the workforce as integral to achieving greater competitiveness. Such enhanced skills were essential in an increasingly technological world that valued the ability to think and analyze; basic reading, math, and writing abilities were no longer sufficient. To many Americans, education reform—particularly more demanding requirements concerning what students should know, which would result in more competent workers—was imperative for the economic good of the country.[5]

Education Reform in the 1980s

Support for reform during the 1980s issued from many quarters—par-ticularly from state governments, but also from boardrooms, living rooms, and the White House. The result was a widespread effort throughout the country to study education reform and enact effective measures to attain a high-quality education system.[6] At least 300 committees, commissions, and boards formed across the nation to study the issue shortly after the release of *A Nation at Risk*.[7] During the several years after the report's issue in 1983, states passed around 3,000 education reform measures, including fifteen comprehensive pieces of state legislation. Indeed, during the mid-1980s, state officials passed more regulations and laws for education than they had during the prior two decades combined. Ranging from Florida's Raise Achievement in Secondary Education Act and the Hart-Hughes Education Reform Act in California—both passed in 1983—to the Comprehensive Reform Act of 1984 in Tennessee to the School Improvement Act of 1985 in Massachusetts, the extensive state laws varied somewhat in content but, overall, they reflected similar approaches to education reform.[8]

The centerpieces of the 1980s state reform measures were enhanced graduation requirements with greater focus on academic subjects; a longer school year and school day; higher teacher salaries; required teacher testing and more demanding degree requirements for teachers; student testing (often making passage of tests a prerequisite for student graduation and an element in determining school ratings and financial rewards); extracurricular eligibility tied to academic performance; and expanded pre-kindergarten and kindergarten programs. The widespread adoption of these central measures attests to the common mindset held across the country as to how to improve the nation's schools. Between 1980 and 1990, forty-two states imposed more rigorous graduation requirements with respect to academic courses. This represented a proactive reaction to the proposals in various national reports, particularly to the National Commission's recommended "new basics" curriculum outlined in *A Nation at Risk*. Meanwhile, forty-seven states enacted student testing programs by 1990 and thirty-nine required teacher testing (up from only a few states that demanded teacher assessment in 1980). As one reformer concludes, these 1980s reforms allowed Americans "to focus on just raising our expectations."[9]

In addition, state officials directed vast amounts of funds toward financing newly instituted and previously existing education programs. Nationally, the amount of spending per year on each student rose 48.3 percent during the 1980s (a figure which takes into account adjustments for inflation). An economic upswing after the recession of 1981–1982 made such large increases in public education funding possible.[10]

Yet notwithstanding the commitment to educational excellence reflected in the substance and financing of the 1980s measures, the reform approach during the 1980s had shortcomings. Reforms enacted during the decade were regulatory and "top-down" in nature: state and local administrators imposed requirements and guidelines on educators. These centralized, bureaucratic measures resulted from the circumstances of 1980s reforms. Often, the primary drivers of reform were those outside the education system—business leaders, elected officials, and other citizens. Educators frequently resisted the changes, and as a result, did not contribute to the dialogue concerning the substance of the reforms. Thus, the regulations were the tools available to non-educators to impose new requirements. Such a regulatory approach also reflected the public's loss of confidence in those educating America's children; citizens supported measures that took control out of educators' hands. In addition, regulations offered policymakers the means to quantify whether reforms were working.[11]

The second primary shortcoming of the 1980s reform movement was the rudimentary nature of much of the testing and curriculum standards that were put into place. Reformers at the time emphasized the important aim of raising the bar at the bottom of the educational ladder to a higher level. The minimum that students were expected to know had previously been set far too low. As a result, examinations often tested basic skills instead of more advanced knowledge and skills. Reform measures also frequently did not provide a well-tailored, enhanced curriculum or effective systems to hold teachers, schools, and districts accountable for student achievement. It soon became apparent that these deficiencies diminished the effectiveness of the 1980s reform measures and resulted in educator disenchantment, criticisms of "dumbed-down" tests, and a lack of clarity regarding reform objectives.

In addition, groups representing teachers and administrators balked at the premise behind the reforms and at their substance generally. Union organizations representing school principals, school boards, administrators, and teachers ranged in their positions from lukewarm to wholeheartedly opposed to the measures. One standard reply was that the claims of an educational crisis were exaggerated and that the real problem with education was insufficient funding, particularly of teacher salaries. The American Federation of Teachers—particularly its leader, Albert Shanker—did endorse calls for reform, most notably reform in the teaching profession. But the largest and most politically influential teachers union, the National Education Association, opposed the movement and its initiatives aimed at teachers, such as performance pay and more-exacting teacher qualifications. Its members repeatedly attempted to throw up roadblocks in front of reform efforts.[12]

Despite this resistance, after the implementation of the 1980s reforms, there arose an increased recognition of the need for radical change in the nation's approach to public education. Reformers came to realize that minor changes would do little to address the pressing necessity for an overhaul of the existing system. A broad-based group of reformers began demanding that the status quo in public education was no longer acceptable. Two major movements resulted: the accountability movement and the choice movement.[13]

Education Reform in the 1990s

While various less-comprehensive reforms continued during the 1990s (such as reductions in class size and continued increased spending per pupil), advocates of accountability and choice pressed a more holistic approach that challenged the basis and structure of the public education system. The central idea behind the choice movement is that if schools are subject to market forces—meaning their clients (students and parents) will go elsewhere if schools do not perform adequately—then the quality of schooling will improve. Poor schools will not survive, since parents will choose to send their children and thus the money for educating those students to more successful schools. Various forms of choice have developed. Two of the most prominent include charter schools and vouchers. Charter schools lie within the public school system, are free from various regulations, but are accountable for student achievement. Voucher programs take many forms, but commonly they allow parents of a child in a low-performing school to send their child to a higher quality public school or private school. The government then redirects the funds for that child's education away from the failing school to the chosen one. In contrast, the accountability movement—in its most basic sense—focuses on setting high standards that spell out what children should know and testing students to ensure that they learn the material. Educators possess freedom as to how they attain high student performance, but they are also held accountable for results.[14]

Advocates have at times maintained that the two movements are antithetical, yet choice and accountability are complementary in various core aspects. As Chester Finn notes, promising school reform lies at the intersection of the idea of choice and competition with the idea of standards and accountability.[15] For example, the central principles of the accountability movement apply in the context of choice, since schools must show that they are successfully teaching students, or market forces will direct money away from their campuses. Moreover, the superior quality of the tools presented in this book became apparent in the context of the accountability movement in striving to help schools improve their performance, but the tools are equally applicable in the charter and voucher context. For example, the need to use data to determine which schools are working and the reasons why is integral to both frameworks;

otherwise, educators and policymakers working within the accountability movement or the choice movement are "flying blind," since they are not aware of how their students are performing, whether currently used educational programs are effective, or what practices would result in higher student achievement.

Because the effectiveness of data and best practices presented in this book became clear through working within the accountability framework, an overview of the accountability movement indicates why these tools are integral—and why the need for them is immediate.

The Accountability Movement

By the late 1980s, various school reformers realized that two major shifts needed to occur. First, reform efforts needed to evolve from a focus on the process of education to a focus on results. State legislators and policymakers increasingly saw the value of empowering educators by giving them local control over how to achieve desired outcomes. "What is urgently needed in the next phase of school reform is a deep commitment to make teachers partners in renewal, at all levels," stated Ernest L. Boyer, president of the Carnegie Foundation, in 1988. "It's time to recognize that whatever is wrong with America's public schools cannot be fixed without the help of those already in the classroom." The following year at an education summit in Charlottesville, Virginia, President George H. W. Bush and state governors advocated "decentralization of authority and decision-making responsibility to the school site, so that educators are empowered to determine the means for accomplishing [educational] goals and to be held responsible for accomplishing them." Many reformers readily accepted the call for site-based control since they recognized that local control better enables schools to meet the individual needs of their unique students.[16]

A second, and related, major shift in reform in the 1990s was a stress on accountability systems. Educators might be given large latitude in

deciding how to teach their students, but they would be held accountable to produce results, meaning high student achievement.[17]

As a result of the accountability movement's focus on educational
outcomes—particularly student achievement outcomes—reformers
across the country worked to clearly set out what students should know
at each level of their education, often termed the "academic standards"
that students should meet. The so-called "standards movement" resulted
in a vast restructuring of education policies in states across the nation.
The American Federation of Teachers—which issued a series of reports
evaluating the quality and effectiveness of academic standards in all fifty
states, Washington, D.C., and Puerto Rico—reported that by 2001, all of
these jurisdictions either had or were developing academic standards.
Also by 2001, thirty states (including the District of Columbia) had high-
quality standards in the core subjects of math, English, science, and
social studies at the elementary, middle, and high school levels. In 1995,
only thirteen states had such clear, specific educational standards. Also,
by 2001, thirty-eight states had begun to align their standards and assessments.[18]

Likewise, states have increasingly held students and educators
accountable for student mastery of the material in state standards. In
2001, over half of the states (twenty-seven) required or were in the
process of requiring students to pass an exit exam aligned to state standards in order to graduate from high school, an increase from nine states
that had such a requirement in 1995. One increasingly prevalent reform
goal—a quest that the establishment of standards has made possible—
has been the abolition of social promotion, meaning the advancement of
a student to the next grade level even though the student lacks the skills
or knowledge for such promotion. By 2001, seventeen states had adopted
anti-social promotion legislation, an increase from three states in 1996.[19]

Proponents and opponents of the accountability movement have
been and continue to be vocal. Debates about the benefits of the
accountability movement are not settled. Further, many states' accounta-

bility systems still remain relatively weak. *Education Week*'s 2004 grading
of state standards and accountability systems found that while forty-
nine states (all except Iowa) had state standards in core academic subjects, only ten received a grade of A- or higher for the quality of their
accountability and standards systems, while twenty received a C+ or
lower. In a 2002–2003 ranking by Princeton Review that considered four
aspects of state accountability systems—alignment of high-stakes tests
with academic content standards, test quality, openness with respect to
test policies and procedures, and the consistency of education policy
with state goals—almost 30 percent of states received a score of 65 or
lower out of 100. Likewise, a 2004 study of thirty states' tests, standards,
and accountability policies conducted by the Thomas B. Fordham Foundation and AccountabilityWorks found that state accountability systems
across the country are, on average, only mediocre. Thus, millions of students attend schools that still lack challenging accountability systems
and quality standards.[20]

Notwithstanding present weaknesses, the public, including teachers
and parents, recognizes the promise of accountability systems based on
standards. In a 1999 survey, 92 percent of principals and 73 percent of
teachers endorsed standards-based education reform. In a 2000 survey,
70 percent of the public and 65 percent of parents agreed that students
should be required to pass a state test before graduating even though
they had passed all of their classes.[21]

Further, students in states with comprehensive, well-structured, and
long-term accountability systems have made substantial academic gains
—gains that give credence to the public's support for accountability.

Accountability Success Stories:
The Key of Comprehensive, Fine-Tuned State Systems

Maryland, Massachusetts, North Carolina, and Texas have all increased
student achievement through well-conceived accountability systems. As

Achieve, Inc. reported in a 2002 study of Maryland, Massachusetts, and Texas: "Their policies are working. Their students are learning more." As a result of their successful approach, the standards and accountability systems in these states ranked among the top in the country in 2003 rankings by Princeton Review and *Education Week*.[22]

Student performance on the Massachusetts and Maryland state assessments improved notably since the 1990s, and corresponding gains by their students on the "nation's report card"—the National Assessment of Educational Progress (NAEP)—confirm students' academic gains. High performance has continued in recent years. In 2003, greater numbers of tenth graders in all ethnic groups passed both the English and the math components of the challenging Massachusetts state assessment on their first attempt than in any year since it was first administered in 1998. African American, Hispanic, and Asian students made particular gains. Likewise, the percentage of students passing the state math and English assessments rose in all grades in 2003. Nationally, Bay State white fourth graders scored among the top five in the country on the 2003 NAEP reading and math tests and 2002 NAEP writing test. The state's African American students were first in the country on the NAEP writing assessment and sixth in the country on the NAEP reading and math tests.[23]

Similarly, in Maryland, students who attained a satisfactory level on the state assessment increased approximately fifty percent between 1993 and 2000. On the NAEP during the 1990s, Maryland eighth graders scored among the most significant gains in the country. Maryland's strong record has continued into the twenty-first century. In 2004, the second year of a new state test, the Maryland School Assessment, scores increased in both math and English. Gains by certain student subgroups were particularly promising. The percentage of African American third graders who performed proficiently in third grade reading increased sixteen points while the percentage of economically disadvantaged fifth graders who performed proficiently in math increased by ten points.

Meanwhile, Maryland's Hispanic fourth graders performed third best in the country on the 2002 writing NAEP and tenth on the 2003 math NAEP, while its white fourth graders scored in the top ten nationally on both the NAEP writing and reading exams.[24]

Likewise, students in North Carolina and Texas attained "greater combined student achievement gains in math and reading [on the NAEP between 1992 and 1996] than any other states," according to a 1998 study commissioned by the National Education Goals Panel. These were sustained and significant improvements.[25]

North Carolina's strong record continues. State education leaders have established challenging education goals, performance targets, and priorities for the state to be *First in America* by 2010. These include the goal to have 90 percent of students in grades 3 through 8 pass state reading and math exams. In 2002–2003, 79 percent of students passed both tests, up from 74 percent in 2001–2002—a rate of progress indicating that the 90 percent goal is attainable by 2010. North Carolina students, meanwhile, are among the top performers on the nation's report card. Hispanic students scored among the top ten nationally in the NAEP 2002 writing and 2003 reading tests, and were second in the nation in the NAEP 2003 math assessment. North Carolina's African American students performed second highest in the country in math and sixth highest in writing on NAEP tests, while its white students scored the highest among all states on the NAEP math test, sixth in the NAEP writing test, and seventh on the NAEP reading test.[26]

Texas students attained similar academic gains over the last decade on both the state achievement test and the National Assessment of Educational Progress. Between 1994 and 2002, student performance on the state reading, writing, and math assessments cumulatively improved by 30 percent, with even larger gains of 44 percent, 39 percent, and 40 percent respectively by African American, Hispanic, and economically disadvantaged students. And Texas students have continued to score high marks on the new, more-demanding state assessment first administered in 2003. On national assessments, Texas' African American students were the top performers in the country on the 2003 math NAEP. Texas' white students scored among the top five in the nation on the 2003 math NAEP and 2002 writing NAEP, while Texas' Hispanic students scored among the top eight on those two tests.[27]

What spurred significant academic gains in these four states? Researchers at Achieve, Inc. and RAND concluded that comprehensive, long-standing standards-based reforms were a key factor that enabled these states to improve student achievement. North Carolina and Texas instituted their reform framework in the early 1980s, Maryland and Massachusetts in the 1990s. The reform policies of these states include clear standards, local flexibility, and accountability for student performance. In addition, consensus among the business, education, and government sectors has proved essential to effective efforts. As the Achieve study concludes, "impressive gains came about because the state reforms did what they were supposed to do: provide incentives and support to help schools and classrooms change instruction for the better."[28]

Moreover—and central to the message in this book—the Achieve researchers found that educators improved their instruction in Maryland, Massachusetts, and Texas because they employed student achievement data to guide classroom instruction. As explored further in chapter 2, the effective use of data is key to improving educational quality. Data enables educators to pinpoint needs and specifically target instruction. Data also empowers educators to locate and employ effective practices of high-performing schools.[29]

Spurring Improvement and Initiative:
The Federal No Child Left Behind Act

Although reform movements in certain states have been intense, comprehensive, and effective, among the most notable evolutions of education policy has occurred at the federal level. Traditionally, the federal government has remained rather hands-off with respect to elementary and secondary education. Because of a strong belief commonly held by Americans that education policy should be made at the local level—and thus governed by those whose children attend the local school—the federal role has usually been circumscribed to providing a relatively small percentage of funding (typically to targeted groups, such as children from poor families and disabled students).[30] The percentage of educational funding paid by the federal government has increased in recent years: from about 4 percent of total spending on education in the country in 1959–1960 to around 7 percent in 1999–2000.[31]

In 2001, by an overwhelming vote (381 to 41 in the U.S. House of Representatives) with strong bipartisan support, Congress passed the federal No Child Left Behind Act, which President George W. Bush signed into law in 2002. Proposed and advocated by President Bush, the legislation represents the most sweeping overhaul of the federal system supporting K–12 education since 1965.[32]

Of central concern to the present work are two points with respect to the No Child Left Behind Act. First, the framework of the Act is modeled in large part after the North Carolina and Texas approach toward accountability. President Bush—who placed efforts to improve public education at the center of his agenda as governor of Texas—saw the effectiveness of the sustained and comprehensive Texas approach and desired children across the nation to reap the same benefits. Thus, the No Child Left Behind Act is built on a strong, proven foundation.

Second, the Act promotes the use of student achievement data and proven, scientifically based educational practices to attain targeted, effective reforms. The legislation thus endorses the same truth that this book promotes: only through using hard data concerning how students are performing can we pinpoint what is working and replicate it; and only by replicating such identified and proven educational techniques will all students benefit from an excellent education.

The central elements of the No Child Left Behind Act are the requirements that each state establish challenging standards in math and reading (and in science by 2005–2006); set annual goals for what constitutes Adequate Yearly Progress (AYP) that will enable all students to reach proficiency under the state academic standards no later than the 2013–2014 school year; and annually test all students in the third through the eighth grade in reading and math by the 2005–2006 school year to determine if they are proficient. Schools that do not meet AYP goals are subject to state accountability measures, which increase in severity the longer a school fails to meet its goals. These include imposing measures for school improvement; requiring corrective action, such as replacing certain staff members; and restructuring a school, such as by making it a charter school. States, not the federal government, design or choose their own assessments and define what constitutes proficiency. But the requirement that each state participate in the National Assessment of Educational Progress, which indicates how a state's students performed vis-à-vis students in other states, is meant to ensure that the state-established standards and tests are challenging. A sample of fourth and eighth graders in each state must take the NAEP once every two years and the results of the test must be made public. There is no federal penalty for performance in the NAEP other than public chastisement for low performance. In addition, to enhance teacher quality, the Act requires school districts to only hire highly qualified teachers after the beginning of the 2002–2003 school year and to ensure that all teachers regardless of their hire date are highly qualified by the close of the 2005–2006 school year.[33]

The approach of the Act toward student improvement is aggressive, and granting the states power over their assessments and proficiency goals is conceptually correct. However, the public must demand accountability from the states. In particular, the public needs to insist that states set high goals for student achievement and aggressive timetables for attaining those goals between now and 2014. Otherwise, states will likely succumb (as many already have) to the temptation to insulate their schools from sanctions for poor performance. Devices adopted by states include lowering the scores that constitute passing marks, changing the definition of when schools need improvement, and delaying for years challenging gains in student achievement (meaning that very large gains will be necessary close to the 2014 deadline in order to attain 100 percent student proficiency).[34]

Under No Child Left Behind, the public possesses the tools to hold states and school districts accountable. States and districts must provide parents and the public with report cards detailing how schools and the state are progressing toward their goal of 100 percent student proficiency. The report card must convey how students are performing as a whole, and—to ensure that all students are achieving—the report must disaggregate (report separately) student performance data by ethnicity, race, gender, migrant status, disability status, English proficiency, and status as economically disadvantaged. This disaggregation forces educators to look beyond overall scores to focus on their lowest-performing students. And this reporting puts valuable, enabling data into the hands of parents and the public. With such information in hand, parents and the public can ensure that states and educators are reaching their goals and can demand better performance if they are not.[35]

Further, the No Child Left Behind Act encourages the discovery and dissemination of effective educational practices for a variety of purposes integral to the central aim: improving the academic achievement of all students. These include practices that promote school improvement, spur the achievement of disadvantaged children, reduce the dropout rate, increase the number of high school graduates, incorporate technology into the educational process, and make charter schools effective.[36] Thus, the Act does not just demand compliance from states and local school districts in exchange for federal funding; it also encourages the spread of information and innovation to improve the performance of educators and students.

A foundational principle that drives all of these provisions is a simple, but revolutionary aim of the Act: for all students to experience an excellent education. Students who traditionally have been left behind—particularly minority students and students in poverty—especially benefit from this heartening commitment. Indeed, as Columbia law professors James S. Liebman and Charles F. Sabel conclude, the No Child Left Behind Act can serve as a vital instrument to "revivify and give new direction" to the civil rights movement in its quest to ensure equal educational opportunities for children of all races.[37]

Unfortunately, the shortsighted vision of compliance—of minding the law merely to "get by" and thus receive federal support—dominates the mindset of many and distracts from the promising goals of the Act. One issue in particular illustrates this tendency: the claim that the federal government is not providing enough funds to states to implement the legislation. Complaints on this issue are widespread. In the months leading up to June 2004, according to the National Conference of State Legislatures, more than twenty states had asked for more federal funding, considered ending participation in the No Child Left Behind Act, or requested changes to the law—although by July 2004, most of these protests had quieted down.[38]

The funding debate is clouded by arguments concerning what amount would constitute "full funding" of the Act, with those on different sides of the debate pointing to different figures. However, certain numbers are certain—and they indicate an unprecedented level of federal support that is targeted to cover states' costs of implementing the No Child Left Behind Act. Since President Bush took office in 2001, federal education funding for grades K–12 has increased over 40 percent. Federal funding for Title I of the No Child Left Behind Act—the largest program under the Act—has risen from $7.9 billion in fiscal year 2000 to $12.3 billion in fiscal year 2004.[39]

Further, the requirements that the Act places on states to test students and to publicly publish the information are both fully funded. As detailed further in chapter 2, through federal and private funding, states can publish their education data on the internet for free at www.schoolresults.org. And findings of the General Accounting Office in May 2003 confirm that the federal government is providing ample funds to cover the states' costs of implementing the Act's testing requirements. A state may choose to impose a more involved and expensive testing regimen, but that is the choice of the state, and thus the additional costs are the state's responsibility.[40]

The other requirements—for states to work toward all students being academically proficient and to ensure teachers are highly qualified—simply require states to do what they should be doing—that is, provide a quality education to all children. As John G. Augenblick, a respected analyst of school finance systems who has consulted with many states, notes, schools and states would have had to pay many of the costs frequently associated with the federal law even if the No Child Left Behind Act had not been enacted because states had committed to improving student achievement prior to passage of the federal Act.[41]

Further, attaining 100 percent student academic proficiency is not a mandate of the No Child Left Behind Act, meaning that the federal government will not penalize states that fail to achieve the goal by 2014. As the Education Trust well states in a response to a 2004 report commissioned by the Ohio legislature, "Federal funding under NCLB is not contingent on student performance levels." Thus, "So long as Ohio measures the achievement of all students against state standards, publicly reports disaggregated results, and commits to undertake improvement in schools not making AYP, Ohio will be in compliance with the student achievement provisions of the law."[42]

As Hayes Mizell has commented, states and localities have had the responsibility and opportunity to ensure that all children receive a quality education; some states and localities have delivered, but many have not.[43] As a result, the federal government is now contributing additional money and resources to further the cause. In return for the investment, the federal government is asking for results—results that will particularly benefit minority students and students in poverty who, prior to this, had often been underserved and left behind.[44]

Thus, what the No Child Left Behind Act provides at its core is a commitment to a heartening goal that no other society has ever committed to: academic proficiency by all students in the United States. To reach that goal, the Act also supplies a road map to strategies to enhance student achievement. The road map involves pinpointing strengths and weaknesses through student performance data and promoting the discovery and use of educational best practices that are proven to spur high academic achievement.[45] It is this vision and use of the Act that this book promotes.

Where U.S. Education Is Today: Gains, Shortcomings, and an Urgent Call to Push Ahead

Since the arrival of the twentieth anniversary of *A Nation at Risk* in 2003, many in the education reform field have considered what has been accomplished during the intervening years. The verdict is largely pessimistic and dispirited. The effort and money invested have been vast: Americans expend close to $400 billion each year on education; the total since the publication of *A Nation at Risk* may approach $5 trillion. Reformers often conclude that there has been little positive achievement. Yet, the discouraging aspects of public education regularly overshadow the fact that there have been many positive developments as well. Various states, districts, and schools have made significant gains—and others can learn and benefit from their success.

Weaknesses are undoubtedly still numerous and wide-ranging.[46] Three weak spots are of particular concern and are interrelated: the continuing racial and socioeconomic gap in student performance, the unacceptably high dropout rate, and high schoolers' poor academic performance and lack of improvement.

Education Trust reports that, although minority students improved their academic performance during the 1990s (as measured by NAEP data), they continue to lag behind their white counterparts. Likewise, students from poor families consistently trail the achievement of economically better-off students. The gap increases as these minority and economically disadvantaged students continue through school. According to a 2001 Education Trust report, as they finish fourth grade, Hispanic and African American students and students from poor families are two years behind their classmates; by the end of eighth grade, this gap expands to three years; and by twelfth grade, to four years. The gap continues into college, with 47 percent of Hispanics and 46 percent of African Americans attaining bachelor's degrees within six years of high school graduation, as compared to 67 percent of white students, according to the National Center for Education Statistics. Only about 54 percent of students in poverty (whose families earn less than $25,000 per year) attain a bachelor's degree within six years, as compared to 77 percent of students from families with annual income in excess of $70,000.[47]

A second major shortcoming in United States public education is the excessively high dropout rate. Although figures vary from study to study, estimates from September 2003 by Dr. Jay P. Greene of the Manhattan Institute calculate the national high school graduation rate to be 70 percent, meaning nearly a third of high school students fail to graduate. Only around half of Hispanic, African American, and Native American students complete high school, compared to 72 percent of whites and 79 percent of Asians nationally. In 1970, the United States led all other nations in the percentage of teenagers who completed high school. Almost thirty years later in the late 1990s, the United States was far from the lead, with its rate of secondary-school completion somewhat below the average among the democratic, industrialized countries that compose the Organization for Economic Cooperation and Development.[48]

A third weak link in public education—and one surely related to the high number of dropouts and the relatively low performance of eco-nomically disadvantaged and minority students—is the low academic performance of high schoolers. On the NAEP, even while the achieve-ment of fourth and eighth graders has been rising, the performance of twelfth graders has remained flat or gotten worse. On the 2002 NAEP reading test, for example, twelfth graders' reading scores dropped in nearly every proficiency level. The percentages of twelfth graders who could read at a basic or proficient level in 2002 were lower than in 1998 and 1992.[49]

Those who conclude that there has been little progress seek to pin-point why. Answers run the gamut, and usually reflect the practical or political perspective of the speaker. The National Education Association, the largest teachers union, concludes that mediocre government support of educators' efforts threatens education. Others point to established education interests such as teachers unions as the primary blockers of reform. Those in education have an interest in maintaining the status quo, as Chester Finn has noted, since they have a guaranteed income and a captive audience of students, but have not been forced to produce results. The consequence, according to Terry Moe, is that the two move-ments with the potential to make large strides toward true reform—choice and accountability—have faced vehement teachers union opposition. The outcome has been accountability and choice regimes that are weak and lack substance.[50]

Those who fault entrenched interests for stalling progress likely are right to a great degree. As co-author Tom Luce discussed in a previous work, *Now or Never: How We Can Save Our Public Schools*, the "Iron Tri-angle"—meaning the established interests in education (including state legislatures, state education agencies, and numerous education associa-tions)—continually opposes a radical revamping of education. The strength of these interests and their ability to frustrate valuable reforms remains considerable.[51]

Yet, the reasons for a lack of reform cannot be placed entirely on their shoulders. We undoubtedly have much farther to go to improve the structure and content of our education system. The notion that state accountability systems are relatively weak, as a whole, is correct. The goal of high-quality instruction in every classroom is far from being met. Children from poor families and minorities all too commonly are subject to education of low quality and, thus, score desperately below national achievement averages.[52]

In light of these weaknesses in our education system, it is easy to become convinced that reform efforts have been for naught. Critiques of public schools and the conclusion that reforms have failed (or at least stalled) emanate regularly from scholars and journalists.[53]

Still, there have been improvements since *A Nation at Risk*—and in some cases, there have been dramatic advances. Only a few states had academic standards when *A Nation at Risk* was published in 1983; the measure of improvement in education was how much money a state was investing in its schools, not whether its students were learning. The shift since that time has been notable: now all states have or are developing standards-based accountability systems. The quality of these systems varies greatly, but state adoption of the accountability approach and state efforts to make improvements are major achievements. States with some of the lowest student attainment scores and poorest populaces—such as those in the South—have been particularly focused on improving their education systems.[54] And some states, like Maryland, Massachusetts, North Carolina, and Texas (as discussed above), have experienced significant gains as a result of comprehensive, well-structured, and sustained reform efforts.[55]

Even those students in challenging circumstances—such as those in inner-city schools with a high percentage of economically disadvantaged and minority students—have improved their performance. Chapter 4 spells out the advances various urban districts are making—advances that became clear through the comprehensive study of student performance data and best practices undertaken to determine The Broad Prize for Urban Education. Others, such as the Council of the Great City Schools, confirm these gains.[56]

In addition, the implementation of the No Child Left Behind Act is spurring all states to press ahead. The U.S. Department of Education has approved accountability plans submitted by all fifty states—meaning that the plans comply with the law's requirements for challenging academic standards, assessments, and timelines for adequate yearly progress toward the goal of all students being academically proficient. Undoubtedly, some operational details still need to be worked out in each state. Additionally, as noted above, the public must be vigilant in holding the states accountable to reach the valuable aim of 100 percent proficiency. But, as states press forward in their implementation, they demonstrate their commitment to the effective reform approach laid out in the Act.[57]

Subsequent chapters of this book spell out some of the best evidence that there has been significant improvement in sectors of the United States education system. Those who view the country's education system or a state's public schools as a whole can miss the fact that amidst an average- or a low-performing group of schools lie examples of excellence. These schools and school districts have discovered the tools that work, and they are implementing those tools to great effect. Indeed, the tools these exemplars employ directly address central weaknesses of our educational system, including the academic achievement gap, dropout rates, and high school academic performance. These tools enable educators to provide students with an excellent education in a broad range of settings: from preschools to high schools, and from large urban districts serving economically disadvantaged populations to small rural districts suffering from a lack of funds. Thus, the evidence presented here is both an encouragement to those who have made great gains and a challenge to those who are not investing in effective reforms. It is also an instruction manual for those who are striving for improvement but do not know how to move ahead. These tools specifically demonstrate how the education reform movement in our country can reach the valuable—but up to now, elusive—goal of enabling all children to perform at high levels.

The starting point is determining what works by using hard evidence of how students are performing and what programs are reaping results. The foundational tool of employing student performance information to guide educational decisions and spur student achievement underlies all effective practices presented in this book. Thus, we focus first on the significance of educational data and how to most effectively use it.

2

Employing Performance Data:

Its Empowering, Enabling Effect

The importance of using data to make decisions in schools and
school districts cannot be overstated.

Sharon Lewis,
The Council of the Great City Schools

In the hands of caring parents and teachers, information is a
powerful tool for education reform.

Rep. John Boehner of Ohio,
Chair, House Committee on Education
and the Workforce

Mention the topic of student academic performance data to people, and their eyes are likely to glaze over. But the subject could not be
more central in our efforts to improve our schools. Employing information on how students perform over time to determine where educational
achievement is taking place (and where it is not) is critical. With such
data, we can see where students' strengths and weaknesses are, make
informed decisions about how to attend to students' academic needs,
and know which programs are proven to be effective in spurring student
achievement and which ones are not. Without such information, any
effort that we make to improve the quality of our children's schooling or
to spur their achievement will be frustratingly ineffective.[1] Thus, effective use of student performance data has a crucial twofold effect. First,

using such information enables us to get past opinions on how we should reform our schools, and instead base our policies on hard evidence. Second, it enables us to educate our students using proven programs in tailored, effective ways.[2]

The first and fundamental step to improving our education system is employing student performance information to determine our students' achievement levels as well as what effective programs should be put into place to optimize students' academic performance. Indeed, the use of such performance data is a central, unifying theme of this book. The tools presented in each chapter are proven to work—meaning they spur student achievement in schools regardless of how challenging the circumstances. Hard data substantiates their results. As the tools presented in each chapter make clear, through such active use of educational data, information on student performance becomes much more than simply the results of tests. Such information becomes the indispensable basis for what various educational scholars term "data-driven decision-making."[3]

Not just any information on student performance can serve this empowering purpose. Educators will attest that they are inundated with data on how students are performing. As Cathy Lassiter, director of Leadership and Capacity Building at Norfolk, Virginia Public Schools, notes, "In past years, you had nothing to really go on except for the grade the student earned in the class." Today, "we have so much data available to us that the challenge is to really know what you are looking at and to know what to do with it as a result of learning . . . from the analysis of data."[4]

Fortunately, evidence clearly points to the type of information that enables us to spur student achievement: privacy-protected records that link the performance of each student over time. Termed "longitudinal student data," such information allows us to assess whether students have increased or decreased their mastery of a subject, whether a school is effectively educating students, and what practices and programs are raising achievement levels. Such longitudinal data is thus much more useful than traditional "snapshot" data, which only records a student's achievement at a particular time.[5]

The aim of this chapter is to present specifically how we can most effectively use student performance information as an empowering tool to make our schools first-rate and to enable our students to perform at their highest potential. First, in order to establish how critical the effective use of student performance information is in our efforts to improve public education, we first discuss the importance of educational data—particularly privacy-protected, student-linked longitudinal data—in further depth. We then explore how policymakers at the state and federal levels as well as those concerned about education throughout the country are increasingly stressing the need to rely on such hard data to drive effective education reforms. Our third section lays out specific examples of how schools and reformers are employing data-driven decision-making. Lastly, we present how specifically to structure data systems and employ the information produced by these systems. We first describe the importance of every state establishing a high-quality educational data system and what the components of such a high-quality system are. We then present tools available to enable educators, policymakers, parents, and the public to use the educational data produced by these state systems to improve student performance.

The Importance of Quality Data Concerning Student Performance

Prior to the standards-based accountability movement that spread across the nation over recent decades, school quality was determined almost entirely in terms of inputs, such as teachers' qualifications and how many books were in the school library. As the focus on educators' accountability for student performance intensified in the 1980s and 1990s, states, districts, and schools increasingly included student per-

formance measures—particularly standardized test scores—in their cal-
culations of school quality. Educators and those involved with education
policy and reform came to recognize a truth from the corporate world.
As Joseph M. Tucci, chairman of the Business Roundtable's Education
and the Workforce Task Force, well states, "You can't manage what you
don't measure."[6]

Three negative outcomes commonly occur as a result of the growing
use of student performance information in the field of education. First,
educators often have felt inundated by reams of figures concerning their
students' performance, as they have not had guidance as to what those
figures mean and how to use them. Second, often educators have used
their data solely to meet state and district reporting requirements. As a
result, they have missed the opportunity to use the data to drive school
improvement. Third, because educators, parents, and education reformers often have reacted to student performance information rather than
use it proactively, discussions concerning data commonly have been
unpleasant and have involved excuses and accusations.[7]

Fortunately, there is an increasing realization that student performance information provides an indispensable tool for analysis to propel
school improvement. When educators and others associated with a
school study students' performance over time, they then can make targeted, tailored changes in how they teach those students. The result is
higher student achievement.[8] The 2001 school improvement plan for
Pueblo, Colorado District 60 demonstrates educators' increased recognition of the importance of data-driven decision-making:

> Benefits of data-driven decisions are to provide evidence that the
> effectiveness of the educational system can be demonstrated through
> students. Data-driven decisions are allowing educators and students
> to follow the corporate example of being results-oriented and
> demonstrating continuous improvement. In the past, decisions in
> public education were based on intuition and [so-called] best prac-

tice. Appropriate decision-making occurs only when the proper data are available to the decision-makers who constantly ask the question, "How do we get there?"

Data-driven decision-making is emerging as a powerful tool to address educational accountability in today's high-tech world. The bottom line for school districts is improved student learning.[9]

One primary reason that educators, parents, and reformers more commonly view performance data as a positive tool rather than a punitive reporting device is that an increasing number of states and districts are using privacy-protected, student-linked longitudinal data systems to track the performance of students over time. Such longitudinal data match individual student information concerning enrollment, test scores, program participation, course completion, and graduation over several years. This differs dramatically from the less illuminating snapshot data that states and school districts have traditionally generated, which only indicate student information at a particular time. Unless we have information concerning a student's performance over time in a particular school, then we cannot ascertain whether that school is effectively educating that student or how to enhance student performance at that school. Thus, the benefits of longitudinal data are numerous. While parents gain a more accurate picture of their child's academic progress and are able to distinguish whether their child's school is effectively teaching its students, educators can identify those areas where they are enabling students to achieve and ascertain those areas that need improvement. Consideration of only students who have attended the school for years means that educators cannot blame poor performance on recent transfers. Further, as detailed below, statewide longitudinal data systems enable educators to locate highly successful schools with similar student demographics and learn what practices they use to spur high student achievement. Similarly, such longitudinal systems give researchers and state policymakers information on what policies are working.[10]

Although the many benefits of longitudinal student information are clear and its use is becoming increasingly common in the field of education, many states and educators do not yet employ it. Indeed, the quality of educational data systems varies dramatically across the country. One factor that contributes to this situation is the historically weak reputation of education research.

Student performance information is a foundational element of educational research, providing the basis from which researchers perform analyses and make conclusions. Unfortunately, four primary factors have hampered the education research field. First, historically, the status of the field has been weak. The reputation of educational research has suffered from low-quality studies, lack of objectivity, and contested findings, particularly when compared with research in fields such as medicine and the physical sciences. Consequently, policymakers and educators have felt free to ignore research results. Second, education research holds some challenges that research in other areas does not as a result of the complex nature of learning and teaching and the multifaceted practical and ethical considerations involved in education. Third, scientific research in education historically has been underfunded by state agencies, the federal government, foundations, and universities. In 1997, a report by a presidential commission noted that under 0.1 percent of the total funds spent on education in the United States funded research. This figure stands in sharp contrast to the investment of 23 percent of the total dollars spent on non-prescription and prescription drugs in drug testing and development. Recently, the federal government has placed much greater emphasis on the necessity for rigorous education research (as detailed below), but a historical lack of attention has hampered the field. Lastly, there commonly has been a disconnect between educational researchers' studies and the practices that educators employ. As a result, research results often are not used to benefit students and teachers.[11]

One outgrowth of weaknesses in the education research field has been frequent inattention to the need for quality information when deciding how best to teach students. People striving to spur higher achievement by students commonly make decisions that are not founded on hard information, and thus are not based on student need or on evidence that a chosen approach works. The result has been a disconcerting shift from one seemingly promising education reform to another—each lacking substantiating evidence that they are effective—without attaining the ultimate goal: gains in student achievement.[12]

Fortunately, a growing number of educators, researchers, and policymakers at the state and federal levels now stress the importance of employing educational data to drive improvement. These groups are insisting that only programs proven to raise student achievement be used in our classrooms. This attention has heightened the importance of hard evidence in educational policy and practice, particularly at the federal level.[13]

The Rise of Evidence-Based Reform

In 2003, a committee of the National Academies of Science finalized a design for an independent organization, the Strategic Education Research Partnership, that will facilitate collaboration among states, researchers, and school districts on education research efforts. The ultimate aim of the Partnership is to empower educators by presenting them with agreed-upon findings about what is working in education, so that they can employ these practices in their classrooms. Similarly, in 1997, the National Education Knowledge Industry Association (NEKIA) formed to further the cause of quality knowledge in the field of education; its members include federally supported research laboratories, clearinghouses, and technical assistance centers. In 2004, the Mid-continent Research for Education and Learning and the Education Commission of the States released "A Policymaker's Primer on Education Research: How to Understand, Evaluate and Use It," funded by the U.S. Department of Education. The Primer's goal is to help policymakers incorporate education research into their decisions.[14] Each of these organizations and publications make clear that data-driven, evidence-based research is increasingly at the forefront of education reform.

The public appears to support this focus on evidence and data in education: in a 2003 Business Roundtable poll, a majority of parents and other members of the public supported requirements for states, districts, and schools to report performance results for all students and for sub-groups of students (as required by the No Child Left Behind Act), such as by socioeconomic status, language proficiency, and race, to ensure that all children are learning.[15]

A similar interest in data in education is driving the policies of various states; as detailed below, a number of states have instituted longitudinal data systems. Although data system quality differs markedly among the states, there is generally an increased focus on the central role such systems play, particularly in light of the reporting requirements states and districts must meet under the No Child Left Behind Act.

Some of the most noticeable shifts to a focus on data-driven reform have occurred at the federal level. Terming this "The Emerging Era of Knowledge Utilization," James Kohlmoos, president of NEKIA, noted in January 2003 that federal policy concerning education research and distribution of research results had undergone more changes in the previous twelve months than in the preceding thirty years or more.[16]

Two major pieces of recent education legislation—the No Child Left Behind Act of 2001 (NCLB) and the Education Sciences Reform Act of 2002 (ESRA)—bring to the forefront the requirement that federally sponsored educational programs must be proven to work by "scientifically based research." Such research, according to an ESRA definition, must involve a rigorous, objective, and systematic methodology and also be supported by findings.[17]

The No Child Left Behind Act requires the use of such scientifically based research in numerous federally supported programs, particularly those that concern reading instruction. The Act—which mentions scientifically based research 111 times—plainly places knowledge garnered by data-based education research as the central stimulus behind national efforts to leave no child behind, as James Kohlmoos notes. Information on student performance lies at the center of such research. Further, the quality data that results from such research will grant clear guidance on which educational practices and programs are effective. Only substantiated practices and programs can receive federal monetary support under NCLB.[18]

In addition to stressing scientifically based research, NCLB imposes comprehensive data reporting requirements on states and school districts. School districts and states must produce and disseminate report cards to parents and the public that contain student achievement data disaggregated by certain categories of students according to—for example—race, ethnicity, and disability, comparisons of schools' performance, facts concerning teacher quality, and other school accountability information. In addition, schools must inform parents as to how their child performed on state assessments and when their child has been assigned to or has been instructed for more than four weeks by a teacher who is not highly qualified.[19] In sum, NCLB calls for educators to employ an intensive accountability system that is integrally based on data.[20]

Similarly, the focus of the Education Sciences Reform Act is to identify and use educational practices that work. ESRA thus supports educational research that produces usable results—meaning programs that educators can employ in the classroom—and emphasizes education research as a scientific discipline. The legislation creates a new Institute of Education Sciences, which focuses on enhancing research in K–12 education.[21]

In addition, both NCLB and ESRA promote the importance of data-driven education reform by encouraging states to develop longitudinal data systems. Both laws authorize substantial funding for statewide longitudinal data, although as of summer 2004, none yet had been appropriated by Congress. Under NCLB, the U.S. Department of Education may grant states funding to improve "the dissemination of information on student achievement and school performance to parents and the community" after the states have instituted testing systems for third- through eighth-grade students as NCLB requires. The funding states receive can assist in linking student achievement, attendance, and graduation records over time and can support systems that identify the best practices in education—ones that are proven to work by scientifically based research. Likewise, ESRA provides for competitive grants to states to develop longitudinal student data systems. Recipients of grants must show how the data generated by the systems will support NCLB, improve academic achievement levels, and close the gap between the achievement of various student groups, such as that between white and African American students.[22]

Thus, the comprehensive federal approach to improving our public education system as instituted by NCLB and ESRA is a system based on and driven by quality data, scientifically based research that uses that data to measure results, and the use of educational practices that are proven to work by such data-driven research. Indeed, a bill introduced with bipartisan support in spring 2004 indicates how central data-driven scientific research is now in the federal approach to education. The Knowledge Utilization in Education Act introduced by Representative Rush D. Holt of New Jersey would provide funds for grants to develop research results that are usable in the classroom. The aim is to help bridge the gap between effective research and educators' use of research results as they teach students. NEKIA, a strong supporter of the measure, hopes that the house bill and a companion measure in the Senate will pass in 2005.[23]

The direction and increasingly accepted approach towards effective education reform is thus clear: growing numbers of parents, educators, members of the public, researchers, and state and federal officials view student performance data as a reliable and essential tool to indicate how students are performing, in what areas they need to improve their achievement, and which educational practices are effective in spurring higher performance. But what evidence do we have that such a data-driven approach works—and that educators are using the approach and students are benefiting? Fortunately, we have a great amount of such evidence.

The Proven Efficacy of Data-Driven Education Reform

Studies of districts and schools across the country in a broad range of circumstances produce a common finding: when educators employ data to track student performance, determine student needs, and then address their needs with proven programs, students achieve at higher levels. Numerous compelling examples include the following:

- Researchers with The Education Trust in a 1999 study identified 366 high-performing schools in twenty-one states in high-poverty circumstances—circumstances that traditionally have resulted in low student performance. One key to their success: "monitoring systems ... for providing ongoing analysis of student achievement data." Quality student data also underlies The Education Trust's research, as a presentation title for a follow-up study attests: *Dispelling the Myth Online (DTM 2.0): The Power of Disaggregated Data.*[24]
- A 2003 study of thirty-two San Francisco Bay area schools entitled *After the Test: How Schools Are Using Data to Close the Achievement Gap,* by the Bay Area School Reform Collaborative in California, determined that the schools that were successful in closing the achievement gap between students of different races were testing their students frequently and using the assessment results to tailor their instruction to a much greater degree than schools that retained their achievement gaps. Two-thirds of educators surveyed at the gap-closing schools use assessment and other data several times a month

to hone in on their students' skill weaknesses, and eighteen percent used such data a few times each week. This contrasted starkly with the less than a quarter of teachers at schools that were not closing the achievement gap who used data a few times a month.[25]

- Mike Schmoker, in a 2001 study, showed how teacher collaboration that focuses on the measurement and use of student performance results in five districts in Milwaukee and near Chicago, Detroit, Houston, and Phoenix has driven improved academic performance. "All results—good or bad—are ultimately good, because they provide us feedback that can guide us, telling us *what to do next* and how to do it better," Schmoker has concluded. "Feedback, then, is synonymous with results."[26]

- In a 2003 study in Washington State, the Washington School Research Center selected ten high-performing elementary schools based on students' passing rates on the Washington State assessment test. Based on its study of the practices of these ten high performers, the Research Center concluded that one of the four essential elements of successful schools was their effective use of assessment data. For example, at Logan Elementary in Spokane, the district assessment coordinator, the school principal, and classroom teachers closely analyze the results of the Washington State assessment to note students' strengths and weaknesses regarding specific skills. Teachers then tailor their instruction to specifically meet the needs of their students in specified skill areas.

  Separately, when presenting the results of the study on the Just for the Kids website, the Washington School Research Center stated that monitoring student performance on multiple assessments and using student performance data to inform instruction are key practices that have spurred high student achievement in Washington schools. For example, at one high-performing school, Lind Elementary in eastern Washington, there is a clear focus on using test data to drive student improvement. All teachers at the school study student assessment results to learn and proactively meet those students' educational needs. Educators not only use such data to identify trends in student results, but also to plan instruction, to determine which students are close to failing, and to discern which students need remediation. Kindergarten through third grade teachers study the results of fourth grade assessments to identify how they can better prepare students for fourth grade, while fifth and sixth grade teachers analyze seventh grade test results to tailor their instruction.[27]

- A 2004 study conducted by Rutgers University for Just for the Kids-New Jersey sought to identify the practices that were enabling students at six New Jersey schools to perform exceptionally well on the state's Grade Eight Proficiency Assessment (GEPA). By using the Just for the Kids data analysis tools (discussed in full below), researchers identified the schools that were high performers. They concluded that three clusters of practices contributed to high achievement on the GEPA: one cluster involved an effective curriculum; a second cluster concerned a positive school culture; and a third included a variety of other practices that supported the first two practice clusters. Along with effective leadership and teacher recruitment, the practices in this third cluster included data-based decision-making. All six high-performing schools analyze student assessment results purposefully, and teachers, principals, and supervisors study assessment score reports to pinpoint areas in which entire classes or individual students need improvement.[28]

- The Florida School Report (FSR), which is an initiative of the Council for Educational Change and is affiliated with the National Center for Educational Accountability's Just for the Kids, likewise determined that the effective use of data was a key element in the success of high-performing Florida schools. Results from an FSR best practice study in 2003 led to identification of twenty high-performing elementary schools and seventeen high-performing middle and high schools. Repeatedly, study results cited data-driven decision-making as a critical practice at these schools.[29]

■ Just for the Kids conducted a series of best practice studies that considered the practices at nearly 100 high-performing schools in Texas and the practices at forty average-performing Texas schools over a four year period. JFTK first identified the consistently high- and average-performing schools through the JFTK data analysis approach detailed below. JFTK then pinpointed the practices at the district, school, and classroom level that spur student achievement at high-performing schools. Among these practices were the development and use of student assessments and data systems to monitor school performance and student learning. For example, at high-performing Dowell Middle School in McKinney Independent School District located north of Dallas, virtually all educational decisions are driven by data. Student performance on district benchmark assessments (assessments that the district administers periodically to gauge student progress) and state tests direct teachers' curriculum development, the setting of school goals, and professional development programs. Data also informs which instructional practices and programs teachers employ, how school resources are allocated, which students receive recognition for academic achievement, and the identification of teachers and students in need of extra help. McKinney ISD supports Dowell Middle School's focus on data: over a three year period, the district revised curricula and assessments to facilitate the effective use of data in all district schools.[30]

As the results of these studies make clear, an increasing number of educators and researchers are employing student performance information to enhance the quality of the education they provide students, and thereby foster student achievement.[31] Yet, although there has been increased recognition of the value of data-driven reform, many state data systems remain woefully inadequate. Likewise, the recognition of how essential student performance information is to effective school improvement efforts is far from universal. Too often, educators and others involved in school reform implement programs without knowing the particular strengths and weaknesses of their students. All too commonly, education programs are labeled as "best practices" when these programs are not supported by data that they work. Such an approach is akin to a doctor administering a drug to a patient without any evidence that the drug will treat the patient's symptoms. The result is a frustrating lack of academic improvement, the inability of students to attain their academic potential, and a misapplication of valuable resources. Only through linking school reform efforts to information that clearly substantiates that those reform efforts work will we be able to improve our schools.[32]

What actions can state educators, parents, policymakers, and reformers take to ensure that their state and schools are reaping the advantages of data-driven decision-making? What are the components of an effective state educational data system? And what tools are available to make that data accessible to all and usable as an effective instrument to drive educational improvement? Two replicable and proven sets of tools point the way to attain a high-quality state longitudinal data system and to employ the data generated by that system to its best advantage.

The Key Elements of an Effective State Educational Data System

Although federal education policy promotes quality, longitudinal data systems, educational data at the state level is fragmented and disparate. Fifty different systems of state standards and state assessment regimes result in a labyrinth that can frustrate anyone trying to determine how schools and students are performing. Add to this mix the dissimilar state methods of collecting data—with some states recording comprehensive performance information and others just cursory data—and the result is an incongruent and often frustratingly incomplete dataset. Yet making sense of this data is crucial to ensuring that all students learn and to identifying exemplars of excellence for others to emulate.

Currently, we are in an era where the requirements for data quality have increased (particularly as called for by the No Child Left Behind Act) and where we have a greater awareness of how to effectively employ the crucial tool of student performance data. Thus, as various states press to comply with NCLB, states should look upon the mandates of NCLB as an opportunity to retool and optimize their data systems in order to maximize student learning.[33] Further, although a quality longitudinal data system is not required by NCLB, compliance with NCLB will be much easier in those states with such quality systems.

Fortunately, states are making efforts to improve their data collection. In order to discern the quality and comprehensiveness of state data systems and what steps states can take to optimize their systems, the National Center for Educational Accountability has identified nine essential elements of statewide data collection systems. All with a stake in public education—including educators, parents, and policymakers—can thus employ these nine elements as a guide to determine (1) the current quality of their state's educational data systems and (2) what steps they should take to make their state's data systems ready and vital instruments in raising student achievement.

These nine essential elements include:

1. *A unique statewide personal identification number for each student,* which enables us to see how that student performed over time;
2. *Enrollment data for each student,* including information on each student's school of enrollment, ethnicity, gender, grade level, economically disadvantaged status, and participation in programs such as bilingual education and special education;
3. *State test data for each student,* with the capability to disaggregate the data by individual test question and academic skill;
4. *Data on untested students* to ensure accuracy in the performance profile of a certain school;
5. *Course completion information for each student,* including ad-

vanced courses to indicate each student's preparation level for
college;

6. *SAT, ACT, and Advanced Placement results for each student,* which
   also indicate each student's readiness for college;

7. *Graduation and dropout data for all students;*

8. *Audit process to ensure the accuracy of state data,* involving statistical checks of information school districts submit, criteria for
   identifying when district data may be erroneous, investigation of
   the flagged data, spot checking of data that is not flagged, and
   imposition of penalties on school districts that submit incorrect
   or incomplete information; and

9. *Capacity to link K–12 and higher education data at the student level*
   to show how high school graduates perform in college.[34]

In a survey funded by the U.S. Department of Education, the Council
of Chief State School Officers contracted with the National Center for
Educational Accountability to determine the current status of the educational data system in every state. In other words, which of the nine elements did each state data system have in place? The results of the survey,
conducted in spring 2003 and updated in spring 2004, presented a mixed
picture. Some results were promising: since 1999, fifteen states had incorporated a student identifier, bringing the total number of states with this
crucial element to twenty-three. Notwithstanding these gains, the
remaining twenty-seven states still had no ability to trace student performance over time. Only four states—Florida, Louisiana, Texas, and
West Virginia—had incorporated all nine elements into their state data
systems by spring 2004.[35]

Given the numerous advantages of a comprehensive, longitudinal
data system, why are data systems so weak in various states? One reason
is the traditional lack of attention to the importance of basing education
decisions on data, as discussed above. Yet, as Chrys Dougherty of the
National Center has recognized, various other practical reasons con-

tribute to the failure to implement quality data systems. For instance, state legislators may be reticent to appropriate money to upgrade their state data systems (although the cost is relatively minimal, typically amounting to a small fraction of one percent of a state's education budget). There are also concerns about protecting student privacy when records trace each student's performance over time. Yet states commonly and effectively address privacy issues by encrypting student identifiers, deleting student names, and having researchers agree not to disclose information on student groups composed of fewer than five students. In addition, on the surface, reports of snapshot data—or data that records student performance at a certain point in time, such as on an assessment administered in spring 2003—and reports of longitudinal data may look similar, and thus do not display the vastly more advantageous nature of a longitudinal system. Policymakers thus need to be informed of these advantages and not be fooled by a glossy printout of snapshot data.[36]

The benefits of a longitudinal data system are many, with students standing to gain the most as the information leads to targeted reforms that enhance the quality of the education they receive. In addition, the relative monetary costs of such a system are small. State legislators, educators, parents, and the general public must make efforts to ensure that their states have high-quality longitudinal data systems that incorporate the nine essential elements detailed above.

Employing Student Performance Data to Maximize Student Achievement

Once a state fully develops a quality educational data system (or even when a state has a less comprehensive system), how can we make sense of the data and use it to improve our schools? Using data as a tool to spur academic achievement involves more than the collection of information; it also involves the exacting arrangement and analysis of the information and calls for communicating the information in an understandable, accessible way.[37] The National Center for Educational Accountability has worked for years on how to employ student performance information to promote student achievement gains. As the studies discussed above make clear, others, too, have recognized the value of analyzing data to trace student performance over time and make targeted reforms.[38]

The National Center, operating under its trade name, Just for the Kids (JFTK), has developed a unique data analysis approach in terms of its accessibility and easily comprehensible format. The Just for the Kids approach views data as the beginning—not the end—of the reform process. It employs data to indicate how students are performing in each school, points the way to high-performing schools in similar circumstances as your school, and presents the practices that those high performers in like circumstances to your school are using to attain results—all with the goal of enabling your school to spur higher student achievement. Central to the Just for the Kids approach is the principle that if a school is performing at a higher level than yours with student demographics (for example, the percentage of students in poverty or who are English language learners) that are equally or more challenging than your school's student demographics, your students can reach that level of performance as well. A key outcome of JFTK's analysis is that it clearly establishes that in every sort of student population, every subject, and every grade, there are schools achieving outstanding results. Thus, no matter what the circumstances are of your school—no matter how challenging they are—there are examples of similarly situated schools that are delivering an excellent education to their students. Through the JFTK analysis, you not only become aware of those schools so that you can contact them, you also gain access to the effective practices those schools are using to attain results.[39]

From Washington State to Texas to New Jersey, states across the nation employ the JFTK approach. In addition, the National Center in partnership with Standard & Poor's School Evaluation Services has produced a website, www.schoolresults.org, providing online data tools to aid all fifty states in fulfilling the data reporting and analysis requirements of the No Child Left Behind Act at no cost to states; the project is funded by the Broad Foundation and the U.S. Department of Education.[40]

Research conducted by JFTK confirms the effectiveness of the approach: in a random sample of 168 Texas elementary schools, researchers found that schools that employed the JFTK data and best practice information to set goals, study high-performing schools, or make program or staff changes attained from 3 to 8 percent greater gains in proficiency scores on Texas state assessments in reading, math, and writing between 1999 and 2001 than comparable schools that did not.[41]

As Columbia law school professors James S. Liebman and Charles F. Sabel recently have noted, JFTK acts as an intermediary between the state education agencies that generate data (which they often present in an incomprehensible format to non-statisticians) and educators, parents, and the public by presenting the school performance data and the best practices of high-performing schools in an easily accessible and usable format. JFTK thus "provides parents with the most useful data for building a constituency for reform" while it also "most effectively culls best practices from the successes of the leading schools and districts for use by less successful institutions."[42]

The concern of this chapter is the first component of the JFTK approach: the organization and use of student performance data. The following chapter, chapter 3, presents the second and equally integral component of the JFTK tools: the best practices of high-performing schools.

JFTK data analysis involves six core concepts; each is crucial to the effectiveness of the approach. The resulting JFTK data analysis method is both replicable across the country and easily accessible to individuals, schools, districts, and states.

Step 1: Work with States to Improve the Accuracy and Completeness of Student Performance Data: As noted above, the rigor and comprehensiveness of data systems vary dramatically from state to state. As states—and the districts and schools in those states—augment their data collection and reporting to meet the requirements of the No Child Left Behind Act, it is crucial that they include certain components not specifically required by the federal statute. These elements will enable states, districts, schools, and others to use data as a tool to pinpoint how students are performing at a certain grade level and in a certain school, where improvement is needed, and which are the high-performing schools. Thus, National Center research concludes that effective data collection must incorporate the nine essential elements listed above. Only through these essential elements of data collection can we ensure that we account for all students and that uses of the student performance information in the following steps reflect a true picture of student performance.[43]

Step 2: Track Performance of Students Over Time: As discussed above, assessing how students perform over time holds vast advantages over taking a one-time look at how students performed in a certain year. In addition, it enables us to ascertain which students have attended a school for some time, and which have recently transferred into a school. This information enables us to focus on the performance of students who have attended a school over a number of years as evidence of achievement levels at the school. Just for the Kids analysis, for example, considers students who have been enrolled in a school for three years or more as being "continuously enrolled" at the school; it is the performance of these continuously enrolled students that JFTK analysis focuses on.

Step 3: Compare School Performance on an Apples-to-Apples Basis and Identify High-Performing Schools with Equally or More Disadvantaged Student Populations: Using the data made available through Steps 1 and 2, we can ascertain student performance at each school in each grade and each subject matter. We can then compare student performance at each school with schools across the state whose students performed at a higher level and that have an equally or more disadvantaged student population based on the percentage of economically disadvantaged students and English language learners. This enables us to pinpoint who the top comparable schools are for each grade and subject. For example, the sample Figure 1 below from the Just for the Kids website shows which schools were the top comparable Washington State schools for Kapowsin Elementary in fourth-grade math in 2003. Note that each top comparable school (those listed below Kapowsin) has a student population with an equal or larger percentage of economically disadvantaged students. Yet

Figure 1. Just for the Kids Top Comparable Schools Table

KAPOWSIN ELEMENTARY, BETHEL
2003 Top Comparable Schools for Grade 4 Mathematics

School Name, District Name	Continuously Enrolled Tested Students			School-Wide
	% Met or Exceeded Standard	% Exceeded Standard	# of Students	% Econ Disadv.
Kapowsin Elementary (K 06) Bethel	65.7	40.0	35	28.2
Franklin Elementary (P 06) Spokane	94.4	55.6	36	50.6
Logan Elementary (P 06) Spokane	90.9	72.7	42	74.6
Madison Elementary (P 05) Everett	88.3	58.3	60	47.5
Evergreen Elementary School (K 06) Mead	87.9	62.1	58	36.4
Bell Elementary (K 06) Lake Washington	87.9	54.5	33	38.3
Larrabee Elementary School (K 05) Bellingham	87.1	41.9	30	39.1
Greenacres Elementary (K 05) Central Valley	86.8	58.5	53	51.9
Blair Elementary School (P 06) Medical Lake	86.7	53.3	45	33.5
Wainwright (P 05) Tacoma	85.7	57.1	28	49.9
Keystone Elementary School (P 05) Central Valley	85.7	50.0	28	68.6
Average of Top Comparable Schools	88.2	57.4		
Opportunity Gap	-22.5			
Number in Pool	574			

each of these top performers is enabling their fourth grade students to attain higher levels of performance on the Washington State math assessment than Kapowsin. Over 94 percent of fourth graders at Franklin Elementary passed the state math test, while only 66 percent of Kapowsin fourth graders did so. The difference between fourth graders who exceeded the state performance standard at Franklin Elementary versus Kapowsin Elementary is smaller: 56 percent versus 40 percent. This information not only shows Kapowsin educators and parents specifically how their students are performing, it also gives them the capacity to contact top comparable schools to determine what they are doing in their math instruction to bring about high levels of student achievement.

Step 4: Identify the Opportunity Gap for Each School: Through this apples-to-apples comparison of schools, we can learn the potential achievement level of each school in the near term based on evidence of how others in like or more difficult circumstances are performing. Figure 2 indicates this potential for improvement—termed the opportunity gap—for fourth graders in math at Kapowsin Elementary: there is a 22.5 percentage point difference between the math performance of continuously enrolled fourth graders at Kapowsin and the math performance of continuously enrolled fourth graders at top comparable schools. Thus, educators and parents can easily see that much higher levels of student achievement are possible, and that justifying lower performance on the basis of challenging circumstances is not appropriate. As Figures 1 and 2 make clear, using student performance information to recognize who the top comparable schools are can help inspire lower-performing schools to reach similar high levels.

Step 5: Track School Performance Over Time: Accurate and complete data collection not only enables us to see how a school performed during a certain year, but also how that school performed over time. Figure 3, for instance, indicates the performance of continuously enrolled fourth graders in mathematics at Kapowsin Elementary in Washington State from 1999 to 2003. Educators and parents can clearly see whether student achievement in that grade and subject is increasing or decreasing. Such results would indicate, for example, whether a curriculum that was instituted in 2000 has had a positive effect on student performance; whether teachers are having success in teaching their students or whether they may need additional instructional support; and whether students have improved or are in need of extra help in the subject. Through Figure 3, educators and parents at Kapowsin can see that the performance of their continuously enrolled fourth graders in math increased between 2001 and 2003, and that while Kapowsin fourth graders are not performing at the level of fourth graders at top comparable schools, Kapowsin students are making gains.

Figure 2. Just for the Kids Opportunity Gap Chart

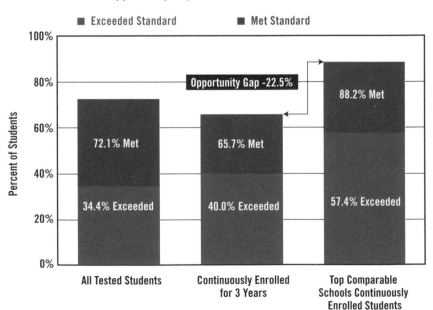

Step 6: Identify Consistently High-Performing Schools Across Grades, Subjects, and Years for Best Practice Studies: Complete and accurate data collection also makes possible the identification of schools that have been consistently high-performing across multiple grades, years, and subjects. (This is distinct from pinpointing the top-performing schools for a single grade, subject, and year in Steps 3 through 5.) Identifying consistently high-performing schools forms the foundation for the vital study of educational best practices. Discussed in detail in chapter 3, such best practice research focuses on schools that are identified as high-performing over a number of years, subjects, and grades and compares these perennial high performers to consistently average-performing

Figure 3. Just for the Kids Multi-Year Performance Chart

KAPOWSIN ELEMENTARY, BETHEL
Multi-Year Summary Chart for Grade 4 Mathematics

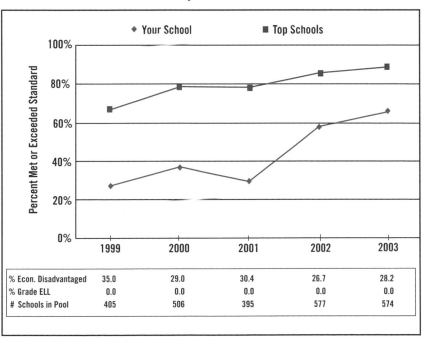

	1999	2000	2001	2002	2003
% Econ. Disadvantaged	35.0	29.0	30.4	26.7	28.2
% Grade ELL	0.0	0.0	0.0	0.0	0.0
# Schools in Pool	405	506	395	577	574

schools in order to pinpoint what the high-performing schools are doing to enable their students to excel.

For such best practice research to accurately reflect the practices of high performers, the identification of which schools have demonstrated consistent high performance must come through a rigorous and reliable approach. These consistent high performers must meet far more stringent criteria than the top comparable schools, which are highlighted because of their comparatively high performance in a single grade, subject, and year. Factors considered in the identification of consistent high performers are (1) the school's performance on the state's assessment test, (2) the demographic characteristics of the student body, including the percent of economically disadvantaged students, and (3) the students' preparation for the school (for example, when analyzing tenth graders, considering the average eighth-grade scores of students the year before entering high school).[44]

The analysis compares the performance of each school in each tested grade and subject to the average performance of demographically similar schools in those same grades and subjects. The school's distance from this average is ranked among schools with similar schoolwide percentages of economically disadvantaged students, and all of the ranks for that school for a single subject—across three years and multiple grades—are averaged to give an overall performance ranking of the school for a particular subject. Those schools whose overall ranks are considered among the best are identified as high-performing in the subject. If they are subsequently identified as high-performing across multiple subjects, they may be selected for best practice research.[45]

Use of the Just for the Kids data at the high-performing Demarest Middle School in New Jersey indicates how accessible and advantageous the JFTK data analysis is. With the effective leadership of Demarest's principal, Dr. Dennis McDonald, teachers employ the JFTK-New Jersey site (www.just4kids.org) to ascertain and print out their school's test scores and examine scores at comparable schools. Demarest students score among the highest in the state. Yet Demarest educators still study schools in New Jersey whose students score close to the level of Demarest students. Demarest teachers contact the comparable schools and visit their campuses in teams to study what they are doing that is effective. Demarest staff also study the best practices of those comparable schools that are presented on the JFTK-New Jersey web site.[46]

JFTK data analysis also shapes the instructional goals of educators at Demarest. Through studying JFTK-New Jersey data, Demarest staff determined that there was a need to enhance the performance of students in expressive writing and language arts. Educators set a goal for greater numbers of students to perform at the Advanced Proficient level on the Grade Eight Proficiency Exam in language arts and tailored their instructional time and attention accordingly.[47]

As the experiences at Demarest Middle School make clear, the effective use of data enables us to see how a school's students are performing and to recognize the level they can attain. Educators, policymakers, and parents are thus empowered by information and can be assured that when they make decisions concerning children's education, their actions will be specifically structured to spur academic achievement by all their students. Two steps—instituting a high-quality state longitudinal data system and then effectively employing the data produced by that system—are thus crucial tools that must form the foundation of our school improvement efforts.

3

Replicating Success: Pinpointing and Emulating High Performers in Education

---

Schools, teachers, principals and child care providers all must have access to the best practices in education if our schools are to be the best they can be.

SENATOR EDWARD M. KENNEDY
OF MASSACHUSETTS

Knowing the right thing to do is the central problem of school improvement. Holding schools accountable for their performance depends on having people in schools with the knowledge, skill, and judgment to make the improvements that will increase student performance.

RICHARD F. ELMORE,
HARVARD GRADUATE SCHOOL OF EDUCATION

AMONG the foremost reasons why we have not seen academic achievement gains by our students is that all too often our students are not being taught with instructional practices that are proven to work. On the surface, this seems surprising. Educators, parents, and policymakers desire for students to succeed. So during an era when states are increasingly imposing high-quality accountability systems that demand achievement by students and hold educators accountable for student performance, why would teachers not exclusively employ educational practices that are proven to be effective? The reasons for this situation are complex, including the traditionally low status of educational research, a lack of quality best practice studies, the complexity of education, and the unfortunate profusion of unsubstantiated programs that claim to be proven "best practices."[1]

One well-documented result of these influences is a gap between the techniques and tools that educators employ in the classroom and the programs and practices that quality research establishes as being effective. Educators are much less likely than those in other professions—such as law or medicine—to use relevant research to guide their practices. One teacher survey from the late 1980s indicated that less than half of teachers believed that education research provided practical suggestions to improve instruction, while a study from the same decade showed that the majority of teachers employed a narrow inventory of teaching practices, and expanded their repertoire only if they received considerable, well-designed training.[2]

This divide between research knowledge and practice has resulted in an unfortunate "revolving door" of reform initiatives in education. A myriad of educational programs and approaches have entered the education scene with great flourish over recent decades, each with bold claims about their ability to improve student achievement, and often with claims that they were proven to work (albeit often supported by flimsy evidence). These approaches have almost invariably fallen flat, and have left the education scene as quickly as they entered. These repeated failures have made many educators, parents, and others involved with schools frustrated and suspicious of approaches that claim to work. Most disastrously, however, these ineffective programs and practices have robbed our students of the high-quality education each of them deserves.[3]

Thus, it is not that educators, parents, and policymakers do not want for students to benefit from the most effective instructional practices, but rather that either (1) educators and others have not been shown and convinced of the practices that are proven to be effective or (2) if they are aware of effective practices, they have not been able to employ them effectively. In short, we need both to increase the knowledge of educators, parents, and policymakers concerning what practices are proven as well as augment their capacity to use those practices effectively. The aim of this chapter and this book as a whole is to meet these two needs.

While other chapters concern proven tools that spur student achievement gains in particular segments of the education system—such as in urban districts, early childhood education, and high schools—this chapter presents a general approach to improve educational quality and, as a result, drive higher student performance in all schools at all levels of K–12 education. This chapter lays out a systemic framework of proven practices that allows educators to employ those effective practices throughout a school system, at the district, school, and classroom levels. This Best Practice Framework and the tools associated with it are usable and replicable by any school system in the country, regardless of student demographics, geography, or grade levels.

Further, the determination and use of effective educational practices discussed here represent "step two" of data-driven decision-making presented in chapter 2 of this book. Repeatedly, those who successfully employ student performance information to drive student achievement gains point to two primary ways that they use student data: first, to demonstrate how their students are performing and to identify their specific strengths and weaknesses, and, second, to shape their educational program in order to meet the specific needs of their students. As Tom Williams, former headmaster of the high-performing Healthy Start Academy in Durham, North Carolina, well states, "The point is what you do with the results, not the excuses you make to cover for them."[4]

This chapter presents precisely what to do with the results of student performance data and how specifically to drive higher student performance. First, to make clear how the tools we present here address a pressing need in our public schools, we discuss how central the use of proven educational practices is to making our schools better but how, tragically, there has traditionally been a weak link between proven programs and classroom instruction. We next explore the encouraging increased focus on the discovery and application of proven educational practices—and how various organizations are trying to bridge the gap between educational research and classroom instruction. Lastly, we present two tools developed by the National Center for Educational Accountability's Just for the Kids that specifically address the pressing needs of pinpointing what high-performing schools and districts are doing to spur student achievement and enabling others who are not high performers to benefit from those practices. The first tool is a rigorous and replicable research process for identifying the best practices of high-performing schools and districts; the second is a best practice framework that effectively communicates the results of best practice studies and facilitates systemic adoption of proven practices at the district, school, and classroom levels.

The Central Importance– but Weak History–of Proven Instructional Practices

Various studies indicate that only a small fraction of educational practices that are proven to be effective are routinely used by educators. The implications of this failure could not be more critical to our efforts to provide every student with a first-rate education. As Mike Schmoker has well argued, until we respect and incorporate the most effective practices for teaching and school improvement, we limit the potential achievement of every student and every teacher. Our goal of enabling every student to attain his or her highest aptitudes through an excellent education simply will remain out of reach.[5]

Why is there a lack of use of proven, research-based educational programs? Or, as one frustrated father recently asked an education reform leader, "Why is it that I can go to the doctor and receive a simple, research-based diagnosis on how to lower my cholesterol, yet when I ask my son's teachers to provide a research base for their recommendation on how to correct my boy's speech impediment, I get no clear answer?"[6]

There are multiple reasons for this situation. Among the most prominent of these reasons is the historically weak status of education research, as discussed in chapter 2. The weakness of the educational research field has particularly damaging effects on the quality of instruction our students receive. As the National Research Council recently concluded, "In no other field are personal experience and ideology so frequently relied on to make policy choices, and in no other field is the research base so inadequate and little used." Several factors have inhibited the potential of education research, including underinvestment in research by the federal government and others, a lack of coordination and focus among the numerous researchers and research studies, and the complex, dynamic nature of education.[7]

In addition, transforming valuable research findings into educational practice in the country's more than one million classrooms is difficult and daunting. Classroom teachers and educators at the school and district levels determine what students experience in classrooms, but getting information to them—as well as convincing them of the value of that information—is challenging. Unlike other countries such as Japan or France, the United States has no centralized structure to communicate educational research findings and train educators in how to apply that knowledge.[8]

Further, often education researchers and education practitioners operate in separate, unrelated spheres; research undertaken is often not related to the needs of practitioners and little communication concerning research findings takes place between the two groups.[9]

Into the void left by the weak education research field and into the midst of the complex education environment have rushed waves of programs claiming to be proven as effective in raising student achievement. These unsubstantiated programs and educators' personal predilections have commonly dominated instructional practice policies—all to the detriment of student learning. In a 2003 study, the National Research Council concluded that, while extensive education programs and policies are continually undertaken, these efforts usually are instigated without adequate evidence to guide their development, implementation, and enhancement over time.[10]

Such a knowledge gap affects all students and all schools—but particularly harms students and teachers in low-performing schools, for educators in these schools clearly know the improvement gains they must attain under state and federal accountability systems, but have scarce knowledge as to how to accomplish the task.[11]

Promising Signs: A Growing Demand for Practices that Work

Fortunately, we may be heralding a new era in education reform; increasingly educators, policymakers, parents, and citizens are calling for educational practices that are well researched and backed by data that attests to their effectiveness. These parties view information on what works and what does not—and why—as vital knowledge as they strive for their schools to meet ever more demanding performance goals under state accountability systems. Even more importantly, they realize that knowledge about the efficacy of programs is crucial to ensuring that all children benefit from a quality education. Further, citizens have become progressively more attuned to the intimate tie between children's performance in school and their later contribution to the civic and economic health of the country. This general recognition is resulting in a call for proven educational strategies to garner student achievement gains.[12]

As discussed in chapter 2, the federal No Child Left Behind Act of 2001 (NCLB) and Education Sciences Reform Act of 2002 (ESRA) both stress the importance of scientifically based research in educational practice. NCLB requires educators to employ educational practices that are supported by scientifically based research, while a principal focus of ESRA is the enhancement of the connection between scientifically based research and classroom practice. Meanwhile, NCLB's challenging goal of having all students academically proficient by 2014 is causing states and schools to strive to locate proven, effective instructional strategies that will spur student achievement gains.[13]

As a result of these influences, both private and governmental efforts are promoting the value of evidence-driven decisions that focus on the critical concern: enhancing student and school performance.[14]

- In 2002, the U.S. Department of Education's Institute of Education Sciences established the What Works Clearinghouse in order to provide educators, researchers, policymakers, and the public with a reliable and credible source for scientific evidence concerning what educational programs and practices work. The Clearinghouse provides publicly available reviews of educational research on selected topics, such as effective math curricula or effective reading instruction for beginning readers.[15]
- In 2004, the U.S. Department of Education established a Teacher-to-Teacher Initiative, one of whose main purposes is to keep teachers abreast of the latest research concerning instructional strategies that are proven to work.[16]
- The National Governor's Association released *Reaching New Heights: Turning Around Low-Performing Schools—a Guide for Governors* in 2003, which advises governors to ensure that schools implement research-based instructional improvement strategies.[17]
- Since beginning a new contract with the U.S. Department of Education in 2001, the nation's ten Regional Educational Laboratories have focused on transforming low-performing schools into high performers. To accomplish this, lab personnel are putting increased effort into studying, understanding, and disseminating instructional practices that are proven to work.[18]
- In 2003, a committee assembled by the National Institutes of Science presented its vision for a Strategic Education Research Partnership (SERP), which would concentrate on research that serves the practice needs of teachers.[19]

One outgrowth of the increased attention on evidence-based reform has been a profusion of "best practice studies," which generally focus on locating high-performing schools, determining what they are doing to drive student achievement, and sharing those practices with others. For example, in 2000, the Public Schools of North Carolina published *Closing the Achievement Gap: Views from Nine Schools,* which described the practices employed by high-performing schools—including those closing the achievement gap between African American and white students—that serve large numbers of minority and economically disadvantaged students.[20] Also in 2000, the Heritage Foundation published *No Excuses: Lessons from 21 High-Performing, High-Poverty Schools.*[21]

The following year, the Education Research Service released the results of the School District Effectiveness Study, which discussed key practices used by six districts serving significant numbers of low-income students that had attained considerable student achievement gains over five years.[22] Two years later, in 2003, Robert J. Marzano synthesized thirty-five years of research on the best practices used by effective schools in his *What Works in Schools: Translating Research into Action,* while the Learning First Alliance's Wendy Togneri presented the practices used by high-poverty districts that were improving student performance in *Beyond Islands of Excellence: What Districts Can Do to Improve Instruction and Achievement in All Schools.*[23] In 2004, the Maryland State Department of Education released its *Study of Higher-Success and Lower-Success Elementary Schools,* which, like Marzano's publication, synthesized various studies' findings concerning the practices that effective schools use.[24]

These studies, organizations, and initiatives all reflect a promising and significant development in our nation's efforts to improve our schools. Increasingly, there is a focus on (1) pinpointing what is working and why, (2) disseminating information to educators concerning these practices, and (3) encouraging educators to adopt these effective tools. One particularly hopeful finding of this research is that various schools with student populations in challenging circumstances (for example, a high percentage of students in poverty) are performing at high levels, and that the methods they are using to attain high achievement are quite replicable.[25]

There are many benefits of this focus on proven practices. For instance, with the assurance that the practices that they have in hand are proven to work, educators and policymakers should be more willing to make needed changes and persist with proven reforms, even when gains in student achievement do not immediately result. Evidence thus gives decision-makers in education confidence that they are teaching students in the most effective way—confidence that was sorely lacking during the era of "revolving door" reforms that we experienced in previous decades. Such hard evidence of what works should also quell ideological debates that have plagued education for decades—and that, all too often, have harmed students' education.[26]

Although this increased attention on proven practices is a welcome development and many of these efforts have produced valuable findings, the abundance of information produced by best practice studies and initiatives is often overwhelming and unaccompanied by clear direction on how to put the information into practice. "There is a huge volume of unconnected and undigested material available, and no authoritative source of carefully screened and vetted research knowledge," as M. S. Donovan, A. K. Wigdor, and C. E. Snow conclude in a 2003 National Research Council report. "As a consequence, even the most promising research-based curricula, the most effective programs, and the most important insights into human learning are often little known and have little effect on U.S. schools."[27] In this environment, one need is imperative in order for students to garner the full benefits from effective educational practices: educators, parents, and policymakers need an easy-to-understand, usable source of best practice information that both clearly communicates what is enabling certain schools to succeed and clearly explains how others can adopt these same practices to the same effect. Thus, such a source must not only present information that is immediately applicable in their local school, it must also incorporate tools and evidence that clearly show users how to put the practices into action at their school.

Second, although the focus on proven practices is worthwhile, the methods researchers use for selecting which schools are high-performing and what their effective practices are varies widely in approach and quality. As the National Research Council and the U.S. Department of Education stress, the process for determining research results is vital, and must be trustworthy and proven—otherwise, a weak methodology compromises the study results. What standards should such study processes meet? More specifically, how can a researcher or educator structure a study to reliably determine the effective practices of high-performing schools?[28]

The tools presented in this chapter meet these two needs. First, we present the rigorous—and replicable—process developed by the National Center for Educational Accountability's Just for the Kids to locate and study the effective practices employed by highly effective schools across the country. Second, we discuss the Just for the Kids Best Practice Framework. Various efforts, such as the Institute of Education Sciences' What Works Clearinghouse and the National Research Council's Strategic Education Research Partnership, represent valuable efforts to promote the application of research findings in the classroom. However, the Best Practice Framework presented here is unique in content, layout, and focus. No other best practice tool provides such an easily accessible, state-specific source of best practices at the classroom, school, and district levels. And no other tool provides the ability for cross-state comparisons of what high performers are doing across the country. We present the Just for the Kids best practice study process and the Best Practice Framework not only to promote their use (at www.just4kids.org). We also seek to encourage others to adopt a similar, rigorous study structure when they investigate high-performing schools and to use a similar organizational framework when they communicate their best practice findings.

Pinpointing the Keys to High Performance:
The Importance of a Rigorous, Exacting Research Process

Walk into any classroom or into any school or district administrator's office and one thing is startlingly clear: that educator has a complex job that involves many responsibilities and tasks. How do we sift through this multifaceted workload to determine what specifically an educator is doing to foster academic achievement by students? Only a rigorous, exacting study will allow us to pinpoint exactly what practices make the difference between a high-performing school or district and one that is average- or poor-performing. Such a research process must involve the investigation of a large cross section of both high-performing schools and those that are not high-performing to determine—through scrupulous examination of data and on-site investigations—what the high performers are doing to drive high student achievement.

Through a four-year best practice study of hundreds of school systems located across the country, Just for the Kids has developed a rigorous, encompassing process to determine what differentiates the practices employed by high-performing versus average-performing schools and districts in states across the country.[29] Central to the integrity of the process is the strong link it makes between best practices and data concerning student performance. No other study, to our knowledge, uses student performance data as such an integral element to determine exactly who the high-performing schools and districts are and how specifically their performance differs from average performers.[30] Further, the process is replicable; any study that is trying to determine what spurs high academic performance can effectively employ this four-step approach.

Step 1: Compare High-Performing Schools and Districts to Average Performers: The Importance of a Control Group: Rather than comparing high-performing schools and districts to low performers, the better approach is to compare those schools and districts that are excelling with those that are average-performing. This allows for the identification of specific factors that high-performing school systems incorporate at the district, school, and classroom levels that allow students to excel. In addition, the inclusion of average-performing school systems as a control group is crucial for the study to be valid and useful. In the absence of control groups, researchers simply cannot ascertain whether a given practice or program influences performance levels, and thus whether it is a factor that is driving high performance.[31]

Step 2: Apply Strict Criteria Regarding Which Schools and Districts to Include in the Study: The study should base school and district selection as a high performer or average performer on student achievement data to a significant degree. As discussed in chapter 2, criteria should be demanding and include, for example, how students continuously enrolled in the school or district for at least three years performed vis-à-vis continuously enrolled students at other schools or districts; how the school or district compares to similar schools or districts in the number of students who score at a proficient level on state assessments; and whether there was a certain minimum number of continuously enrolled students in each tested subject, grade, and year. Researchers should then further cull the pool of average- and high-performing schools and districts in order for those studied to represent the geographic and demographic spectrum of the state or area under study. This culling takes into account the economic status, language proficiency, and ethnicity of students at each school and district as well as the location of the school and district. It also includes further examination of student performance.[32]

Step 3: Conduct Rigorous, Thorough Site Visits to Both High- and Average-Performing Schools and Districts and Perform Document Collection: Researchers should visit high-performing and average-performing schools and districts to conduct interviews and focus groups with district, school, and classroom educators. At times, these conversations also include school board members, community members, parents, and students. It is also crucial for researchers to gather documents in order to pinpoint effective practices. By analyzing in detail what schools and districts with high student achievement are doing that those with average student achievement are not, researchers can make specific, targeted conclusions for others to emulate.

Step 4: Study and Specify Best Practices at the Classroom, School, and District Level: Researchers increasingly stress how important a systemic approach to education reform is. Because the quality of education that a student receives is influenced by educators at the district, school, and classroom levels, we must ensure that educators at all three levels are using effective practices in order for students to receive a high-quality education.[33] Without effective action at the district and school level, classroom teachers bear an unsustainable burden to improve student achievement on their own. In addition, only at the district level can administrators ensure that students experience an aligned, quality curriculum from kindergarten through twelfth grade. The study, then, should focus on practices that district-, school-, and classroom-level educators employ to ensure sustained student performance.

Much best practice information gives educators general principles to follow, but the process outlined here allows us to determine specific practices to employ and helps us to understand the relationships between those practices. Through a rigorous process that includes demanding school selection procedures, a control group of average-performing schools, and the study of practices at the district, school, and classroom levels, we can determine precisely what high-performing schools and districts are doing to reap results.

A Framework for Accessing and Applying Proven Practices

A rigorous process for ascertaining what high performers are doing to get results is crucial. But how do we ensure that educators use the results of high-quality best practice studies for the benefit of our students? As noted above, this central quest of linking research with practice drives significant and well-directed efforts, including the federal Institute of Education Sciences' What Works Clearinghouse and the National Research Council's initiative for a Strategic Education Research Partnership. Likewise, the Best Practice Framework developed by Just for the Kids directly addresses this essential need of making proven best practices immediately accessible and applicable to educators throughout the country—and does so in a unique template format that clearly communicates the relation between various practices and the tools available to put them into use.

After studying over three hundred school systems across the country using the exacting procedure outlined above and undertaking various national studies including The Broad Prize for Urban Education (detailed in chapter 4), Just for the Kids was able to distill areas of instructional practice common to high-performing school systems around the nation. These findings form the organizational structure of the Best Practice Framework: a highly usable template that is being employed in various state and national studies to present best practice findings. For example, as of July 2004, researchers associated with Just for the Kids in eight states—Arkansas, California, Colorado, Illinois, New Jersey (beginning in 2005), Tennessee, Texas, and Washington—either had already employed or were in the process of employing the Best Practice Framework to present the practices that distinguish high performers in their states (see http://www.just4kids.org/bestpractice/).[34]

Thus, the Framework enables us to study the best practices of high-performing schools and districts in a particular state, as well as conduct a cross-state comparison of practices. The Framework also facilitates systemic reform by clearly portraying how best practices at the district, school, and classroom levels intersect and support each other in high-performing school systems. In addition, the Framework enables us to locate high-performing schools and districts that are similar to our own school and district in terms of student demographics and identify the specific practices those high performers are using—including documents and strategies that the schools and districts employ to successfully implement the practices.

Four central, interrelated elements structure the Best Practices Framework that appears in Figure 4:

- Five organizing themes;
- Three levels of school instruction, at the district, school, and classroom levels;
- The specific practices that high-performing school systems employ in these five thematic areas at the three levels of school instruction; and
- The supporting influences that determine how specifically a certain practice will be applied in a specific school system.

The Five Organizing Themes

Studies of hundreds of school systems across the country enabled researchers at the National Center for Educational Accountability/Just for the Kids to pinpoint five central themes around which high-performing schools and districts focus their instructional practices.

1. *Curriculum and Academic Goals:* Practices in this theme enable high-performing school systems to establish clear, specific academic goals that apply to all students in every grade of their education. All educators agree upon these learning goals and are held accountable for enabling each child to reach them.
2. *Staff Selection, Leadership, and Capacity Building:* These practices facilitate the selection and development of high-quality teachers and instructional leaders, including district leadership, school principals, and teacher leaders.

Figure 4. The National Center for Educational Accountability
Best Practice Framework

Best Practice Framework
Based on the Study of Consistently High-Performing School Systems

	MANAGING CONTINUOUS IMPROVEMENT		
Organizing Themes	District Practices	School Practices	Classroom Practices
Curriculum & Academic Goals			
Staff Selection, Leadership, & Capacity Building			
Instructional Programs, Practices, & Arrangements			
Monitoring: Compilation, Analysis, & Use of Data			
Recognition, Intervention, & Adjustment			

MANAGING CHANGE

LOCAL INFLUENCES, RELATIONSHIPS AND COMMUNICATION

RESOURCE ALLOCATION

CORE BELIEFS ABOUT TEACHING AND LEARNING

3. *Instructional Programs, Practices, and Arrangements:* Practices in the third theme concern the provision of tools—such as instructional materials, adequate instructional time, and technology—that enable educators to reach the academic goals set by the district.

4. *Monitoring: Compilation, Analysis, and Use of Data:* Practices in this theme demonstrate that high performers employ the crucial tool of student performance data to determine how students are performing, to pinpoint each student's specific academic strengths and weaknesses, and to know what instructional techniques and materials are effective.

5. *Recognition, Intervention, and Adjustment:* These practices concern how educators in high-performing schools and districts use the information from student performance data to recognize the academic needs of each student and provide immediate and intense intervention to attend to those needs.[35]

Three Levels of School Instruction

The Framework presents practices used in the five thematic areas at three school levels: the district, the school, and the classroom. Educators at the district, school, and classroom levels must each employ distinct yet complementary best practices. Also, there must be a distribution of responsibility among educators at the district, school, and classroom levels to accomplish educational goals and to avoid overburdening classroom teachers with too much responsibility for student performance. For instance, successful staff selection and capacity building occurs (1) through district selection and development of effective instructional leaders who are carefully matched to all district schools; (2) when these instructional leaders are joined by instructional specialists and master teachers to ensure that each teacher in each district school is using effective teaching strategies; and (3) when classroom teachers meet with others who teach the same grade or subject matter to coordinate curriculum and instructional strategies. This three-tiered approach ensures that district and school administrations foster excellent instruction and that teachers deliver high-quality teaching.[36]

The Practices

The grid of boxes that form the bulk of the Framework are areas for insertion of the "meat" of each best practice study: the specific practices (organized by theme and school level) that the studied high-performing school systems are using to garner high student achievement.

Supporting Influences

Although the core elements of best practices are shared by high-performing school systems, the specific way that high performers carry out effective practices will vary depending upon such factors as local influences, the allocation of resources in the school system, and the malleability of a given district to make necessary changes. For example, educators' attitudes concerning how to most effectively work together may vary from district to district; thus, one school district might schedule a shared meeting period for teachers to discuss curriculum, while another may establish an electronic discussion board to serve the same purpose. Although contextual circumstances influence the most effective way to enact each practice in a given school or district, they should never form excuses not to enact the practices.[37]

The Best Practice Framework thus provides a structure for communicating what high-performing school systems are doing to get results. This usable organizational tool supplies access not only to a listing of best practices, but also to a full set of tools that facilitate enactment of the practices. For example:

- *Tools for Implementing the Practices:* You can access specific descriptions of what the practices entail, case studies of particular school systems that employ the practices, and documents and strategies that enable those high performers to successfully apply the practices.
- *Self-Audit Tool:* The Framework includes a "self-audit" tool for each practice, which is composed of twenty questions that identify whether your school system is effectively employing a particular practice. The self-audits can be taken by an individual or by a group—and group audits reflect both individual and a group's aggregate responses.[38]

The Best Practice Framework in Action

Although various state and national studies employ the Just for the Kids Best Practice Framework, the use of the Framework is perhaps best developed in the Just for the Kids Texas Best Practice Study. We discuss the Texas Framework here and present it in Figures 5 through 9 to demonstrate how the Just for the Kids Best Practice Framework operates as well as the full range of tools available through the Framework.

The presentation and use of the Texas Framework makes two things clear: first, that the practices educators employ at the district, school, and classroom levels in high-performing school systems in each of the five thematic areas complement, interact, and support each other and, second, that the specific ways schools and districts implement practices differ, since local influences and educators' choices affect how students are taught in each school and district.

The Just for the Kids Best Practice Study of high-performing schools and districts in Texas represents the results of studying almost 100 high-performing schools and forty average-performing comparison schools throughout the state over a four-year period. The findings represent a rich, detailed, and sizeable set of results on what Texas schools and dis-

Figure 5. The Best Practice Framework for Texas High-Performing School Systems

Best Practice Framework
for Just for the Kids — Texas

Based on the Study of Consistently High-Performing School Systems

Organizing Themes	District Practices	School Practices	Classroom Practices
Curriculum & Academic Goals	Define clear and specific academic objectives by grade and subject	Center school plan on explicit improvement of specific academic objectives	Ensure teaching content is based on specified academic objectives
Staff Selection, Leadership, & Capacity Building	Provide strong instructional leaders, highly qualified teachers, and aligned professional development	Select, develop, and allocate staff based on student learning	Collaborate in grade/subject level teams focused on student work
Instructional Programs, Practices, & Arrangements	Provide evidence-based instructional programs	Ensure the use of evidence-based programs, practices, and arrangements in every classroom	Use evidence-based programs, practices, and arrangements
Monitoring: Compilation, Analysis, & Use of Data	Develop student assessment and data monitoring systems to monitor school performance	Monitor teacher performance and student learning	Monitor student learning
Recognition, Intervention, & Adjustment	Recognize, intervene, or adjust based on school performance	Recognize, intervene, or adjust based on teacher and student performance	Recognize, intervene, or adjust based on student performance

LOCAL INFLUENCES, RELATIONSHIPS AND COMMUNICATION

RESOURCE ALLOCATION

ORGANIZATIONAL KNOWLEDGE

CORE BELIEFS ABOUT TEACHING AND LEARNING

tricts are doing effectively to drive high student achievement. These study results led to the determination of the fifteen specific practices that fill in the boxes in the Best Practice Framework for Texas High-Performing School Systems.

As with all best practice study results that are presented using the Framework, three levels of information are available for each of these fifteen best practices, including (1) a detailed explanation of what the practice involves (which summarizes information gleaned from a broad group of high performers); (2) a guide to determine whether a particular practice is being implemented in your district or school and, if so, whether it is being implemented effectively; and (3) specific examples and usable evidence from high performers that are successfully employing the practice. The principle behind presenting such specific evidence is familiar to educators, for they know that among the most effective ways to empower students to improve is to show them what excellent work looks like. The same lesson applies to effective teaching: showing educators what takes place in a high-performing school system is a powerful device for improving the quality of the instruction educators deliver.[39]

A Detailed Explanation of the Practice

A detailed explanation of each best practice—a description assimilated from various high performers who are effectively employing the practice—clearly communicates what the practice entails. For example, the explanation in Figure 6 describes how Texas high-performing school districts provide instructional leaders, highly qualified teachers, and quality professional development.

A Description of Effective Implementation of the Practice

Often, schools and districts believe that they are implementing a practice. They may be to a certain degree. But there is a big difference between

Figure 6. Detailed Explanation of a Best Practice

Theme: Staff Selection, Leadership, and Capacity Building

School Level: District

Practice: Provide strong instructional leaders, highly qualified teachers, and aligned professional development

What does this practice involve?

After clearly identifying the district curriculum, the district must then ensure that the schools are equipped to successfully deliver that curriculum. By ensuring that school leaders have the knowledge and skills to provide the leadership for curriculum delivery and that the necessary support for this work is in place, the district can confidently hold all schools accountable for results.

Provide Strong Instructional Leaders

Knowledge of the powerful effect of instructional leadership on student performance drives the recruitment and selection of the principal at each school. Rigorous and on-going training programs with an emphasis on how to use data to drive decision-making support and develop the instructional leadership of the principal. As a result, both the authority and responsibility for school improvement are placed directly in the hands of the principal.

Provide Highly Qualified Teachers and Aligned Professional Development

Personnel recruitment and selection as well as professional development plans and expenditures are focused on the academic goals. District budget allocations and expenditures demonstrate a direct link to academic goals. There is a continual commitment to using student data for focusing those expenditures. Competitive grants and external partnerships—carefully coordinated to support established improvement planning—increase the district's resources to improve instruction.

Figure 7. Description of Effective Implementation of a Best Practice

Theme: Staff Selection, Leadership, and Capacity Building

School Level: District

Practice: Provide strong instructional leaders, highly qualified teachers, and aligned professional development

What does this practice look like in high-performing districts?

Missing the Mark	On Target
Personnel are hired with little consideration of the skills necessary to meet academic goals.	Personnel selection and evaluation are aligned to stated academic goals.
Little training and development are available to help leaders reach academic goals; school leaders are focused primarily on management of the building.	There is ongoing training and development of instructional leaders; school leaders focus primarily on delivering stated academic goals.
If support is offered, support staff have not necessarily been successful with comparable student populations.	Educators are supported by instructional leaders who have been successful with comparable student populations.
Professional development is too general, not tied to academic goals or student achievement data.	District professional development is differentiated, focused on specific academic goals, and tied to student achievement needs.
No monitoring system is aligned to professional development.	The implementation and impact of professional development is routinely monitored.

incorporating a practice and incorporating it effectively. Thus, a second tool available for each practice listed in the Framework and exemplified in Figure 7 is a comparison of the actions high performers take to implement a practice effectively versus actions that "miss the mark," meaning they do not allow a school system to fully benefit from the practice.

Specific Evidence from High Performers

What if our school system is not employing this practice or our district or school is using this practice, but could be doing so more effectively? Then we can turn to descriptions of how specific high performers successfully implement the proven practice. The Best Practice Framework includes the names and demographic information of high-performing schools or districts that effectively use each practice. We can contact those high performers directly to find out how they are successfully carrying out a particular practice. In addition, in the Best Practice Framework, we can access materials such as Just for the Kids case studies that explain how those schools and districts employ the practice; documents that enable the schools and districts to successfully carry out the practice; and links to data charts that indicate how students at those schools and districts perform.

For example, if our district notes that it needs to improve its staff selection and capacity building, we can investigate districts listed under that practice, as noted in Figure 8. If about a fifth of students in our school district are economically disadvantaged (the percentage of students who receive free or reduced-price meals), then the success of Cypress-Fairbanks Independent School District in Houston, Texas, may be of particular interest. We can investigate the evidence presented for Cypress-Fairbanks, which includes descriptions concerning the district's Leadership Academy, professional development, and teacher self-monitoring (excerpts of which are in Figure 9)—and then we can strive to incorporate similar strategies in our own school system. In addition, we can contact educators at Cypress-Fairbanks to gather information as to how they effectively select and build the capacity of staff.

Figure 8. Information on High-Performing Schools and Districts That Employ a Best Practice

Theme: Staff Selection, Leadership, and Capacity Building

School Level: District

Practice: Provide strong instructional leaders, highly qualified teachers, and aligned professional development

High-Performing Districts

Brazosport ISD

Free / Reduced Lunch: 34.5%	Enrollment: 13,247	Freeport

Brownsville ISD

Free / Reduced Lunch: 92.8%	Enrollment: 42,541	Brownsville

Clint ISD

Free / Reduced Lunch: 88.6%	Enrollment: 7,918	Clint

Cypress-Fairbanks ISD

Free / Reduced Lunch: 21.8%	Enrollment: 67,441	Houston

Pasadena ISD

Free / Reduced Lunch: 57.3%	Enrollment: 43,476	Pasadena

Richardson ISD

Free / Reduced Lunch: 33.8%	Enrollment: 34,655	Richardson

Spring Branch ISD

Free / Reduced Lunch: 53.1%	Enrollment: 32,540	Houston

Evidence   JFTK District Report

Figure 9. Specific Evidence of How High Performers Employ a Best Practice

Theme: Staff Selection, Leadership, and Capacity Building

School Level: District

Practice: Provide strong instructional leaders, highly qualified teachers, and aligned professional development

Excerpts of Evidence from Cypress-Fairbanks ISD

Leadership Academy: Cypress-Fairbanks ISD has developed a year-long Leadership Academy for teachers (with at least four years of experience) or administrators who aspire to the principalship or other leadership role. The Academy addresses the[ir] competencies. . . . Candidates must submit three references, a letter from a supervisor who will serve as a mentor, an application form, and a resume to be considered for the program.

Professional Development: Professional development for teachers in Cypress-Fairbanks ISD is closely linked to student achievement goals. During the first six weeks, teachers must indicate the source of their performance measures, students' targeted needs, their personal goals, the instructional strategies they plan to use, and other capacity building activities in which they plan to engage.

Self-Monitoring by Teachers: Teachers must self-monitor their student performance goals throughout the year. In November and again in February, they share their progress and ongoing plans with a colleague.

A final self-evaluation reflecting on the impact of data analysis and different strategies is completed prior to their summative conference.

As the Cypress-Fairbanks ISD illustration indicates, the information made available through the Best Practice Framework equips teachers, schools, and districts with specific steps that they can take to implement each practice, along with contact information for high-performing schools and districts if they need further information.

We are at a heartening crossroads in education reform, as more educators, researchers, and governmental initiatives place an increasing focus on locating and using practices that are proven to work. The Best Practice Framework and the rigorous process for conducting best practice studies presented here can serve as empowering tools to bring the substantial benefits of proven practices to full effect. Clear evidence points to ways to provide all students with a quality education. It is up to us to follow through by putting these proven methods to work.

4

Overcoming the Gaps in State Data and Student Achievement: The Broad Prize for Urban Education

---

> The expertise and contribution made by the NCEA to the inaugural Broad Prize from its incipient states to its culmination was invaluable. NCEA gave us the ability, using state accountability data, to substantiate the essential link between high standards and results in student learning.
>
> ELI BROAD, FOUNDER, THE BROAD FOUNDATION

> This [Broad Prize] approach to identifying high performing school districts, combining publicly available achievement data with other important improvement evidence such as closing the achievement gap, will help to focus public education in urban centers on what matters most.
>
> STEVEN FLEISCHMAN, EDUCATION QUALITY INSTITUTE

IN OUR EFFORTS to make our schools excellent, two goals are paramount and interconnected: first, we must raise the achievement level of our students; second, we must close the achievement gap—meaning the gap between the achievement level of white, affluent students and that of minority and economically disadvantaged students (see chapter 1). We cannot reach these goals unless we successfully address the pressing and unique needs of urban schools. Although the 100 largest school districts represent less than 1 percent of all school districts in the country, they educate almost a quarter of all public school students, about 30 percent of all students from low-income families, and 40 percent of non-white students (as of 2001–2002).[1]

Unfortunately, student achievement in urban schools as a group has been perennially low. As the Council of the Great City Schools reported in 2004, student performance in reading and math in sixty-one urban school systems across the country is below national and state averages, even though students in these urban districts recently have made achievement gains. In addition, dropout rates in urban districts are disturbingly high. Given the large proportion of our country's children—particularly of minority and economically disadvantaged children—who attend urban schools, improving the level of student achievement in these districts is critical.[2]

How do we do so? The answer is straightforward. The first step is to employ student performance data to locate high-performing urban districts that face similar demographic and economic challenges as other urban districts. Studies, such as those by the Education Trust and the National Center for Educational Accountability, establish that there are high-performing schools and districts with high percentages of economically disadvantaged and minority students throughout the country. Likewise, various groups—including the Council of the Great City Schools—are studying achievement trends in the nation's largest urban districts.[3] The second step is to discern what these high-performing urban districts are doing to garner results. Then, other urban districts can adopt those proven strategies for attaining high achievement in urban schools. As we have seen in previous chapters, this approach works and makes simple sense: if we want to succeed, we should learn from and emulate those in similar circumstances who are succeeding.

Yet there are various challenges to this approach in the context of urban school districts. First, how do we determine who the high-performing urban districts are when the districts are spread across the country? Each state has its own assessment and system of academic standards; these tests and standards vary in format, content, and difficulty. Thus, the same score on two states' achievement tests does not necessarily indicate the same level of achievement. As a result, we are unable to compare the performance of students in, for example, New Jersey with those next door in Pennsylvania or with those across the country in California. The nation's only currently existing report card—the National Assessment of Educational Progress (NAEP)—is valuable in providing revealing data of national trends, but is based only on a sample of students and provides results on a statewide basis. In 2002, NAEP began a promising effort, the Trial Urban District Assessment (TUDA), which compares the performance of students in urban districts across the country. But the TUDA currently only reflects the performance of a sample of students in a relatively small number of districts (six districts in 2002 and ten in 2003, including the District of Columbia).[4] In sum, the patchwork of state standards, assessments, and data collection systems and lack of a national examination for all students have hampered the ability of researchers and educators to determine how students across the country are performing, to make comparisons of performance between states, and to locate excellent schools and districts throughout the nation from which others can learn.

A second challenge poses similarly complex obstacles: even if we are able to discern who the high-performing districts are, how do we determine what specifically they are doing to spur student achievement?

These challenges faced The Broad Foundation—founded by Eli and Edythe Broad—as it established a groundbreaking award in 2002: The Broad Prize for Urban Education.[5] The Broad Foundation created the $1,000,000 annual Broad Prize—the largest public education award in United States history—to recognize urban districts that have shown great improvement in student achievement and simultaneously have reduced achievement gaps among ethnic groups and between low-income and non-low-income students. The goal is to motivate other urban districts by showing them the high level of educational performance they can achieve and to provide specific successful educational practices used by the winner and finalist districts that other districts can employ to attain improvement. The Prize awards $500,000 to the winning district and $125,000 to each of four finalist districts to fund college

scholarships for over 100 high school seniors from low-income families—students who otherwise might not have such an opportunity.[6]

The beneficial outgrowths of The Broad Prize are numerous and
wide-ranging. First, the research process conducted by The Broad Foundation and the National Center for Educational Accountability (funded
by a Broad Foundation grant) furthers our knowledge of how urban districts across the country are performing by analyzing more data for
more school districts than previously has ever been analyzed collectively.
Second, The Broad Prize process revealed several particularly high-performing urban districts, which were chosen as finalists during the Prize
competition in 2002 and 2003. The performance of these districts can
serve as benchmarks for others. Third, the analysis portrays how districts
can attain high performance. Strictly structured site visits revealed that
all finalists employ similar strategies (which are replicable by others) to
attain educational improvement, notwithstanding different state educational standards and assessments. Lastly, the process used to determine
who the high-performing urban districts are and their best practices is
applicable in a wide array of studies, whether of urban or non-urban
schools. Thus, educational researchers and policymakers can employ the
proven approach used in the Prize process to structure other analyses in
order to gain a valid picture of performance and improvement trends
across the country.

This chapter lays out the process for awarding The Broad Prize for
Urban Education and the practices that the high-performing Broad
Prize finalists employ to attain high performance with two central goals:
first, to share specifically how we can ascertain how our school districts—both urban and non-urban—are performing across the country
(not just in a particular state) and, second, to empower urban school
districts with information concerning specific measures they can take to
improve their performance. The chapter considers three interrelated
subjects in turn: the process developed to determine which urban districts out of all districts nationally merited being recognized as the high-

performing Broad Prize finalists and winner; how this investigation revealed that high-performing urban districts across the country employ common strategies to garner high student achievement; and what those specific practices are.

A Rigorous, Encompassing, Replicable Process

Researchers for The Broad Prize established a process that involves the most rigorous, thorough investigation of urban education—indeed, of public education generally—in all fifty states ever undertaken. The process is replicable in other studies, whether they concern hundreds of school districts across the country or a few districts in multiple states. However, The Broad Prize process is not a magic bullet. Data from various states is sparse and longitudinal data—meaning data that follows a student over time—is becoming increasingly available but is still meager in numerous states. So researchers structured The Broad Prize procedures to operate within the data universe as it stands today in the most effective way possible.

Three key elements ensure the validity and reliability of the Prize process: (1) using educational experts throughout the process to advise and make award decisions; (2) strictly controlling data analysis to compare districts against demographically similar districts in their state— meaning against those districts with similar percentages of economically disadvantaged students; and (3) conducting a thorough, structured investigation of finalist districts through site visits to ascertain firsthand the educational strategies they employ.[7]

Experts Employed Throughout the Process: Three primary groups composed of distinguished education and business leaders assist researchers in structuring and awarding the Prize.

- A *group of advisors* comprised of statistical experts and those experienced with the investigation and development of best practices guide

National Center researchers throughout the process, including in the preliminary gathering and analysis of statistical data concerning urban districts.

■ A twenty-member *Review Board* of educational leaders also provides judgment and expertise as to how to collect and analyze dissimilar district data. A determination of what characteristics qualifies a district as urban, and thus a nominee for the Prize, resulted in a list of 106 nominee urban districts in 2003 based on these districts' student demographics and geography.[8] The Review Board thoroughly reviews a broad array of data, including district performance on state assessments, how each district performed in light of the percentage of district students from low-income families, and the performance trend of the district over several years. The Board then chooses the five Prize finalists.

■ Later, after teams of educators and researchers conduct site visits of the finalist districts, a *Selection Jury* composed of twelve nationally recognized business, education, government, and nonprofit leaders reviews many categories of information—including data from site visits—and chooses the winner of The Broad Prize.

Data Analyzed on an "Apples-to-Apples" Basis with Student Poverty Levels as a Primary Factor: Two key elements drive the use of data in The Broad Prize process. First, researchers and the Review Board—as they analyze the nominee urban districts and pick the five finalists—concentrate on publicly available data supplied by each state's department of education and only compare each nominee to other districts in their state (meaning only to districts that were subject to the same educational assessments and standards as the nominee). Researchers' use of such publicly available data from each state ensures that the data for every district in a state is from the same test and includes the same categories of information; this standardization enables researchers to compare the performance of all districts within each state. Second, a primary focus is on whether each nominee district performs above or below its expected performance level and improvement rate over time, with the expected rate based on the performance and improvement levels of other districts in the state with a similar percentage of economically disadvantaged students (as determined by the percentage of students reported eligible for the federal program of free or reduced-price school meals). The focus on each state's data and the comparison of each district with those in their state that have student populations with similar economic demographics ensures that comparisons are not being made between results in different states, which by their nature are incompatible because they are based on different standards and tests. It also averts a cross-state comparison of the substance of state tests and standards, which differ in stringency and content. Further, because the income level of a student's family has traditionally been a dominant non-school influence on a student's academic achievement, the analysis focuses on the economic demographics of each district.

Highly Structured Site Visits:

- *Team and Protocol:* In order to grant the Selection Jury a comprehensive picture of the five finalists, researchers conduct three-day site visits of each finalist district to collect information concerning district practices and policies. The site visit teams include professors, school principals, senior district teachers and leaders, and researchers; many on the teams have received national recognition. Each site visit follows an identical schedule and includes requests for identical information. The protocols, developed by Just for the Kids, an affiliate of the National Center, strictly guide the entire site visit as the team investigates the educational practices used by the finalist districts.

- *Content:* Each site visit involves over thirty hours of interviews. In 2003, each visit resulted in the collection of over 100 documents from each district as evidence of what that high-performing urban district was doing to enhance teaching and learning. At each of the five finalist districts, researchers interview the superintendent, assistant superintendent for curriculum and instruction, union president, school board president, representatives of parents and businesses involved with the district, and other senior district personnel. In addition, the site visit team visits one high school, one intermediate school, and one elementary school in each district; at each of the three schools, researchers interview the principal and teachers. Team members also observe classroom instruction and collaborative staff meetings at each school. After the completion of all five site visits, a team of National Center researchers evaluates all of the gathered best practice evidence and gauges its quality against predetermined guidelines.

A Common Approach to Attaining High Performance: Standards, Monitoring, and Accountability

A primary element hindering progress in efforts to improve our schools has been the conflicting schools of thought on how to spur student performance. For decades, reformers have pinned their hopes on various, at times conflicting, approaches to school improvement, ranging from reliance on a particular curriculum to reduced class sizes to increased spending per pupil (see chapters 1 and 3).

Perhaps one of the most significant findings to result from the nationwide Broad Prize study is that high-performing urban districts across the country employ a similar approach to bring about student achievement. During the site visits for the inaugural 2002 Broad Prize competition, the similarities between the methods used by the five finalist districts became clearly apparent; study of the five high-performing finalists in 2003 (which included three districts that were also nominated in 2002) indicated that they too employed these same basic components to spur achievement. All seven of these districts—located across the country in disparate settings ranging from Boston to Atlanta to Long Beach, California—consistently employ accountability systems and emphasize that all students, regardless of their circumstances, are able to perform at a high level if they experience a challenging curriculum, high-quality instruction, effective monitoring of their performance through assessments, and extra attention in areas of weakness to bolster their performance. The results of The Broad Prize research thus reveal that standards and accountability have become the accepted and effective approach of high performers across the country.

Hence, each of the 2003 Broad Prize finalists:

1. Defines clear and specific *academic objectives* by grade and subject;
2. Provides strong *instructional leaders*, highly qualified *teachers*, and aligned *professional development;*
3. Selects or develops *instructional materials and programs* based on scientific evidence;
4. Regularly *monitors* school and student performance; and
5.   *Rewards, intervenes, or adjusts* its school support based on student performance information.

Indeed, each of The Broad Prize finalists applies these best practices consistently and extensively, and thus portrays how central such practices are to attaining educational excellence—and how other districts could benefit by adopting them.[9]

Specific, Replicable Findings: How High-Performing Urban Districts Are Spurring Student Achievement

Among the reasons most commonly cited for urban students' relatively low achievement levels and their high dropout rates is the unwieldy size of many urban districts, which makes providing each student with a high-quality education a challenge. Another purported reason is that a high percentage of students educated at urban districts are often students in poverty and minority students, both factors that have traditionally resulted in low student performance. Yet the finalists and winners of The Broad Prize establish that these are not limiting factors: these districts are among the largest districts in the country and all have high percentages of economically disadvantaged and minority students. The 2003 Prize finalists included Boston Public Schools (Massachusetts), Garden Grove Unified School District (California), Jefferson County Public Schools (Kentucky), Norfolk Public Schools (Virginia), and the 2003 Broad Prize winner, Long Beach Unified School District (California). Ranging in size from 37,000 to 97,000 students, these five districts educate on average 68,000 students—much larger than the national average district size of about 2,800. The five finalists were among the largest districts in the country, ranking between 29th largest and 131st largest of the approximately 15,000 districts nationwide. At least 45 percent of the students at each district are economically disadvantaged (they qualify for free or reduced-price school lunch), and in four of the five districts, more than 70 percent of the student body is non-white.[10]

Notwithstanding the demographics and size of these districts, their students are attaining notably high and sustained student achievement levels. What are these districts specifically doing to attain such high-performance from their students?

Educators at the finalist districts provided Broad Prize researchers with detailed descriptions of the methods they employ to spur student achievement and supplied the materials they use to carry out their approach. Their practices are numerous, rich in content, and replicable in other districts. The practices are spelled out in full at www.nc4ea.org and www.just4kids.org/bestpractice. In this chapter, we provide an overview of findings in each of the five areas of best practice, and briefly describe a sample of specific evidence in all five areas.

Three points should be kept in mind. First, these five practice areas are interrelated and support each other. For instance, the high-quality instructional leadership at each finalist district cannot be effective unless the leadership knows specifically what their students are supposed to learn, as spelled out in clear academic objectives set by the district for each grade and subject. Second, as with all effective strategies in education, local circumstances will influence how each district most effectively puts each practice to use. As the evidence presented below makes clear, the specific method that each finalist district uses to carry out each practice varies. But the end result is the same: high student achievement. Third, implementing change and getting promising results involves commitment and, at times, struggles and frustration. Garden Grove Unified School District Superintendent Laura Schwalm notes that the "real challenge" is not setting up new, effective practices, but "breaking down old systems that have been institutionalized for decades that really have not probably served us as well as they should." As she leads her high-performing Garden Grove district, Schwalm also stresses that "you've got to not lose your momentum when you get stuck" in your efforts to improve student achievement. Rather, you need to assess why you are stuck, "pick yourself up with renewed energy and go forward."[11]

Area 1: Curriculum and Academic Goals: The District Clearly Defines What Students Should Know in Every Subject and Grade

One key to success at each of the high-performing Broad Prize finalist urban districts is that the district clearly knows what the end goal is for each student in each subject and in each grade. Thus, educators at the district level—as well as educators in each district school and classroom—are very familiar with what each eighth grader should know in math by the end of the school year and what each third grader should be able to accomplish in reading. All teachers know what they are to teach and what their students are to learn. This sounds like common sense: in order to accomplish certain goals, you should know what those goals are.

Unfortunately districts all too commonly ignore this vital component of clearly laying out academic objectives.

These high-performing districts take the standards—meaning the specific academic objectives that students must attain in each grade and subject—set by their state as a base, and build their own district academic objectives. For example, in its Citywide Learning Standards, Boston Public Schools clearly defines what each student in its district should know in each grade and each subject. Located online at http://boston.k12.ma.us/teach/curriculum.asp, a separate Grade Level Summary for each grade lists specifically what students should know and be familiar with in English language arts, history and social studies, mathematics, science, and technology. For example, sixth graders will cover the topic "Systems in Living Things" in science and should then be able to:

- Describe the hierarchical organization of multicellular organisms from cell to tissue to organs to systems to organisms.
- Identify the general functions of the major systems of the human body (digestion, respiration, reproduction, circulation, excretion, protection from disease, movement, control, and coordination) and describe ways that these systems interact with each other.[12]

After establishing the standards, the districts then clearly communicate these learning objectives to each educator in the district. Norfolk Public Schools "unpacks" the state standards—meaning the district breaks each state standard down into usable, easily comprehendible pieces—in order to give teachers a clear understanding of what the state requires. Cathy Lassiter, director of Leadership and Capacity Building at Norfolk Public Schools, explains that "where there is one, two, and three parts of a standard from the state of Virginia, Norfolk has a Norfolk A, and a Norfolk B, and a Norfolk C." This enables teachers "to read and look at the state standard and then look at Norfolk's interpretation of that standard," which gives them specific guidance as "to how they should teach it."[13]

Likewise, in one concise, twenty-five page document, Long Beach Unified School District unpacks the California algebra standards for its teachers and provides them with sample problems and tasks that indicate student mastery of each standard. For instance, as displayed in Figure 10, one item breaks down the state's requirement that algebra students be able to verify that a point lies on a line and work with linear equations, and indicates what students should be able to accomplish when they have mastered this standard.[14]

Figure 10. Excerpt from Long Beach Unified School District Algebra Standards 2003

Standard	Unpacked	Level of Cognition	Proving Behavior	Task Analysis
7.0 Students verify that a point lies on a line, given an equation of the line.	Verify a point lies on a line, given an equation of a line.	Verify evaluation	Which ordered pair is a solution of $x + y = -3$ A. (-3,-3) B. (-2,1) C. (-1,-2) D. (6,-2)	Evaluate equations Order of operations Coordinate plane properties
Students are able to derive linear equation by using the point-slope formula.	Derive linear equations by using the point-slope formula	Derive synthesis using application	Find the equation of a line which has a slope of -2 and goes through the point (-1,3). Find the equation for the line that passes through (-2,5) and has a slope of -2/3.	Point-slope formula $y = mx + b$ slope is change [in] y to change in x

Once the finalist districts have established objectives and communicated them to teachers, the districts provide the teachers with materials that enable them to reach these goals, such as targeted and rich curriculum pacing guides and documents and videotapes that communicate examples of effective ways to teach each objective. Jefferson County Public Schools fosters students' ability to meet the state standards, Kentucky's Core Content of Assessment, and teachers' ability to enable students to do so through district Core Content Guides for each grade and subject. The excerpt from the Core Content Guide for eleventh grade history presented in Figure 11, for instance, identifies which state standards a teacher can integrate when teaching a topic such as the Great Depression. The Guides also indicate activities that students can undertake to master the content, and resources such as textbooks and online materials that the teacher can use to convey the subject matter.[15]

Area 2: Staff Selection and Capacity Building: The District Builds Strong Instructional Leaders and Highly Qualified Teachers, and Provides Effective Ongoing Training

Each of the high-performing Broad finalists clearly realize not only the importance of having well-defined goals through clear academic objectives, but also the central necessity of having educators who have the capacity to empower students to reach those goals. All of the identified high-performing urban districts build up the capacity of their staff in three vital ways: first, they develop and support strong instructional leaders, including each school's principal; second, they hire and support highly qualified teachers; and, third, they provide high-quality professional development that is closely aligned with the staff's instructional needs.

Figure 11. Excerpt from Jefferson County Public Schools Core Content Guide for Eleventh Grade History, Reconstruction to the Present

THE GREAT DEPRESSION AND THE NEW DEAL

Topic	Core Content	Activities	Resources
The Great Depression * Causes * Stock Market Crash (3 days)	Recognizes that cause-and-effect relationships can be analyzed by looking at multiple causation (e.g., individual influences, ideas and beliefs, technology, resources). (5.1.3)	Write on the board (or on the overhead) the terms—depression, slump, and recession. Ask students to speculate on how those terms might be arranged from less to more severe and explain why.	1. *The Americans*, McDougall Littell. Chapter 14, Section 1.
			2. http://www.mcdougallittel.com
	Explains how natural disasters may affect decisions relative to human activities (e.g., adopting building codes, buying flood insurance). (4.4.3) [cont'd]	As a class brainstorm reasons as to why the economy of a wealthy and booming nation (1920's U.S.) might become stagnant. [cont'd]	3. CD Rom Grolier Multimedia Encyclopedia.
			4. *The Century*, Peter Jennings and Todd Brewster. Chapters 3 & 4. [cont'd]

Strong Instructional Leaders: Selection and Support

1. Selection

A school principal's primary responsibility is to be an instructional leader. The selection of these instructional leaders in the Broad finalist districts is structured and targeted. In choosing a principal, these high-performing districts employ a comprehensive and focused recruitment and interview process. Of particular concern is whether the candidate has been successful in raising student achievement with students who are similar to the students at the district's schools, the strategies the candidate would use to raise student achievement, and how the candidate would employ data in this process. An excerpt from the Norfolk Public Schools principal interview questions presented in Figure 12 indicates this focus on instruction and achievement.[16]

The high-performing Broad finalist districts also foster the development of instructional leaders. Boston Public Schools prepares ten to fifteen fellows each year in school leadership and management in its Boston Principal Fellows program. Funded by The Broad Foundation and the U.S. Department of Education, the program involves a 12-month, intensive residency program during which each fellow works under one of the district's strongest principals and benefits from additional coursework, seminars, and teaching by community leaders and educators. Fellows receive a Massachusetts Initial Principal License and (with some personal expense) a master's degree or certificate of advanced graduate studies after completing the program. They also receive a salary in exchange for their commitment to work with Boston Public Schools for three years after completion of the program. Fellows are considered for principal positions in the district, although they are not guaranteed a position.[17]

2. Support

The Broad finalists provide tailored, ongoing, and high-quality support to all principals, both new hires and experienced veterans. Norfolk Public Schools, for example, established a Principal Mentor Program in 1999–2000 that provides three years of mentoring for new principals by distinguished retired principals. During new principals' first year in their position, they attend monthly workshops that focus on skills such as developing and communicating a school vision; building deep knowl-

Figure 12. Excerpt from Norfolk Public Schools Principal Interview Questions

PRINCIPAL INTERVIEW QUESTIONS

1. *Give us three examples of promising/best instructional practices used by teachers and why do you think those particular practices are important to support the acts of quality teaching and learning?*

Look Fors

- Using powerful research-based strategies (identify similarities and differences; summarizing and note taking; reinforcing efforts and providing recognition; homework and practice; nonlinguistic representations; cooperative learning; setting objectives and providing feedback; generating and testing hypotheses; questions, cues and advance organizers)

- Using writing as a power strategy; writing across the curriculum

- Integrating science and social studies in communication skills

- Frequent assessment to drive instruction

- Differentiation based on assessment/student needs (address needs of reluctant learner-gifted)

- Small group instruction/flexible groups based on need

- Active student engagement in real-life problems

- Use of technology to support teaching and learning

- Aligning teaching material and personnel resources to support student needs

edge about instruction and how to foster student learning; and effectively employing accountability systems. Follow-up with their mentors during the principals' second and third year augments the strong foundation set in this first year.[18]

In addition, the high-performing districts ensure that principals' professional development and meetings among principals focus on curriculum and instruction—primary elements for spurring student achievement. As Norfolk Public Schools Superintendent John Simpson explains, principals' development meetings and administrative meetings in the district center on "some instructional focus." Instead of business concerns and announcements, the meetings concentrate on "moving the district forward" academically. Likewise, Long Beach Unified School District focuses its professional development for district elementary and middle school principals on literacy.[19]

Highly Qualified Teachers: Recruitment, Induction, and Support

In addition to high-quality instructional leadership from principals, central to the Broad finalists' attainment of high student achievement is their excellent teaching corps. These high-performing districts stress finding teachers that fit the needs of particular district schools; aggressively recruit and train superior educators; and then provide ongoing and effective support and professional development to teachers.

1. Recruitment and Hiring

Boston Public Schools created the Boston Teacher Residency Program in 2003 based on the medical residency model. Teacher residents work under a master teacher in a classroom for an entire school year and take courses tailored to specific district needs. The intensive training ensures that the residents will possess the skills and experience needed to teach effectively from their first day as a classroom instructor. Funded by a coalition of twelve family foundations based in Boston, the program provides residents with $10,000 for living expenses, enables them to participate with no charge for tuition if they teach in the Boston Public Schools for three years after completing the residency, and grants residents the option to earn a master's degree through the program.[20]

2. Induction

Long Beach Unified School District requires first-, second-, and third-year teachers to undergo intensive professional development, including a seven-day institute that focuses on academic standards. The novice teachers learn what the district standards are, how to create lesson plans around these standards, and how to recognize which assessments test mastery of the standards. The teachers also learn how to "unpack" the standards—or break them down into pieces—and then construct an entire teaching unit around these various "unpacked" pieces.[21]

3. Professional Development

Professional development for educators has the reputation of being a waste of educators' time and a source of big paychecks for outside consultants.[22] In the high-performing Broad finalist districts, professional development has the opposite effect: training is targeted and highly productive in eliciting effective instruction and, thus, student achievement gains. District personnel use student performance data to determine what instructional programs would most benefit teachers and, as a result, advance student performance. The programs concentrate on teaching and often provide opportunities for educators to practice their classroom instruction techniques. For example, Boston Public Schools improves teachers' instruction through a coaching program. Classroom teachers, instructional coaches, and the school principal work as colleagues to determine how students learn best, what instructional practices are most successful, and what teachers are doing effectively and ineffectively. The principal and coaches at each school determine how to allocate coaches' time and set the school's professional development goals to address areas of academic weakness revealed by student performance data.[23]

Area 3: Instructional Programs: The District Employs Proven Academic Programs

All of the high-performing Broad Prize finalists display similar, effective approaches to the instructional materials their districts employ: these districts only implement programs that will enable their students to meet the academic objectives that the district has clearly set out. Hence why these districts establish their academic goals *before* establishing their academic programs. In addition, to ensure that the instructional programs are well-tailored to empower their students to meet these objectives, the districts employ student performance data so that they can pinpoint what the specific needs of district students are. In Jefferson County Public Schools, for instance, the district ensures that the instructional materials that each school selects are aligned with state standards as well as with that school's comprehensive school improvement plan. In addition, the district stresses that schools must study their disaggregated student performance data to ensure that the chosen instructional materials directly address the academic needs of their students. Likewise, Long Beach Unified School District undertakes a thorough district textbook adoption process that includes committees' evaluation of state adopted instructional programs to determine which is best aligned with district academic objectives and student needs in Long Beach.[24]

These high-performing districts also share another focus in their instructional material selection process: they only implement instructional programs that are proven to bring about academic achievement gains among groups of students that are demographically similar to their own district's students. As Cathy Lassiter of Norfolk Public Schools explains, "we look at what the research says about those particular instructional materials . . . most importantly, have they been used and been successful with children who are similar to the children we serve at Norfolk Public Schools?" Likewise, Boston Public Schools based its successful effort to implement a standards-based education in each classroom—what the district terms Whole School Improvement—on research of high-performing schools in high poverty circumstances across the country.[25] In sum, Broad finalist districts focus on whether instructional programs are backed up by evidence that they work. As discussed in chapters 2 and 3, the federal No Child Left Behind Act requires educational programs to be proven by evidence that they bring about achievement. The high performance of the Broad finalists indicates the significance and rightness of this requirement.

In addition, the successful Broad finalist districts pilot the instructional programs in their own district to ensure that the programs are effective with their students. For example, Boston, with the support of a local education foundation, piloted a reform model in twenty-seven schools that focused on improving instruction so that students could meet standards. District Superintendent Thomas Payzant closely watched the performance of those schools under the program, and only after seeing their success (and further refining the program) did Boston Public Schools expand the program to all district schools under its Whole School Improvement program. Garden Grove similarly pilots all of its instructional materials in each of its schools; the district receives feedback from teachers who use the materials and then submits a recommendation to the district's board of education.[26]

Once these high-performing districts put an instructional program into place, teachers throughout their districts receive the support needed to implement the curriculum effectively and, thus, can enable students to meet district academic objectives. A common tool is a chart or rubric that lays out the connection between the instructional program and academic objectives. For example, Norfolk Public Schools developed a "Connecting the Pieces" document, a one-page overview for each grade, that shows how the district's instructional programs, practices, standards, and assessments fit together. First-grade teachers, for example, can follow the chart to see what instructional strategies work best to help their first graders master a particular academic objective, and what assessment can best determine whether the students have mastered it. Similarly, Long Beach Unified School District employs pacing charts for third-grade mathematics that indicate how instructional materials, standards, classroom activities, and assessments interrelate, as illustrated by the excerpt in Figure 13.[27]

The districts also create and provide numerous other types of support and classroom tools. Long Beach's high school teachers noted a need for a common set of high school materials in reading and writing beyond that provided by available instructional materials, so they created a handbook that guides students in, for instance, how to take notes and prepare for an exam. Now all high school students across the district use this common guide.[28]

Area 4: Monitoring and Assessment: The District Consistently Employs and Monitors Student Performance Information and Teacher Performance to Reach Goals

Of central importance to all of the Broad finalist districts is their comprehensive and highly relevant system of assessing and monitoring student and teacher performance. These districts employ information on the current performance of their students and teachers to illuminate what specifically the district can do to enable students to perform at a higher level. Three elements are central to the assessment and monitoring approach in these high-performing districts: a complete and accessible district data system of student performance information; ongoing monitoring of student and teacher performance through benchmark

Figure 13. Excerpt from Long Beach Unified School District Pacing Chart for Grade 3 Mathematics

HOUGHTON MIFFLIN MATHEMATICS AND ASSESSMENT PORTFOLIO STUDENT WORKBOOK (APSW)

Chapter	Standard and Sub-concept	Houghton Mifflin Lessons	Vocabulary	New Content Lessons	Manipulative Activity Powerpoint or Imovie	OEM	Assessment Portfolio Student Workbook
5	Numeration: Multiplication Concepts	Do You Remember and Try These, 1, 2, 3, 4, 5, Quick Check, 7, 8, 9, 10, 11, Quick Check, Chapter Review (246-247), Chapter Test (248), Test Prep Cumulative Review (241)	multiplication array factors product commutative property	1, 6, 9, 11	Manipulatives for sets Number Lines Color Tiles Practice Game, "Multiplying Dots!" p.233 NLVM: Rectangle Multiplication	*310	62

assessments and teacher evaluations; and the use of student performance information to set goals, evaluate progress toward achieving them,
and adjust instructional practices to spur that progress.

The Broad finalist districts employ their systems for collecting and
using student performance data as integral tools to drive student achievement gains. Their data collection systems incorporate the characteristics
of an effective data system outlined in chapter 2. For example, their systems employ a unique identifier for each student so that the district can
trace student performance over time and disaggregate reports by numerous student characteristics, such as students' length of enrollment in the
district, their gender, and whether they are economically disadvantaged.
The No Child Left Behind Act requires such disaggregation; the way that
the Broad finalists employ this disaggregated data makes it clear why this
disaggregation requirement is such a positive one for our children. As Jefferson County Public Schools Superintendent Stephen Daeschner
explains, as a result of using longitudinal student performance data and
disaggregated data, "the district knows what's going on over years: are you
gaining, are you losing, are you getting better within [certain areas]?"[29]

In addition, the districts make their data system an accessible, valuable tool to educators throughout the district. My BPS-Assessment in
the Boston Public Schools provides teachers and principals with the
online capability to customize reports to answer specific inquiries, such
as how did the African American students in my class perform on the
language arts questions of the Massachusetts assessment?[30] Officials at
Boston Public Schools note,

> Perhaps the most significant impact of MyBPS to date [2004] is the
> ability for individual teachers to view student assessment data for
> their own class and for principals and instructional teams to view
> performance data for their entire schools. In an easy point and click
> environment, teachers can even view their own students' writing
> prompts on the MCAS test, the state's high stakes exam.[31]

A second common characteristic of these districts toward data and monitoring is their ongoing evaluation of teacher instruction and student achievement. In Long Beach, district staff follow detailed guidelines as they conduct "focused instructional walkthroughs" at schools to evaluate teachers and administrators. These walkthroughs serve to gather data not available elsewhere about teaching techniques and student learning. Likewise, Boston Public Schools requires schools to test all students in reading, writing, and math three times each school year, and analyze the results of those tests. The district specifies the content of some of these benchmark assessments, while others are compiled by teachers in a subject, grade, or other small group.[32]

A third characteristic of monitoring and assessment shared by these districts is their effective use of student performance information. The districts use the data to determine what district academic goals should be, whether students are reaching those goals, and how to adjust teachers' instruction to spur student achievement. For example, Boston Public Schools requires each school to base their school improvement plan on analysis of student performance data, although each school can determine which assessments to use (in addition to the state mandated assessment) and how to use data analysis to help form its plan. The district stresses that careful analysis of performance data is vital to enabling each student to improve academically.[33]

Area 5: Rewards and Intervention: The District Recognizes Success and Takes Action to Address Performance Weaknesses

A fifth area of practice is also central to the Broad finalists' success: rewarding those schools that achieve student performance goals and providing assistance and intervention to schools that display weaknesses in student performance. This follow-through by the districts ensures that schools will receive due recognition when they succeed and they will receive needed support when they are struggling. Because these high-performing districts employ student performance data effectively, the districts clearly know when rewards are merited and when intervention is required.

Although we more commonly hear about how districts assist or sanction schools when student achievement is poor, the Broad finalists realize that rewards for high performance are just as integral to eliciting student achievement. These rewards include monetary incentives, awards, and other types of recognition. Schools in Long Beach Unified School District that are recognized as a National Blue Ribbon School, a California Distinguished School, or a Title I Achieving School receive $10,000 to $25,000; school personnel decide how best to devote the funds to address school needs. In addition, Long Beach provides recognition to district schools that have attained continuous academic improvement over numerous years; these schools receive various awards from the school board and the district has flags painted on walls at these schools designating them as "star schools." Norfolk Public Schools encourages effective teaching through annually awarding a Teacher of the Year and an All-City Teaching Team. Boston Public Schools likewise understands the importance of recognizing principals whose schools attain high performance; principals at schools that make considerable achievement gains in English language arts and math receive incentive bonuses.[34]

The Broad finalist districts also realize how vital support is to those schools and students who are not meeting achievement goals. They rely on disaggregated student data to determine which students need extra help to improve their performance. As Pat Todd, executive director of student assignments at Jefferson County Public Schools, describes, "the best intervention begins with a good diagnosis of what students are able to do," so the district puts "a heavy emphasis on the use of disaggregating your data" to see how schools, classrooms, and individual students are performing.[35]

Once they determine which students and educators need further support, the districts use various, well placed intervention programs that serve as a spur to student achievement, not a punishment for falling short. Schools are certainly held accountable for student performance; in Boston Public Schools, schools undergo intensive review each year and a particularly thorough review every four years to ensure that students are meeting academic progress goals.[36] These high-performing districts fulfill the demands of these accountability systems in part because the districts support low-achievers in hands-on, effective ways.

The districts determine which are the struggling schools and focus resources on them. Long Beach determines which schools are low-performing, "focus schools" each year, and then devotes district office personnel who have expertise in the relevant content area to those schools to give hands-on support. Norfolk, likewise, assigns supplementary literacy and mathematics teachers to low-performing middle schools. The district also allocates remediation funds to schools with the aim of affecting those students who did not pass the state test or did not master core curriculum objectives.[37] These effective districts keep thorough records of the intervention that each student receives; this provides staff, for example, in Long Beach, with a grade-by-grade intervention summary for each student, which guides current and future decisions on interventions for that student.[38]

Once these districts spot the students that need extra help, the district provides intensive intervention programs as early as possible and continues the extra support until the student can perform on grade level. Norfolk Public Schools, for instance, focuses resources on ensuring that children in kindergarten through third grade can read on grade level. The district supports Virginia's Early Intervention Reading Initiative by devoting additional literacy and math teachers to schools where students need extra attention. Boston Public Schools provides its lowest-performing students in third, sixth, and ninth grade with a fifteen-month program that fosters their achievement; students experience summer school, a full school year with double-blocked periods (or extra time) in math and reading in which they work with specialists, and, if a student needs it, another summer school session. Superintendent Thomas Payzant describes the effort as "very, very successful." Likewise, incoming ninth graders in Garden Grove who are at risk—meaning their math or reading score is below the 20th percentile—take part in a ninth-grade academy, which involves a group of teachers (one English, one math, one science, one study skills) designated solely to those students and after-school mentoring by that cadre of teachers. Meanwhile, Garden Grove students in third, sixth, and ninth grades who lack grade-level literacy skills are provided with extensive literacy training, with the goal of enabling them to be on grade level by the next year.[39]

The preceeding descriptions represent only a sampling of the rich store of best practice information from Broad finalist districts available online (www.nc4ea.org and www.just4kids.org/bestpractice). Yet this overview of the common approach taken by Broad finalists to attain high student achievement indicates how all districts can provide a high-quality education to students. The specific way that each district should best implement these core practice areas will differ depending upon local circumstances, yet the basic building blocks are shared, proven, and replicable.

The Broad Prize, in sum, provides much needed direction to researchers, educators, policymakers, and parents. The Prize process grants researchers, who have long bemoaned the inability to ascertain how school districts across the county are performing, with a method to make this determination. Likewise, the Broad finalists' effective practices provide educators, parents, and policymakers with vision and direction to attain stellar results. Most importantly, as we apply the advances from The Broad Prize, the real winners will be our students as they benefit from a superior education.

5

Ensuring School Readiness: Making Significant Gains in Early Childhood Education

_____

When kids enter behind—and poor kids do, and minority kids do—they don't catch up. If we know that, then why don't we start earlier?

LINDA ESPINOSA,
NATIONAL INSTITUTE FOR EARLY EDUCATION RESEARCH

It's not just that "no child is left behind." It's how they come to us at the beginning.

DUNBAR BROOKS,
MARYLAND STATE SCHOOL BOARD MEMBER

RECENT BRAIN RESEARCH and studies of academic performance make the connection clear: children's intellectual development as well as their social and emotional growth during their earliest years is critical for their later academic success. Likewise, children who begin school behind their peers—meaning they lack certain academic building blocks and cognitive skills when they begin kindergarten—may never catch up and will likely get further behind as they proceed through school.[1] Personal and societal costs from a lack of school readiness are high: those children who fall behind experience frustration and, as a result, all too often drop out of school. On average, a high school dropout results in lost lifetime productivity and wages and other costs ranging from $470,000 to $750,000 (in 1997 dollars).[2]

As many as one third of children beginning kindergarten suffer from this "preparation gap," according to a 1991 National Survey of Kindergarten Teachers conducted by the Carnegie Foundation for the Advancement of Teaching.[3] Those children who start behind are predominantly from poor families or are minorities. Data from a recent U.S. Department of Education study of around 22,000 students display this great "inequality at the starting gate" according to children's socioeconomic status and race: before beginning kindergarten, children from the highest socioeconomic group scored 60 percent higher on cognitive skills than children from the poorest group, while African American children's average math achievement was 21 percent lower than white children's and Hispanics' math performance was 19 percent lower than whites'.[4] Likewise, studies demonstrate that, on average, children from low-income circumstances begin school a year to a year and a half behind children from middle-class families in cognitive skills, including language.[5]

Further, children who lack school readiness place an intense and often insurmountable burden on elementary and secondary schools. Among their many educational duties, all schools have the responsibility under the No Child Left Behind Act to ensure that every student is academically proficient by 2014; in elementary school, this means that every child must be able to read at grade level by the end of third grade.[6] Yet many schools are handicapped as numerous kindergartners who enter their doors do not possess the building blocks to be ready to learn.

Strong bipartisan cooperation on the issue of ensuring children's school readiness attests to its incontrovertible importance. In 1990, President George H. W. Bush and the National Governors Association, headed by Arkansas Governor Bill Clinton, established the Goals 2000, which were later signed into law in 1994 by President Clinton. The first goal concerned school readiness: "by the year 2000 . . . All students in America will start school ready to learn."[7]

The reasons for children's lack of school readiness and the preparation gap among children are multiple and varied. Disadvantaged children are often exposed to fewer words, fewer books, and fewer literacy activities—such as having a book read or a story told to them—in their homes than more economically fortunate children. Further, children from more affluent families are more likely to have attended preschool, particularly a high-quality preschool, than disadvantaged children.[8]

Although there are various causes for a lack of school readiness, promising research over recent decades has dramatically advanced our understanding of how the brain develops in a child's earliest years and what types of experiences prior to kindergarten translate into later school success. One central, hopeful conclusion is that children—particularly children in disadvantaged circumstances—who participate in a high-quality preschool program experience greater academic achievement and school success than those children who do not.[9]

So how do we ensure that excellent preschool education is available to each young child?[10] The task may seem daunting, but the goal is obtainable if we have the political will to accomplish it. The principles that would guide the effort to provide high-quality pre-kindergarten programs are the same that we have seen in chapters 3 and 4 concerning how best to educate children in grades K–12: we must effectively use data to identify those who are succeeding in providing a high-quality preschool program and in making it accessible, determine what they are doing to be successful, and emulate them.

Our focus here is to lay out the keys to one early childhood education effort that data establishes is reaping substantial gains for disadvantaged children in numerous states across the country: preschool programs anchored in the Language Enrichment Activities Program (LEAP) curriculum. Our aims in discussing these programs that use LEAP are threefold. First, we seek to highlight four principal elements of the programs' success:

- Employing a *high-quality, language-rich curriculum;*
- Ensuring *excellent teaching* through training and mentoring;

- Using *collaboration* among various educational, civic, corporate, and governmental groups to expand access to high-quality programs for all disadvantaged children in certain geographic areas; and
- Employing *data* concerning children's social, emotional, and academic development to continually monitor and enhance the programs' quality and effectiveness.

Our second goal is to demonstrate that—although each of these four elements is often stressed as individually important—it is the combination of all four that produces a high-quality and accessible early education program. Our third aim is to emphasize how the success of the preschools using LEAP and each of the factors leading to their success are replicable in diverse settings in every state. Thus, we aspire for others not to just recognize the value of LEAP and the efforts surrounding the program, but for others to build on its success through employing LEAP or similar language-rich curricula, high-quality teachers, a thorough data and monitoring system, and broad collaboration efforts to benefit our country's young children.

In order to demonstrate how the LEAP program approach integrates recent research on effective early childhood education and addresses pressing needs to enhance preschool quality, our discussion first concerns study findings regarding early childhood education and the quality of preschool education in our country. We then explore LEAP and each of its four keys to effectiveness.

The Key of a High-Quality Preschool Curriculum: Spurring Academic and Social-Emotional Development

Four fundamental findings undergird the conclusion that a high-quality preschool program enables children, particularly disadvantaged children, to attain higher academic achievement and success in school. First, brain and cognitive research demonstrate that young children have a greater capacity to learn—and garner greater benefits from learning—than was previously thought.[11] Second, studies also establish the broad and long-term benefits of quality preschool programs, including, for example, higher achievement scores, increased graduation rates, and fewer criminal arrests. As a result, the cost-benefit of such programs to society is large: every dollar invested in high-quality preschools generates $4 to $7 in returns from—among other things—decreased costs for special education and grade retention, increased individual earnings, and reduced crime.[12]

Third, we now also have an expanded view of the type of preschool program that is "developmentally appropriate." Increasingly, those in the early childhood education field recognize that an effective program incorporates and interrelates play and free exploration with academics. The resulting view of early childhood education is more multifaceted and realistic. The challenge is to determine how best to combine and balance educational and fun activities. Teaching academic skills to preschoolers is most effective—some would argue that it is only effective—when children are engaged, entertained, and enabled to develop their interests.[13]

Fourth, studies clearly establish that a preschool program must be of high quality for children to garner these positive benefits, and what the components of a high-quality program are.[14] Of all the academic components of a preschool curriculum, teaching young children the skills that will enable them to read is particularly important during the pre-kindergarten years. Much research establishes that young children's acquisition of fundamental pre-literacy skills is vital to their ability to read well later. The ability to read effectively is a critical foundation for success in various academic areas, because being able to read well leads to reading more and, thus, the acquisition of more knowledge across various academic subjects.[15]

Although the central importance of a quality preschool experience for our children is clear, the condition of pre-kindergarten programs in our country is varied.[16] Head Start, the largest federally funded pre-school program (serving 900,000 children in poverty in 2003), is a success story in many ways. The program provides valuable, comprehensive services, including nutritional services, health care examinations, immunizations, meals, and parental involvement opportunities. In addition, participation in Head Start enables children to develop social and emotional skills needed for school. Further, Head Start has placed an increased focus on enhancing children's early literacy skills as required by the 1998 Head Start reauthorization. This focus appears to be having heartening effects. While research in the late 1990s indicated that Head Start children were not attaining gains in certain crucial pre-literacy skills, a nationally representative study of children who entered Head Start in 2000 found that children experienced gains in vocabulary, writing skills, and (to a lesser extent) letter recognition, but only very slight gains in math skills. Yet, as researchers noted, students who had experienced Head Start still performed far below national norms. How can we enable these students—who typically enter Head Start with skills far below the national average—to catch up with their peers so that they are ready for kindergarten? Some preliminary studies of Head Start centers in New York conducted as part of the Head Start Quality Research Consortium indicate that Head Start children can make markedly larger gains in crucial pre-literacy skills if they experience a research-based curriculum that focuses on literacy. This research supports the goal of this chapter: enabling all disadvantaged children to benefit from a high-quality, language-rich preschool curriculum.[17]

There is an increasing focus nationally on maintaining all of Head Start's valuable social, nutritional, and medical services while further enhancing the program's academic components. As discussed below, various Head Start centers in Texas, for example, have stressed for years the academic quality of the program—and, by doing so, have attained stellar results. Likewise, at the federal level, both houses of Congress (in the bills reauthorizing Head Start, which have yet to be passed as of July

2004) and the Bush administration place particular emphasis on enhancing the academic components of Head Start and teacher quality to ensure that children are ready for kindergarten.[18]

Since the 1980s, states' involvement in early childhood education has increased dramatically. In the 2001–2002 school year, forty states funded forty-five preschool programs, which differed as to how well they were funded, which children had access to them, and what their quality standards were. Some of these state supported programs—such as the New Jersey Abbott District program offered in the state's poorest districts—provide particularly strong pre-kindergarten schooling, especially when compared with programs funded by other states.[19] Unfortunately, notwithstanding the strength of some state-funded early childhood education, "state preschool programs are failing the nation's children," according to a 2003 study by the National Institute for Early Education Research (NIEER). In addition to inadequate funding, the quality of state preschool programs is unfortunately quite low overall. There are a few bright spots of preschool quality, such as demanding teacher certification requirements in Oklahoma and the comparatively high-quality standards in Arkansas, Illinois, and New Jersey's Abbott District program. But as NIEER expresses, the general low quality of these programs across the country is cause for concern and should be remedied: "Without quality, children will not receive the educational benefits that states seek to provide, and some children may even be harmed."[20]

How can we provide high-quality preschool programs to all our young children? The LEAP approach and its adoption across the country provide a replicable model.

The Background and Success of a Language-Rich Curriculum

Beginning in 1989, through the vision and encouragement of Texas Instruments Chairman Jerry R. Junkins, the Texas Instruments Foundation sought to improve the educational performance of children from low-income families in the Dallas, Texas, community. The Foundation joined forces with Head Start of Greater Dallas in 1990 to establish a model preschool, the Margaret H. Cone Head Start Center, for ninety four-year-old children in a predominately African American neighborhood known as Frazier Courts. The Center is next door to federal housing projects in one of Dallas's most economically depressed neighborhoods, which is plagued by high rates of crime and unemployment. When the Cone Center was founded in 1990, families served by the Center had an average income of about $7,000, 39 percent of the parents of children at the Center had graduated from high school, and single parents headed 90 percent of Cone Center households.[21]

The Foundation funded enhanced services—more than usually available through a Head Start center—during the Center's first two years of operation (1990–1992), including a full-time staff that included two social workers and a nurse practitioner, extended hours, a year-round program, increased staff salaries and benefits, and a parent employment program. These enhanced services benefited many, and Cone children experienced gains in various developmental areas. But crucially, after two years of the enhanced social services, Cone children were not making gains in cognitive and language skills. After attending the Cone program, they were still beginning kindergarten with ability levels developed far below expected levels for their age, according to the Batelle Developmental Inventory. Indeed, the Cone children were no more ready for elementary school than those who had not benefited from Cone's services. After completing kindergarten, Cone children's scores on the Iowa Test of Basic Skills (ITBS) were consistently at the 20th to 30th percentile. The TI Foundation recognized that it had to do more to address the Cone children's academic needs.[22]

In 1993, the Foundation asked the Southern Methodist University (SMU) Learning Therapy Program to develop a curriculum that would promote the development of the Cone children's cognitive and language abilities. Nell Carvell of SMU created the Language Enrichment

Activities Program (LEAP), a research-based and age-appropriate program that is interactive and congruent with Head Start's focus on social and emotional development. Carvell recognized the vital importance of exposing these children from poverty—whose home life often lacks books, conversation, and pictures—to language richness. Before creating LEAP, Carvell tested the Cone children using the Peabody Picture Vocabulary Test and found that most were around eighteen months behind in their development of oral language. They also lacked awareness of sentence structure and an age-appropriate vocabulary. To address these needs, LEAP concentrates on developing children's vocabulary, listening skills, phonological awareness, fine motor skills, and knowledge of math and science concepts. Children are not seated at desks; rather the day involves enjoyment and play as children learn from self-initiated and group activities as well as multisensory experiences around the classroom. Although teachers are not circumscribed in how they communicate the materials, a LEAP instruction guide provides teachers with a model, ideas, and assistance. The curriculum and materials cost approximately $1,000 per classroom, and teachers can receive teacher training and course-training materials for approximately $900 per year. A dual-language LEAP curriculum is also available for Hispanic children.[23]

Soon after the implementation of LEAP, it became clear that the curriculum was enabling Cone children to be developmentally ready for academic success in kindergarten and later grades. Children who took the ITBS in 1990–1992 after their year at Cone—prior to the implementation of LEAP—scored in the 20th to 30th percentile on average. After Cone children began experiencing LEAP, their average ITBS scores from 1995–2001 jumped to the 60th to 70th percentile. Cone children have continued to perform consistently between the 60th and 70th percentiles on nationally standardized tests.[24]

The academic gains that Cone children experience through the LEAP curriculum continue into elementary school. Children who attend Cone who then attend the local Dallas Independent School District elementary school—Frazier Elementary—outperform their peers at Frazier who have not had the benefit of LEAP. In spring 2001, 85 percent of third graders who had experienced the LEAP curriculum at the Cone Center could read at or above grade level on the Stanford 9 test as compared to 66 percent of Frazier third graders who had not attended Cone. Likewise, in 2002 on the Stanford 9, 90 percent of Cone third graders could read at or above grade level versus 74 percent of non-Cone third graders. In 2002, 100 percent of third graders who had attended Cone and then kindergarten through third grade at Frazier passed the Texas state reading assessment. Partially as a result of the Cone students' excellent performance, Frazier elementary earned the Texas Education Agency rank of "Exemplary" in 2002—an outstanding accomplishment considering that over 92 percent of Frazier's students are from low-income families (2003 percentage).[25]

Expanding LEAP Across Texas and the Country

In 1996—after seeing three years of notable student performance gains by Cone students who experienced LEAP—the Texas Instruments Foundation desired for other low-income students around Texas to benefit from similar high-quality programs. The Foundation enlisted the Lyndon Baines Johnson School of Public Affairs to study how to encourage others across the state to replicate the model. The result was a funding proposal for the state: *Texas Ready-to-Read Grants: An Extension of the Texas Reading Initiative.* With support from Texas First Lady Laura Bush and Governor George W. Bush, in 1999, the Texas legislature appropriated $17 million to fund enhanced early childhood pre-reading programs based on the LEAP/Cone model. The measure represented a significant commitment by the state to systemic deployment of a language-rich, research-based curriculum to environments serving young children across Texas.[26]

In addition, the proven success of LEAP at the Cone Center has led various groups across the country to seek out and adopt the program. As of May 2004, approximately 65,000 children have benefited from the LEAP curriculum in over 1,500 Head Start and public school classrooms.

Preschool educators in approximately forty Texas towns and six large Texas cities employ LEAP. This number includes over 500 classrooms in Dallas and about 100 classrooms in both Houston and Austin.

In addition, over 500 predominantly disadvantaged preschoolers in Tuscaloosa County, Alabama, experience the LEAP curriculum. Their gains under the program were apparent after only one year: children in classrooms that employed the curriculum increased their score on the DIAL-3 assessment of developmental skills from an average of around 31 to 32 percent at the start of the school year to an average of around 58 percent at the end of the school year.

The California Reading and Literature Project implemented the program in 125 classrooms in California in 2002, while fifty classrooms in Caddo Parish in northern Louisiana used LEAP during the 2003–2004 school year. Likewise, children in Maine and Virginia began to take part in the curriculum during the 2002–2003 school year at pilot sites. In addition, Head Start agencies and school districts in Alaska, Florida, Georgia, Kansas, Oklahoma, Pennsylvania, and Washington have purchased sets of the curriculum.

Four Replicable Keys to
High-Quality, Accessible Preschool

What are the key elements of the LEAP curriculum that have brought about substantial gains in children's cognitive and language skills? And what are the keys to the widespread adoption of this quality preschool program? Four primary components have led to these outstanding results: a high-quality, language-rich curriculum; high-quality teacher training and support; community collaboration to make the program accessible to all needy children; and the use of data to ensure program effectiveness and to enhance the program in targeted ways.

1. A Quality, Language-Rich Curriculum

One of the most important—and repeatedly cited as among the most lacking—aspects of early childhood education is the quality of the curriculum.[27] As a National Research Council report concludes, an effective preschool curriculum incorporates lessons and objectives across a broad range of developmental and content areas. The curriculum also must reflect the latest research on how preschoolers learn best and what they should be learning.[28]

LEAP does so, particularly with its focus on pre-literacy development for disadvantaged children. As Nell Carvell, LEAP's creator explains, "LEAP is based on 'developmentally appropriate practices' that also provide opportunities for children from impoverished backgrounds to 'play' with the alphabet and numbers, and learn about books and literacy so they can enter kindergarten performing at an appropriate academic level." LEAP thus exposes disadvantaged children to language richness through books, conversation, stories, and numerous, enjoyable exercises that the children participate in throughout the day. The curriculum revolves around seven areas involving language, such as Language with Stories, which focuses on interactive listening to stories read from books; Language with Sounds, which develops phonological awareness through identification of rhyme, words in phrases and sentences, compound words, and syllables through repeating, clapping, and tapping; Language with Math and Science, which fosters children's learning of basic math and science concepts; and Language with Letters, which focuses on naming the letters of the alphabet and pre-writing fine motor development. Teachers interweave these seven areas of competency into ten thematic subject areas, such as Seasons and Weather and Self and Family.[29]

Each activity incorporates both enjoyment and developmental

growth. For example, children discover what the letter /r/ sounds like and that certain words begin with /r/ by pulling various objects from a bag that all begin with the sound /r/. The bag may contain, for example, a radio, a rabbit, a ring, a roller skate, a robot, and a ruler. Children name each object as they pull it out of the bag. The teacher and children then say the names of all of the objects together. The teacher points out that the objects all start with the same sound and then instructs the students on how to say /r/. The teacher then asks them to repeat the names of the objects that they pulled out of the bag (which are still displayed on a table), and for them to name the sound that each word starts with. The teacher may then have the children sit in a circle and play "Riddle me Ree, I see something that you can see, and it starts with /r/."[30]

Children also learn math and science concepts in an enjoyable and age-appropriate way. For instance, children place cut out shapes of clouds, the sun, and raindrops on a bulletin board-size calendar to indicate the weather for that day. The teacher and children discuss what the shapes are called and what rain, snow, and sunshine look and feel like. At the end of each week, the teacher asks the students to count how many days of sun (or rain, or clouds) they have experienced that week—and then to count how many days of sun (or rain, or clouds) they have had that month. The children may sing songs associated with weather, such as, "It's Raining, It's Pouring," and the teacher may read related books to them, such as *Rain Makes Applesauce* or *It Looked Like Spilt Milk.*[31]

2. High-Quality Teacher Training and Support

Although an outside observer may simply see the enjoyment of the children as they engage in these activities, the way in which these activities are taught is crucial for children to benefit from them. As Amy Wilkins, executive director of the Trust for Early Education, states, "The single best way to help better prepare children for school is to ensure that each classroom is staffed by a well educated teacher." Nationwide, many chil-

dren in preschool—perhaps most of them—are not instructed by qualified teachers. Preschool teachers' salaries are quite low; as a result, many
early childhood educators leave the profession. And likely, many who are
interested in the profession never enter it because of the low pay. Teachers in state preschool programs, for example, receive a salary that is less
than half the average $43,000 paid to public K–12 teachers. Head Start
teachers are paid about half the amount (averaging $21,000 in the
2000–2001 school year) received by public school teachers. As of 2002,
preschool teachers' average salary was $16,000.[32]

The National Research Council advises that every teacher of three- to
five-year-olds should possess a bachelor's degree with a specialization in
early childhood education and child development. Although some programs—such as New Jersey's Abbott District program—follow this standard, funding challenges and thus low teacher salaries make this
recommendation difficult to carry out in all preschools at present. Only
eighteen states require preschool teachers to have a bachelor's degree. As
of February 2003, less than 20 percent of Head Start teachers possessed a
bachelor's degree.[33] Further, although specifics vary between the Senate
and House bills, pending federal legislation reauthorizing Head Start
would require half of all Head Start teachers (or half of all teachers in
each Head Start center) to hold a bachelor's degree in early childhood
education or a related field by 2008 or 2010.[34]

Although these degree requirements are promising steps toward a
more qualified and knowledgeable preschool teaching corps, funding
and logistical constraints indicate that it may be some time before all
preschool teachers hold a bachelor's degree in early childhood education. In the meantime, how can we ensure that those who instruct our
young children are doing so effectively? Indeed, even those who hold
bachelor's degrees and other credentials may not be instructing children
well.

LEAP teacher training provides a valuable approach to equipping
preschool teachers with the skills they need to effectively instruct young

children; the teacher quality that results is central to LEAP's success. Many preschool instructors at Head Start and in other programs have not received a quality basic education in reading, spelling, writing, and learning strategies. To ensure the effectiveness of LEAP teachers, the Southern Methodist University preschool teacher education program provides thorough teacher training. The program—which includes 40 to forty-five hours of training in lecture and practice format—focuses on teachers' reading and language skills and the application of LEAP materials. The instructors who lead the LEAP teacher training must fulfill some exacting requirements: they must have earned a master's degree, take part in extensive LEAP training, and be experienced as a LEAP teacher. There are three types of training programs: one offers three hours of undergraduate credit from SMU; another offers three hours of graduate credit, and is intended for those who already hold a bachelor's or master's degree; and the third offers a non-credit workshop. About 1,800 teachers and teacher assistants had taken part in LEAP training as of February 2004. In addition, a 2004 federal grant (discussed below) will support the training of an additional 105 early childhood educators during the 2004–2005 school year to effectively use LEAP. The federal grant will also fund a twice-yearly observation of each LEAP teacher's class to pinpoint areas of strength and weakness (such as classroom environment, best teaching practices, and LEAP implementation) and a follow-up conference with the teacher. The information generated by these observations will thus enable teachers to focus their efforts on how to teach more effectively.[35]

In addition, in Dallas preschool classrooms, after LEAP teachers begin instructing children, specially trained mentors provide the teachers with ongoing support and training. As of June 2004, twenty-one mentors serve LEAP instructors in the Dallas Independent School District, sixteen mentors assist LEAP teachers at Child Care Management Services (CCMS) facilities, with another three mentors recently hired by SMU to support CCMS. Various trained specialists at Head Start also serve as mentors. In addition, funds from the 2004 federal grant will enable the majority of LEAP classrooms in Dallas to have a mentor. Further, beginning in the 2004–2005 school year, LEAP mentors serving those Dallas classrooms participating in the U.S. Department of Education grant will have a personal digital assistant (PDA) on hand when they visit each classroom. Mentors will be able to administer child-friendly assessments to each child and access results on the spot. As a result, mentors and teachers immediately can note the strengths and weaknesses each child has at that particular point of the school year, and thus can tailor instruction to meet that child's needs.[36]

The mentoring program has been highly successful in supporting and enhancing LEAP instructors' teaching. Classroom observations and data indicate renewed energy and professionalism in the preschool classrooms. Teachers report feeling appreciated by their peers in the upper elementary grades, and preliminary test scores on the DIAL-3 assessment indicate the children's high level of academic growth. Other than retirement, there has been almost no turnover in the mentor staff.[37]

3. Community Collaboration

Even after a pre-kindergarten program qualifies as a high-quality program featuring well qualified teachers and a strong curriculum, we face yet another hurdle: how to enable as many children—particularly disadvantaged children—to benefit from the program as possible? Access to preschool is a problem at both the federal level—because Head Start does not receive enough funds to serve all eligible children—and at the state level—where inadequate funding and lack of programs in certain geographic areas of a state mean that there are not even enough seats for disadvantaged children, much less for all young children.[38]

One key to overcoming this problem of children's access to preschool is through broad-based community collaboration. Bringing preschool providers, K–12 educators, nonprofit entities, foundations, and business interests together to leverage and focus their knowledge, assets, and efforts can greatly expand the number of children served by early childhood education. In recent years, many private businesses and state funded schools have formed public-private partnerships through which the businesses invest funds in improving the structural and educational quality of preschools. Businesses—especially in states such as Arizona, California, Florida, and Texas, which have fast-growing populations of young people—are increasingly realizing that their investment in pre-kindergarten serves their interest in having a qualified workforce in future years. Other collaborations are working to extend access to quality preschool. Preschool for All in Houston, Texas, which involves over 100 government, business, early childhood, philanthropic, and public education entities, aspires to make quality pre-kindergarten available to all Houston three- and four-year-olds. In addition, collaborations between a state and various early education providers can also be effective, according to a 2003 study by the Education Development Center (EDC). EDC found that when states support coordination of efforts among pre-kindergarten, local child care programs, and Head Start, such partnerships can increase the accessibility and quality of preschool for eligible young children.[39]

One collaborative effort—Dallas Kids—is reaping substantial gains for disadvantaged children in Dallas. This broad-based coalition of early childhood education providers, business interests, higher education providers, researchers, and other community leaders is working to ensure that every Dallas child in poverty enters kindergarten ready to learn. Dallas Kids' goal is to provide every economically disadvantaged child with an early childhood education experience that is research-based and proven; coalition members have identified LEAP as the high-quality curriculum that will enable them to reach this aim. Other parties, including the federal government, have recognized the worth-while nature of Dallas Kids' goals and the beneficial effect of such widespread community collaboration; indeed, the federal government awarded Dallas Kids a $500,000 grant in 2004 to further its efforts.[40]

Dallas Kids was formed through the labors of the nonprofit Foundation for Community Empowerment and its founder, J. McDonald Williams, chairman emeritus of the Trammell Crow Company. The coalition represents a broad cross section of Dallas organizations—organizations that are well-placed to make the coalition's goal of reaching every disadvantaged child a reality. These include the major early childhood education providers, including the Dallas Independent School District, Child Care Group, Head Start of Greater Dallas, and providers of Child Care Management Services, as well as the Dallas Citizens Council (composed of CEOs of the top 250 companies in Dallas), the Dallas Housing Authority, Education First Steps, FaithLEAP Dallas, the Foundation for Community Empowerment, the Greater Dallas Chamber of Commerce, Southern Methodist University, Texas Instruments Foundation, Work-Source for Dallas County, and YMCA of Metropolitan Dallas.[41]

By 2010, an estimated 29,000 three- and four-year-old children from low-income families will live in Dallas County, approximately 19,000 of whom will live in the geographic area served by the Dallas Independent School District (DISD). Within the next five to ten years, the Dallas Kids collaboration aims for 75 to 85 percent of these 19,000 disadvantaged young children in the DISD area to be experiencing the LEAP curriculum. The group will also enable children who live in Dallas County but outside of DISD to experience the high-quality program. In the 2003–2004 school year, over 11,000 economically disadvantaged children experienced LEAP through preschool programs provided by DISD, Head Start, and some CCMS providers. Dallas Kids members thus served 58 percent of the targeted 19,000 children from low-income families in the DISD area—and thereby surpassed the Dallas Kids goal of serving 45 to 50 percent of these children in 2003–2004.[42]

Coalition efforts have also made possible another crucial element of ensuring the academic success of disadvantaged kids in Dallas: the ability to follow the academic performance of children who experience LEAP in preschool throughout their K–12 years in the Dallas Independent School District. As a result of collaborative efforts of DISD administrators and researchers with other early education providers in the coalition, every child who is in a preschool classroom that uses LEAP is assigned a unique, privacy-protected number for record purposes, so that it is possible to track how that child progresses academically from beginning elementary school through high school graduation. Although such linkage of preschool academic information with performance in later grades is rare, it is vital for purposes of ensuring that early childhood education is effective, and to be able to adequately respond to the academic and social-emotional development needs of each child.[43]

In addition to community coalitions, collaboration between early childhood educators and elementary school teachers is also integral to enabling children to progress through their early academic years with success. For example, one critical key to the success of Cone Center children in elementary school is the close working relationship between Cone and Frazier Elementary (the elementary school that most Cone children attend). Communication between teachers at Cone and Frazier is ongoing; Frazier's kindergarten teachers and principal and Cone's teachers and directors meet quarterly. In addition, every spring, Frazier educators receive information about the developmental levels of incoming children who attended Cone. This collaboration—in combination with strong leadership at Frazier, Frazier's use of a quality elementary curriculum that focuses on literacy, and active support from Dallas Independent School District administration—have enabled Cone children to continue their academic success as they progress through school.[44]

4. Use of Monitoring and Data to Ensure Effectiveness

As in all levels of education, the only way to know if a preschool program is spurring children's development is to assess whether it is doing so. Likewise, the only way to know how we can improve a preschool curriculum and specifically tailor it to best meet children's needs is to ascertain which parts of the program are effective and which are not. As scholar David Dickinson attests, "If Head Start and community child-care providers are to take seriously the need to support children's early language and literacy needs, they must have tools that help them assess the quality of their programs."[45]

Debate, however, surrounds the topic of preschool assessment. One contingent argues that assessing preschoolers can garner unreliable results because young children's abilities may fluctuate each day, and their development of skills is sporadic and uneven. Others argue that assessments can decontextualize knowledge and recognition, such as by having a child recognize an emotion through a picture. These are among the foremost arguments asserted by critics of the National Reporting System, an assessment initiated in 2003 of Head Start students' skills in such areas as letter recognition, vocabulary, and math ability. Administered to over 430,000 children during its first administration in fall 2003, the assessment is the largest of preschoolers every undertaken.[46]

Experiences in connection with assessments and the LEAP curriculum have made two principles apparent. First, in order for assessments to generate accurate and useful results, assessments must be child-friendly, child-centered, reflective of children's skill levels, and administered by a person knowledgeable about and trained in the assessment instruments. Assessments used to gauge the effectiveness of LEAP often request children to simply point to a picture that corresponds with what the administrator says. Other assessments may require a child to respond orally. The sample question in Figure 14 demonstrates the child-friendly nature of these assessments. (In order to not compromise the test instrument, this is not an actual question from this instrument.)[47]

Further, in order to obtain reliable, helpful results, the administrator also must be sensitive to the desires or moods of the child that day. Bill D. Ball, a licensed specialist in school psychology who assesses children at various Head Start centers in the Dallas area and consults with the Texas Instruments Foundation, displays this sensitivity:

If a child does not want to participate in the assessment, we don't force the issue. We tell the child "OK." Then we try back in a few days. Children typically agree to assessment the second time they are asked. If a child is sick or is having a rough day, they are removed from the assessment list for that day.

Figure 14. Sample Question Type from Peabody Picture Vocabulary Test, Third Edition

Peabody Picture Vocabulary Test, Third Edition (PPVT-3)*

*Note: this is not an actual item on this test

Examiner says: Point to horse

However, usually, Ball notes, "most children enjoy the assessments," since "they view the assessment as fun, like a game," in which they get focused attention from an adult, and get to select stickers for themselves as a treat after completing the assessment. "The most common problem," according to Ball, "is that once children in a class get to know the assessment administrators, they all beg the administrators to take them next."[48]

The second principle that assessments of LEAP's effectiveness have made plain is that, when properly administered, assessments provide invaluable, enlightening information that can directly benefit young children's development. Indeed, without assessments, the intense need of children at the Cone Center for a language-rich curriculum would not have been apparent. These disadvantaged children would have tragically continued to start school with low cognitive skills. Because the Texas Instruments Foundation employed assessments to gauge the effectiveness of the Cone Center services since its inception in 1990, the Foundation was able to pinpoint where weaknesses were in the program, and tailor a new curriculum—LEAP—to successfully address these children's underdeveloped language and cognitive abilities. In addition, ongoing, regular assessments after LEAP was in place have enabled those with the Foundation, Nell Carvell, and others at SMU to note precise areas of the curriculum that need bolstering or precise skills of the students that need extra attention.

Our understanding of many aspects of early childhood development and education has come a long way in recent years. We now know how important academic and social-emotional development is during the first five years of life to later academic success and, ultimately, earnings and quality of life. We also know the crucial role that quality preschool programs play in ensuring that young children—particularly disadvantaged children—develop those cognitive skills needed for school success.

Our next step is to make these quality programs available to children nationwide. The evidence for how to do so—and what a quality curriculum looks like—is before us through examples like the LEAP program. Employing the central components of a language-rich curriculum, quality teacher training and mentoring, community collaboration, and an effective assessment and monitoring system to continually enhance the program can make a quality—and crucial—early childhood education available to every child.

6

Inspiring and Rewarding Excellence in High Schools: Advanced Placement Incentive Programs

———

Historically, minority students have not performed as well as Anglo students but performance seems to be a function of opportunity, not ethnicity. This includes the opportunity to have superior teachers, the opportunity to be in an environment of high expectations, and the opportunity to have resources for quality instruction.

DALLAS INDEPENDENT SCHOOL DISTRICT, FINAL REPORT, ADVANCED PLACEMENT PROGRAM, 2000–2001

AP . . . , as far as I can tell after 20 years of watching it closely, has done more to improve U.S. high schools than any other program during that period.

JAY MATHEWS, *WASHINGTON POST*

AMONG the educational issues of greatest concern in our nation today is whether we are educating our high school students in a manner that prepares them to perform well in the workplace and in college. Statistics concerning high school graduates' preparation for higher education and well-paying jobs are discouraging, if not alarming. Over 70 percent of high school graduates enter either four- or two-year colleges, yet a minimum of 28 percent of these students enroll immediately in remedial math or English courses—meaning courses that cover content that students should have learned in high school and for which students do not earn college credit. During their years at college, 53 percent of students take one or more remedial math or English classes. The percentages of poor and minority college students in remedial classes are even higher. In addition, college graduation rates are markedly low: only 45 to 49 percent of students who earn ten or more credits in higher education earn a college degree; that percentage decreases to 25 to 37 percent of African Americans and 25 to 28 percent of Hispanics.[1] Meanwhile in our increasingly knowledge-based workplace, most jobs that pay wages sufficient to support a family call for high skills. For instance, gaining and keeping a job in manufacturing—a sector formerly open to those with minimum skills—now demands advanced mathematical skills learned in higher-level courses like Algebra II. Yet at most only half of African American, Hispanic, and Native American high school students take Algebra II while only two-thirds of white and Asian high school students do so.[2]

How do we ensure that our high school graduates are well-prepared for the workplace and higher education? Many factors contribute to students' preparation, or lack of it. But fortunately, recent research and results in classrooms across the country clearly point to a proven, effective key: the rigor of a student's high school curriculum is the best predictor of college success and graduation from college. Likewise, students who take more challenging classes in high school garner higher paying jobs than those students who take a less rigorous course load. The benefits of a challenging high school curriculum for college graduation are particularly pronounced for African American and Hispanic high school students—an especially promising finding as we strive to close the achievement gap between the different races.[3]

Among the most rigorous—and most nationally accepted and respected—courses are Advanced Placement (AP) courses, which educate high school students in college-level material in subjects ranging from math and sciences to English and studio art. If students pass a course exam administered nationally by the College Board, they can earn college credit. Long seen as an avenue for academically advanced, affluent, white students to groom their transcripts for college admissions, Advanced Placement courses are increasingly viewed as a key to driving higher educational achievement by all students, particularly economically disadvantaged and minority students.

But how do we encourage students to participate and succeed in these rigorous Advanced Placement courses? Data clearly points to an effective means for driving higher participation and success in AP courses, especially among minority students and students in poverty: Advanced Placement Incentive Programs. These voluntary programs (1) provide monetary rewards for students, teachers, and principals for success on AP exams; (2) supply enhanced training and support for teachers; (3) prepare middle and high school students for AP courses in later years; and (4) provide extra assistance for students through tutoring and AP preparation sessions. Where Advanced Placement Incentive Programs are in place, AP participation and the number of passing scores on AP exams have skyrocketed—particularly among groups traditionally underrepresented in AP courses and among AP examination takers.

This chapter presents how Advanced Placement Incentive Programs provide a proven tool to bolster the high school academic success—and the later college and life achievement—of students. To establish how central these incentive programs are to addressing key issues in secondary and postsecondary education and the workplace, we first discuss more fully the research establishing the crucial and clear benefits of a rigorous high school curriculum and how students in poverty and minority students often have less access to challenging courses. We then describe the contours and extensive growth nationwide of the Advanced Placement program. Our discussion then centers on the origins and expansion of AP Incentive Programs, including how Congress and state legislatures have embraced these incentive-based programs and how data establishes that AP Incentive Programs work. Lastly, we lay out five interrelated components that are vital to the success of AP Incentive Programs:

- Experienced AP teachers—called *lead teachers*—who support and train other AP teachers as well as teachers of students in earlier grades who are preparing for AP courses (pre-AP teachers of pre-AP courses);

- *Intensive training of AP and pre-AP teachers in subject-matter content;*
- *Extra tutoring and preparation sessions for students;*
- *Financial incentives* for students, teachers, and principals; and
- *Professional management* through an outside, nonprofit organization that vigilantly supports and monitors the process.

A central theme of our discussion is how AP Incentive Programs that include all five of these fundamental components are replicable in school districts across the country.

A Rigorous High School Curriculum: The Importance of Access

Research clearly shows that students who undertake a rigorous high school curriculum generally attain higher levels of academic success, have higher college attendance and graduation rates, and earn greater amounts of money as adults than fellow students who take less challenging high school courses. Students' high school course load is more determinative of whether the students will complete college with a bachelor's degree than the students' test scores, class rank, or grade point average, according to a 1999 study by U.S. Department of Education researcher Clifford Adelman. Adelman also finds that high school students who complete a course beyond Algebra II (such as pre-calculus or trigonometry) more than double the likelihood that, upon entering college, they will complete a bachelor's degree. The positive impact of a challenging high school curriculum on bachelor's degree completion for African American and Hispanic students is particularly pronounced—and is much greater for these minority students than for white students. For example, only 45 percent of African Americans who enter a four-year college earn a bachelor's degree, but 73 percent of African Americans who took a rigorous high school curriculum receive their degree. Adelman's study thus points to how to effectively address the gap in rates of bachelor's degree attainment between whites and minorities. "This is a matter of doing the right thing for minority students: not merely admitting them to college, but making sure that they have the momentum to complete the degrees," Adelman concludes. Otherwise, he notes, "we defraud them."[4]

Likewise, students who ultimately get the highest-paying jobs took the most high school mathematics courses, according to a 2003 study by Educational Testing Service researchers Anthony P. Carnevale and Donna M. Desrochers who analyzed data from a national longitudinal survey. Eighty-four percent of workers in the highest-paying 25 percent of jobs (meaning those earning more than $40,000 a year) have taken Algebra II or a higher-level math class in high school. Over half of this well-paid group has taken a course more advanced than Algebra II, such as trigonometry or pre-calculus. This compares with only one half of young workers who earn less than $25,000 a year who have taken Algebra II or a more advanced high school math course, and 20 percent of these low-wage earners who have taken a higher-level math course than Algebra II. The study also finds that high wage earners are much more likely than low-wage earners to have taken English honors, composition, and literature courses in high school, while low-wage earners more often have taken remedial English or English as a second language.[5]

The way to improve the academic and economic prospects of our high school students, then, is clear: we need to ensure that each student experiences a rigorous high school curriculum. Fortunately, between 1990 and 2000, students increased the number of high school course credits that they earned. According to the National Center for Education Statistics' national High School Transcript Survey, in 2000, students earned 26.1 course credits, of which 15.0 were in core English, science, math, and social studies courses. This was an increase from 1990, when high schoolers took an average of 23.6 course credits, of which 13.7 were in core subjects. These figures, however, do not indicate whether these credits were earned in demanding courses.[6]

Further, a vast opportunity gap in course-taking exists: minority students and students from poor families are underrepresented in advanced courses. For instance, by 1998, 56 percent of Asian and 45 percent of white high school graduates had taken at least one advanced science or math course, but only 26 percent of Hispanic and 30 percent of African American graduates had completed such classes. Hispanic and African American graduates also were less likely than whites or Asians to take advanced English courses. Indeed, one scholar surmises that at least 25 percent of the difference between whites' and African Americans' test scores on the 1995 Third International Mathematics and Science Study resulted from African Americans' less rigorous course taking. Only 30 percent of African Americans in the study had taken precalculus or calculus, as compared to half of white students.[7]

One reason for minorities' lower representation in honors courses— a reason stressed by Sharif Shakrani, deputy executive director of the National Assessment Governing Board—is that Hispanic and African American students are less prone to gain a strong foundation in math during their middle school years. Another reason is that many schools, particularly urban and rural schools serving poor populations, do not offer challenging courses, such as Advanced Placement courses. As of 2002, about 62 percent of schools offered Advanced Placement; many of the schools that did not served minority students and students in poverty. Indeed, both the National Research Council and College Board President Gaston Caperton have recognized the imperative of making access to AP courses more equitable. "By extending AP to many more inner city and rural schools, we can raise the quality of instruction and levels of achievement for students who have historically been underserved," Caperton has stated. "This is an equity issue."[8]

The aim of this chapter is to show how we can successfully address this equity of access issue and spark academic achievement, particularly among minority students and students from low-income families, through Advanced Placement Incentive Programs. At the core of these successful incentive programs is the nationally respected Advanced Placement program.

The Advanced Placement Program

The College Board established the Advanced Placement program in 1955 to enable high school students to undertake college-level work during high school. Courses are offered in nineteen disciplines, ranging from calculus and chemistry to art history and macroeconomics. Participation in the program is voluntary. Students who earn a score of 3 or higher on a 5-point scale can receive course credit or advanced placement at nearly 3,000 colleges and universities (with policies on how much credit students receive varying widely among institutions).[9]

Initially serving solely top-achieving students in a small number of private and suburban high schools, the AP program is now widely adopted and commonly available to any student who has a desire for challenging high school coursework and is enrolled in a district that offers AP. As of 2000, the program was offered in about 12,000 high schools located in every state in the United States, as well as in Canada and 63 other countries. The 1990s witnessed a large growth in the Advanced Placement program: in 1990, 330,000 students took 490,000 examinations; this increased to 760,000 students taking over 1,270,000 exams in spring 2000. By 2003, over one million students took over 1.7 million AP exams. Advanced Placement participation by minority students and economically disadvantaged students, in particular, has increased. Between 1998 and 2002, while overall participation rates rose 48 percent, minority student participation rose 77 percent while participation by students in poverty rose 101 percent. Despite these increases, minority students and students in poverty are still underrepresented in AP courses. For example, African Americans and Hispanics represent

31 percent of high school students nationally, but make up only 17 percent of students taking AP tests.[10]

What accounts for the fast growth and increased interest in Advanced Placement? The program benefits from a strong reputation; as the College Board assesses, "In the midst of debates about the quality of American education, AP is regularly cited as a high-quality program that works." Even critics like Yale professor William Lichten recognize that "all sides give AP approval." Advanced Placement is recognized for its high standards and demanding curriculum. Bob Schaeffer, of FairTest, usually a critic of standardized tests, praises the design of AP: he notes that because the curriculum and standards are well-publicized, AP levels the playing field, since one is confident that all students nationwide are tested on the same curriculum. Likewise, the program provides measurable, nationally comparable results. For each subject, students across the country take the same exam, and grading is done for all exams nationally by a team of graders. Thus, if a student from an economically challenged, inner-city or rural school earns a 3 on an AP exam, that student's performance met the same standard as a student from a well-known elite prep school who scored a 3. The passing score is not only personally fulfilling to the student, but is also a valid indicator of that student's performance level to college admission officers nationwide. As Georgeanne Porter, University of Missouri at Columbia undergraduate admissions director, notes, "the quality [of AP] is unquestioned." [11]

Further, Advanced Placement courses upgrade the rigor of a high school's curriculum. Proponents note how the challenging coursework thus serves to energize inner-city schools. In addition, research establishes that taking an AP course enables students to attain academic success in high school and become better prepared for college, whether they take and pass the AP exam or not. According to the National Center for Education Statistics, high school graduates who took math and science AP courses or math and science courses in another advanced high school program, the International Baccalaureate program (IB), earned a mean GPA of 3.61, while those who took neither AP nor IB math or science courses earned a mean GPA of 2.85.[12]

Likewise, a National Center for Educational Accountability study of Texas students from the eighth grade through college graduation found that minority students and students from poverty who participated in AP in high school performed significantly better in college—in terms of performance on a college readiness exam administered on college entry, first year GPA in college, the number of credits earned during their first

Figure 15. Advanced Placement and Texas Students' College Readiness

AP Enhances Texas Students' Readiness for College

*% of Students Entering Texas Public Colleges
or Universities Who Passed the State College Readiness Exam
or Were Exempt from Taking the Exam*

	Passed an AP Exam in High School	Took, Did Not Pass an AP Exam in High School	Did Not Take an AP Exam in High School
Anglo (37,004 students)	95%	79%	50%
Hispanic (18,019 students)	89%	56%	25%
African American (7,312 students)	87%	50%	17%
Low-Income (15,167 students)	84%	54%	20%

Based on (1) a cohort of students graduating from High School in Spring 1998 and enrolled in a Texas Public College or University by Fall 1998, totaling 67,863 students, and (2) AP Exams in the core academic subjects of English, Math, Science, and Social Studies.

"College Ready" students passed all sections of the Texas Academic Skills Program (TASP) test, or were exempted from taking the TASP.

Source: National Center for Educational Accountability

year of college, and the likelihood of obtaining a bachelor's degree in four or five years—than their peers who did not participate in AP during high school. (See Figures 15 through 17.) For example, 89 percent of the Hispanic high school graduates who had passed an AP exam in high school and who entered a Texas public college or university passed or were exempt from taking a college readiness exam, while only 25 percent of Hispanic graduates who had not taken an AP test in high school passed or were exempt from the test. Likewise, 40 percent of economically disadvantaged students who had passed an AP exam in high school

Figure 16. Advanced Placement and Texas Students' College Performance

AP Enhances Texas Students' Performance in College
Average First Year GPA of Students
at Texas Public Colleges and Universities

	Passed an AP Exam in High School	Took, Did Not Pass an AP Exam in High School	Did Not Take an AP Exam in High School
Anglo (37,004 students)	3.11	2.72	2.35
Hispanic (18,019 students)	2.87	2.42	2.03
African American (7,312 students)	2.81	2.47	1.93
Low-Income (15,167 students)	2.95	2.45	2.01

Based on (1) a cohort of students graduating from High School in Spring 1998 and enrolled in a Texas Public College or University by Fall 1998, totaling 67,863 students, and (2) AP Exams in the core academic subjects of English, Math, Science, and Social Studies.

Source: National Center for Educational Accountability

attained a bachelor's degree within five years of high school graduation, compared to 7 percent of students from poverty who had not taken an AP exam.[13]

Yet Advanced Placement has not escaped criticism. In addition to a primary complaint that the program is not accessible to minority and economically disadvantaged students (as discussed previously), another critique made by the National Research Council is that the Advanced

Figure 17. Advanced Placement and Texas Students' College Graduation Rate

AP Enhances Texas Students' College Graduation Rate

% Receiving BA Degree from Texas Public Colleges and Universities within 5 Years of High School Graduation

	Passed an AP Exam in High School	Took, Did Not Pass an AP Exam in High School	Did Not Take an AP Exam in High School
Anglo (47,647 students)	57%	43%	22%
Hispanic (19,868 students)	47%	26%	8%
African American (7,813 students)	42%	36%	11%
Low-Income (22,028 students)	40%	24%	7%
Total (78,079 students)	57%	37%	17%

Based on (1) a cohort of students graduating from High School in Spring 1998 and enrolled in a Texas Public College or University by Fall 1998, totaling 78,079 students, and (2) AP Exams in the core academic subjects of English, Math, Science, and Social Studies.

Source: National Center for Educational Accountability

Placement curriculum does not provide quality, in-depth learning experiences, but rather presents students and teachers with too much to cover in too little time. The College Board recognizes the breadth-versus-depth challenge, and is working with the National Science Foundation and National Research Council to enhance science courses. Still other critics claim that it is a mistake to make AP courses available to all. Lichten maintains that the College Board focuses too much on participation rates to the detriment of program quality and passage rates on AP exams. Still others claim that only "A" students are able to handle the work. As discussed below, student performance in schools that make AP available to all show conclusively that all students—not just the high-academic achievers—can handle the curriculum with tailored support and effective teaching. A fourth criticism is that AP teachers are of uneven quality and receive little support from the College Board. AP Incentive Programs address this issue directly by providing enhanced teacher training and ongoing, intensive support from experienced, successful AP teachers. Lastly, some complain that devoting resources to college-level courses like AP in high school is misplaced when the fastest growing course areas in colleges involve remedial, high school-level courses. Certainly, we must reduce the need for remedial college courses by ensuring that students gain the knowledge they need for college in their high school coursework. However, reducing the number of AP courses will not help to alleviate the large percentage of students who are unprepared for college; indeed, doing so could likely increase the number of unprepared students. Through open-enrollment, voluntary Advanced Placement courses, students who might not otherwise experience academic rigor in high school are participating in advanced courses—and, in turn, they are becoming well-prepared for college.[14]

Even in light of criticisms, the strong reputation and benefits from AP are clear. In a recent poll of readers of the *American School Board Journal* (who are predominately educators), 80 percent indicated that they desired for more of their students to take AP courses. As these educators understood, Advanced Placement provides foundational benefits for success in high school, higher education, and the workplace. As the College Board has recognized and the U.S. Department of Education has well-stated, "AP courses are valuable to any student planning to attend college, but are of even more importance to students without family experience of college attendance, among peer groups who do not consider education a promising option for the future, or in schools not emphasizing college preparation."[15] It is these students—who are often economically disadvantaged or are minorities—that Advanced Placement Incentive Programs likewise particularly benefit.

The Concept and Origins of
Advanced Placement Incentive Programs

In the early 1990s, the federal government was to build the Superconducting Supercollider in Waxahachie, Texas. One Supercollider board member, Peter O'Donnell, realized that in order to attract approximately 2,000 scientists, physicists, and engineers to the Waxahachie area south of Dallas, it was necessary to improve the quality of the area's schools so that those recruited to the project could be assured that their children would receive a high-quality education. Private schools were distant from the Supercollider site, so Peter O'Donnell and Carolyn Bacon, executive director of the O'Donnell Foundation, developed the idea of Advanced Placement Incentive Programs to bolster curriculum quality and student performance at the public schools, whose performance up to that time had been average. The incentive program concept took the already widely respected and established Advanced Placement program—including its curriculum, standards, and teacher training—and supplemented it with financial incentives. For every student who passed an AP exam in science, math, or English, the AP teacher received a bonus and the school received $100. The student received $100 as a mini-scholarship. In addition, the O'Donnell Foundation paid for training of AP teachers.[16]

The success of the Advanced Placement Incentive Program at nine schools near the Superconducting Supercollider site was clear and substantial. The number of students taking AP exams increased sixteen times from 47 to 770 between 1990—the year prior to the first year of the incentive program in 1991—and 1995. Likewise, the number of students passing exams during this period increased from 43 to 379.[17]

Arguably, the incentive program approach was among the most successful and long-lasting outgrowths of the Supercollider project (which was cancelled by Congress in 1993). As the effectiveness of the incentive concept at the schools near the Supercollider site became clear, officials of the Dallas Independent School District (DISD/Dallas ISD) approached the O'Donnell Foundation in the mid-1990s to request the implementation of an incentive program in the DISD. The demographics of the Dallas Independent School District are challenging: over 90 percent of students are minorities (as compared with a minority population of around 30 percent at the Superconducting Supercollider schools) and around three quarters of DISD students are from poor families (as compared to the statewide average of approximately 60 percent). The average SAT score of DISD students is 850, far below the U.S. average of 1018 (as of 2003). Thus, success with an Advanced Placement Incentive Program in the Dallas Independent School District would indicate that similarly structured incentive programs could be effective in raising students' academic expectations and achievement in even the most challenging of circumstances.[18]

There was initially some opposition to the incentive program in DISD on the grounds that it was "creaming," meaning it would only benefit high-performing white students in the district, and not Hispanic or African American students. Yet supporters—including those at the O'Donnell Foundation—knew that the Advanced Placement program was excellent, that the AP incentive classes would provide high-quality teaching, and that the incentive program would be voluntary and open to all students. It soon became clear after the 1995 initiation of the DISD incentive program that the program exceeded all expectations, not only with respect to increasing AP participation and exam-passage rates but also in closing the achievement gap between minority and white students.[19]

In 1995, the year before the O'Donnell Foundation began its five-year commitment to fund the DISD Advanced Placement Incentive Program in math, English, and science in nine high schools, 139 students from those nine schools passed Advanced Placement exams. In 2000, 754 students from the nine participating schools passed. Gains were particularly dramatic by minority students: after the incentive programs had been in place for one year at the nine high schools, the number of African American and Hispanic students who took AP exams jumped from 53 to 310, and the number of exams taken by African American and Hispanic students increased from 64 to 400.[20]

By 2003, almost all DISD high schools participated in an AP Incentive Program, with ten schools funded through the Texas Instruments Foundation and another five supported by Roger Enrico, former CEO of PepsiCo. In these fifteen high schools—populated largely by minority and economically disadvantaged students—the percentage of AP exam takers is almost double the United States average while AP exam-passage rates in math, English, and science by minority students is three times the United States average (as of August 2003).[21]

Figures 18 through 21, for example, display the notable gains in the number of students passing AP exams in the ten Dallas ISD schools funded, as of 2004, by the Texas Instruments Foundation. Eight of these ten schools were among the nine original DISD schools sponsored by the O'Donnell Foundation's Incentive Program that began in 1996. The two additional schools that joined the program when TI began supporting the program in 2001 are demographically similar to the original eight.

The number of passing AP test scores in these ten schools took a substantial jump during the first year of the DISD AP Incentive Program in 1996 (from 157 to 361), and in 2003 numbered over 1,000. Further, the AP passage rate in these ten DISD schools was over 30 percent higher than the United States and Texas average in 2003. AP performance by African American and Hispanic students is particularly strong: the number of passing exams in AP math, science, and English by African Americans and Hispanics has increased almost six times since 1996, and the AP passage rate by African American and Hispanic students at the ten schools was over twice the national and Texas average in 2003.

The success of the AP Incentive Programs in Dallas has caught the attention of educators and legislators in Texas and throughout the country; as Carolyn Bacon notes, "they look at Dallas and they know that if it

Figure 18. Advanced Placement Passing Scores at Ten Dallas Independent School District Schools, 1990–2003

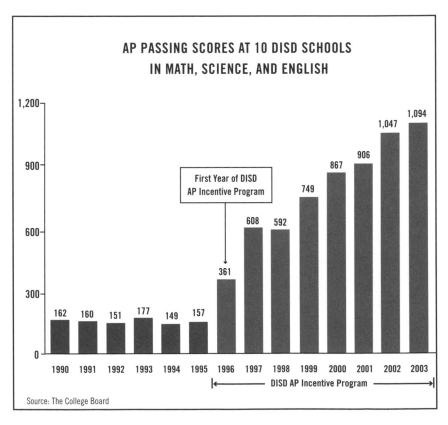

works in Dallas, it can work in their schools." To fill the needs of school districts in Texas who desired AP Incentive Programs and of donors who desired to establish incentive programs but did not have the interest or ability to manage the programs, in 2000, the O'Donnell Foundation created the nonprofit Advanced Placement Strategies, Inc. (AP Strategies). Staffed by some of the country's most successful AP teachers, AP Strategies works with schools, districts, and monetary donors to set up AP and pre-AP Incentive Programs and then supports and manages the programs. The private donor commits to fund the program in a district for five years; the donor can specify which AP subjects will be included in a particular incentive program (such as math, science, and English or studio art and music theory) as well as which district will benefit from the

Figure 19. Advanced Placement Passing Scores per 1,000 Juniors and Seniors, Ten Dallas ISD Schools, Texas, and the U.S., 1995–2003

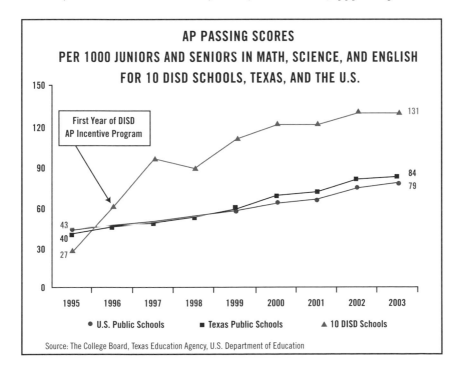

donor's funds. Gregg Fleisher, president of AP Strategies, describes AP Strategies' role as a grant administrator and fiscal agent for the donor and as a partner with the school district in providing curricular and logistical support. The multiple roles work, Fleisher notes, because "we tell the districts going in that our role is to assist you however we can."[22]

As of June 2004, AP Strategies coordinates incentive programs in twenty-six districts across Texas that cumulatively involve twelve different AP subjects, ranging from calculus to biology to studio art. Gains in Advanced Placement participation and exam passage rates have been impressive. In one year—between 2002 and 2003—the students in incentive schools across Texas served by AP Strategies increased the

Figure 20. Advanced Placement Passing Scores at Ten Dallas ISD Schools for African Americans and Hispanics, 1995–2003

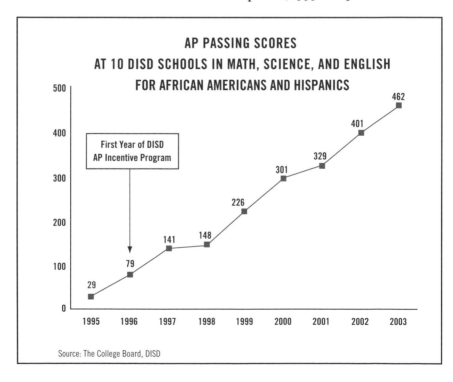

Source: The College Board, DISD

number of passing scores in math, science, English, and social studies exams by 25 percent (from 2730 to 3414 passing exams). In Tyler Independent School District, passing scores on math, science, and English exams have increased 77 percent over two years between 2001 and 2003, after the APS managed incentive program began in 2002. Passing scores at Tascosa High School in Amarillo, Texas, in all AP subject tests have increased 191 percent in three years, after the inception of the incentive program in 2001.[23]

Figure 21. Minority Advanced Placement Passing Scores per 1,000 African American and Hispanic Juniors and Seniors, Ten Dallas ISD Schools, Texas, and the U.S., 1995–2003

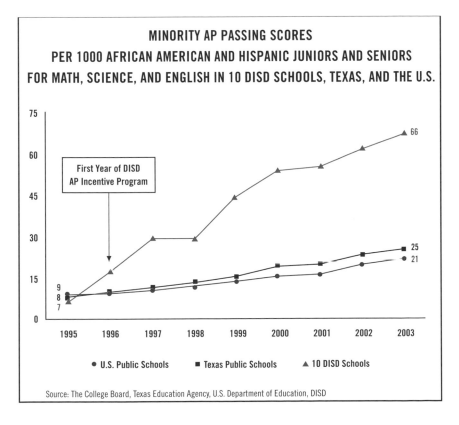

In addition, students and teachers in studio art, art history, and music theory incentive programs currently managed by AP Strategies have generated notable results—and have succeeded in closing the achievement gap between the races on Advanced Placement performance. The O'Donnell Foundation funds AP art and music incentive programs in twenty-eight Dallas area schools (including public and private schools), and has done so since 1995 in nineteen schools. Between 1995 and 2003, AP arts and music exam participation rates increased almost four times in the nineteen schools, and passing scores on art and music AP exams multiplied nearly three and a half times. At these nineteen schools, students take AP art and music exams at almost four times the national average and over four times the Texas average per 1,000 juniors and seniors. Even more notable, students in these schools pass AP exams at nearly six times the national average and almost five times the state average per 1,000 juniors and seniors enrolled. Recognition of the quality of the students' and teachers' work has been abundant: students in the Dallas area AP arts incentive programs earned over $7 million in scholarships in 2002–2003 and two of the twenty AP arts incentive program teachers have received Fulbright scholarships. Further, the passage rate on AP art and music exams by minorities and whites in these incentive schools is nearly equal; in some schools Hispanic students pass more often than whites. These results demonstrate how AP Incentive Programs can enable us to attain a much sought after goal in education: closing the achievement gap between the races.[24]

The incentive approach to Advanced Placement programs has caught on not only in numerous districts across Texas, but also in various state legislatures, state education agencies, and in Congress. Many states have enacted legislation promoting Advanced Placement. Some states support teacher training; others mandate that AP is offered in every high school; and others subsidize examination fees. Kentucky, Texas, and Florida have enacted among the most effective. Kentucky's Commonwealth Diploma Program initiated in 1987 predated the creation of the O'Donnell incentive programs in Texas. Students can earn the Commonwealth Diploma by taking at least four AP courses; students receive reimbursement of their AP exam fees if they pass at least three AP exams. Since 1987, around 9,000 Kentucky high school graduates have earned the diploma. Kentucky schools have significantly expanded their offerings of AP courses, while state agencies make virtual AP courses available over the internet.[25]

In 1993, the Texas legislature passed the Texas Advanced Placement Incentive Program, and fully funded the program in 1997. The Texas program provides schools $100 for each student passing an Advanced Placement exam and pays schools a one-time $3,000 grant for equipment. The Texas program also covers $450 for teacher training, and awards each teacher $250 when they first teach an AP course. The state pays for $30 of each student's $82 AP exam fee. Since 1997, the percentage of schools offering AP courses in Texas has increased markedly; in 1996 only 54 percent of Texas public high schools offered AP courses, a rate which trailed the national average of 58 percent. By 2003, 71 percent of public high schools in Texas offered AP, which exceeded the national average of 66 percent. The number of high school students who took at least one AP exam increased 149 percent between the full funding of the program in 1997 and 2003, while passing scores increased 133 percent during the same period.[26]

Florida enacted a statewide AP Incentive Program in 2001, under which teachers receive $50 for each of their students who passes an AP exam. Teachers in low-performing schools who have one or more students pass an AP exam receive $500. After the incentive program went into effect, the number of students in low-performing Florida schools who were enrolled in Advanced Placement courses increased dramatically—from 4,000 to 7,000 students in one year. Florida now leads the nation in the number of African American students enrolled in Advanced Placement courses.[27]

Meanwhile, there has been bipartisan support for expanding Advanced Placement and Advanced Placement Incentive Programs at the federal level since the late 1990s. In 1997, Democratic Senator Jeff Bingaman of New Mexico and Republican Senator Kay Bailey Hutchison of Texas jointly and successfully worked for the enactment of a federal AP Incentive Program. Then, in 2001, the two senators succeeded in having that program become part of the No Child Left Behind Act. In addition to providing grants to expand opportunities for students (particularly economically disadvantaged students) to participate in the AP program, the federal incentive program provides funds to states to cover all or part of the test fees for AP exams for economically disadvantaged students. This federal AP test fee program has benefited students from low-income families across the country. In the first year of the program, in fiscal year 1998, $3 million was appropriated to thirty-two states that applied for the monies; of these, twenty-three were able to offer AP exams to students in poverty free-of-charge in May 1999; the other nine provided exams to these students at vastly reduced rates.[28]

Future prospects for the federal AP Incentive Program are bright: both contenders for the 2004 presidential election support making AP more accessible. Democratic Senator John Kerry advocates offering AP in every U.S. high school. President George W. Bush called for the expansion of Advanced Placement in schools serving low-income populations in his State of the Union address in 2004. President Bush has also requested to more than double funding for the AP Incentive Program from $24 million to $52 million in fiscal year 2005. His administration also promotes Advanced Placement Incentive Programs for students in poverty as a race-neutral alternative to increasing diversity on college campuses.[29]

These federal and state incentive programs enable an organization like Advanced Placement Strategies to leverage the funding it receives from donors. Because state and federal funds cover portions of the costs of, for example, teacher training and student exam fees, AP Strategies can devote donor funds to other central aspects of the incentive program, such as costs of student preparation sessions, stipends for AP and pre-AP teachers, and financial rewards for successful students and teachers.[30]

The Proven, Replicable Way to Structure
an AP Incentive Program for Success

The proliferation of AP Incentive Programs at the state and federal levels demonstrates the widely recognized value of AP and incentives to increase students' success in AP. The particulars of programs vary widely, with some states paying for AP teacher training, others paying exam fees, while still others pay teachers or schools for student success. These state and federal policies have proven valuable in spurring students' involvement in AP and with supporting teacher preparation. Yet if an educator, potential monetary donor, parent, or policymaker desires to establish an AP Incentive Program in their local school district, how should they structure the program to ensure success both in terms of student participation and achievement in Advanced Placement—particularly among students traditionally underrepresented in AP? The structure of the highly effective incentive programs begun by the O'Donnell Foundation and currently coordinated by Advanced Placement Strategies provides a comprehensive and replicable model; data from student results across Texas prove that the approach works. Five components are vital keys to the AP Strategies Advanced Placement Incentive Program approach:

- *Lead teachers*
- *Intensive teacher training in content*
- *Extra time on task for students*
- *Financial incentives*
- *Professional management*

All components are interrelated and interdependent, notes AP Strategies President Gregg Fleisher: "if you take away one of the components, the whole program won't be as powerful because some of the things that are desperately needed won't get accomplished." Another essential aspect of program success is a multi-year commitment by the district and the donor to the incentive program; Advanced Placement Strategies requires five-year commitments by all involved parties. This assures educators that the incentive program is not just this year's fashion, but rather will continue and will garner results.[31]

1. Lead Teachers

In Advanced Placement and academic courses generally, one fact remains constant: the quality of the teacher is key to the academic success of students. Thus, one significant area of the Advanced Placement program that educators and researchers note needs enhancing is the support and training that AP teachers receive. The College Board has no control over who teaches AP courses or what their qualifications are and does not certify AP teachers. Although teachers benefit from Advanced Placement workshops offered by the College Board and five-day AP summer institutes, this training is not mandatory. According to the College Board, 59 percent of schools do not require their AP teachers to attend. Nationally, in 1999–2000, only around 56 percent of the approximately 100,000 AP teachers participated in the institutes or workshops. As a result, teachers of demanding AP and pre-AP courses often lack training and knowledgeable support throughout the year to optimize their teaching performance. The outcome—particularly for novice AP and pre-AP teachers—can be frustration in a challenging job and disappointing performance by their students on the AP exams. Experienced and successful AP teachers made this need clear to the O'Donnell Foundation when the Foundation set up the Dallas ISD incentive program in the mid-1990s. With the guidance of these AP teachers, the Foundation instituted two fundamental and highly effective components of its AP Incentive Program: lead teachers and intensive teacher training. All of the incentive programs managed by AP Strategies incorporate these two teacher support components to great effect. "The incentive program is so much more than just checks and money to teachers," assesses Dorinda Rickels, a Dallas ISD lead teacher in calculus. "The support system is just as important."[32]

The lead teacher is an expert AP instructor who supports and enhances the teaching of the other AP and pre-AP teachers in the district. The principal criterion for earning the position of an AP lead teacher is that the teacher has a proven, successful record of enabling students to pass Advanced Placement exams. The lead teacher earns full salary and benefits from the school district, plus a stipend from the incentive program donor. The amount of the stipend varies between districts and may range from around $2,000 to $18,000; the stipend for lead teachers in Dallas Independent School District, for example, is $10,000. The number of lead teachers in a district varies depending on which academic subjects are part of a district's incentive program. But generally each district has one English lead teacher, one math lead teacher, and three lead teachers in the sciences: one for each of biology, chemistry, and physics.[33]

Lead AP teachers devote part of their time to teaching—meaning they often teach one AP course—and spend the remainder of their time supporting AP and pre-AP teachers in their district. The job involves more flexibility than if they were teaching full-time, but also more responsibility. Their task is to increase the number of AP exams taken in the district and the number of passing scores on the exams. As a result, lead teachers wear many hats and handle a lot of work. As Fleisher describes, about half of their time is often devoted to their own AP students, while about a quarter of their time is spent visiting and assisting the other AP and pre-AP teachers in schools throughout the district. How lead teachers assist other teachers differs depending upon needs. For example, lead teachers may lend support to other teachers on how to best teach a concept or what material to cover or they may conduct tutoring sessions to illustrate to other teachers how to best help individual students. English lead teachers may help new AP or pre-AP teachers grade essays to demonstrate grading techniques that the lead teacher learned through experience. Lead teachers spend the remaining quarter of their time preparing for student preparation sessions and teacher training (which are explained in more detail below). "They instinctively know what it takes for one student to learn a rigorous curriculum and concepts," notes Carolyn Bacon.

Thus, they "constantly are helping the other teachers figure out how to teach quadratic equations or literature analysis."[34]

In some districts, teachers called "circuit riders" work alongside lead teachers. Like lead teachers, circuit riders travel between district schools. But even more than lead teachers, circuit riders will take over teaching in a class while classroom teachers observe circuit riders' effective teaching techniques. Experience with five schools in Dallas ISD demonstrates the effectiveness of the circuit rider/lead teacher model: after one year of having assistance from both lead teachers and circuit-riding teachers, the five schools combined had 49 students pass the AP calculus exam—a large jump from their combined previous best of 12 passing students.[35]

Advanced Placement Strategies assists the lead teachers with whatever needs the lead teachers have. If lead teachers are strong and experienced with their responsibilities, AP Strategies asks those lead teachers how it can assist and will aid with manpower, materials, or other needs. If lead teachers are less experienced, members of AP Strategies staff—who each have highly successful track records as AP teachers—are available to guide the novice lead teachers in all aspects of their job, from advising them how best to assist teachers to how to juggle their many responsibilities.[36]

2. Intensive Teacher Training in Content

Lead teachers play a crucial role in the second key component of AP Incentive Program success: intensive training of AP and pre-AP teachers in subject-matter content. The National Research Council concluded in 2002 that "many of the teachers who participate in AP professional development activities do so on their own time and at their own expense" and that the professional training in Advanced Placement available nationally is voluntary and limited to two options: College Board regional offices offer one- to two-day workshops and independent agencies offer summer institutes, which are usually five days long. To address the intense need of AP and pre-AP teachers for greater and sustained training, AP Incentive Programs administered by AP Strategies involve a comprehensive, sustained teacher training regimen composed of four parts. AP and pre-AP teachers:

- Attend both a two-day *College Board workshop* and a *five-day summer institute;*
- Meet monthly with all teachers who teach their subject in middle and high school (a *vertical team*) to develop and align curriculum;
- Receive support from AP Strategies staff members through *regular classroom visits;* and
- Participate in two or more *additional days of training* with district AP and pre-AP teachers led by the district's lead teacher in their subject.[37]

Unlike a majority of schools that do not require teacher attendance at College Board workshops and summer training institutes, teacher participation in these workshops and institutes is required in AP Incentive Programs coordinated by AP Strategies. Depending on the incentive program structure in the district, the donor or the district may cover the costs for attending. Although the training AP teachers in other districts receive may be limited to these College Board workshops and national institutes, in the AP incentive districts, these national programs form but one sector of a comprehensive training regimen.[38]

The second component of teacher training—monthly vertical team meetings—serves the crucial purpose of ensuring that students have the necessary academic foundation from earlier grades to succeed in AP courses. "Access is not enough," notes U.S. Secretary of Education Rod Paige. "We need to make sure that more of our students are prepared to succeed in these rigorous courses." Bolstering the rigor and quality of coursework in the pre-AP grades thus advances the goal of making success in Advanced Placement courses more attainable by all, particularly students from poverty and minority students. Various groups, including the College Board through its AP Vertical Teams and Building Success programs and the Charles A. Dana Center's Advanced Placement Equity Initiative at the University of Texas at Austin, are stressing the importance of pre-AP enhancement through vertical teams.[39]

In the AP Incentive Programs coordinated by AP Strategies, vertical teams are composed of teachers of grades seven through twelve who teach the same subject. Led by the AP teacher, the team members work on the middle and high school curriculum to ensure that students learn the necessary building blocks each year in preparation for AP. The vertical team in math, for example, is headed by the high school's AP calculus teacher, and math curriculum from seventh through twelfth grade is aligned so that students enter the calculus classroom well-prepared to grasp the challenging course. As a result of working in vertical teams, teachers gain a clear understanding of one important goal of their teaching: preparing their students for rigorous work in Advanced Placement courses. Their students in turn start setting their sights on success in AP courses as early as seventh grade.[40]

Vertical teams in English, math, and science also benefit from pre-AP curriculum guides and lesson plans developed by master English, math, and science teachers from across the country through the impetus and funding of the O'Donnell Foundation. In 2002, a group of highly successful English teachers collaborated concerning how they successfully taught students to prepare them for AP English. The collection of their materials and knowledge resulted in the *Laying the Foundation* curriculum guides for pre-AP English teachers of grades six through ten. In 2003 and 2004, top science and math teachers collaborated to produce *Laying the Foundation* curriculum guides for pre-AP math teachers in grades six through eleven and pre-AP science teachers in grades six through eleven. These guides represent the first effort to lay out the skills students must master in pre-AP classes to succeed in an Advanced Placement course, to specify at what point skills must be taught, and to delineate at what level students should be performing as they progress through their pre-AP years. Training in the use of the guides is critical to their effectiveness. Demand for the guides and for training has been strong: during summer 2002, for example, 4,000 teachers across Texas were trained in the English guides.[41]

Each guide features a set of concepts that are central to success in that AP subject. Sixth graders learn these concepts, and the concepts are then reinforced in later grades. Pre-AP English students, for example, benefit from lessons that focus on critical thinking, analysis, discussion, and writing abilities; lessons progress in difficulty and depth each year. Likewise, the middle school math guide is organized around conceptual strands that directly connect to the subject matter taught in AP calculus and statistics. The Texas Education Agency has recognized the effectiveness of the *Laying the Foundation* guides by awarding Advanced Placement Strategies a $1.35 million contract to instruct 270 pre-AP English teachers in seven Texas school districts that have a predominantly Hispanic student population.[42]

The third component of teacher training and support involves regular visits by AP Strategies staff members to classrooms taught by AP and pre-AP teachers. These visits provide assistance with teaching techniques, classroom management, and curriculum from AP teachers (now AP Strategies staff members) who have a proven record of success in teaching the subject matter. Staff members particularly concentrate attention on teachers who are novice AP instructors.[43]

Members of AP Strategies know that the crucial characteristic of an effective AP teacher is the teacher's ability to inspire students. Does the teacher make students excited about the subject matter so that they are attentive in class and meet with the teacher after school for assistance? Does the teacher have a good rapport with students? If so, past experience shows that, once the teacher learns the subject matter (a process smoothed with AP Strategies staff support), students will perform very well in that teacher's AP class. For example, Thomas Jefferson High School in Dallas, which has a predominantly Hispanic student body, had never had more than one student pass the AP calculus exam. A young Hispanic teacher was having success in inspiring students in his pre-AP math class, but he had never taught calculus. After the principal appointed that teacher the AP calculus instructor, AP Strategies staff members attended the teacher's class three days each week and met with him before class to go over the content he would cover that day. At the end of his first year, thirteen of his students passed the AP calculus exam—a number surpassing that attained by many wealthy schools. Fleisher approximates that without the support of AP Strategies staff, it likely would have taken the teacher five years to reach the level of proficiency with his calculus class that he attained after one year with AP Strategies support.[44]

Lastly, to expand upon the other training AP and pre-AP teachers receive, AP Strategies encourages districts to set two or more additional training days during each year. These usually take place on district-wide teacher professional development days, and are led by the district's lead teachers, with AP Strategies staff also conducting parts of the training sessions.[45]

3. Extra Time on Task for Students

Students benefit from extra instruction and preparation for AP exams in the incentive programs through both after school tutoring sessions with AP teachers and district-wide preparation sessions on Saturdays. The agreement between the donor, AP Strategies, and the district requires each AP teacher to tutor students after school one hour a week, but most teachers devote many more after school hours to tutoring. If a teacher is not having success with students, AP Strategies may arrange for the district's lead teacher in that subject to conduct the tutoring sessions.[46]

In addition, for each AP subject, a district has three Saturday prep sessions, which usually take place in the spring as students prepare for the AP examinations in May. The sessions typically run from around 8:30 in the morning to around 2:30 in the afternoon. The district's AP teachers and lead teachers, staff members from AP Strategies, and various consultants knowledgeable in the subject matter and hired by AP Strategies instruct and assist students. Students can choose which of various sessions they would like to attend. The calculus prep session, for instance, may have sessions in five different rooms taking place simultaneously, each covering a separate subject (for example, one may concern integrals, and another may concentrate on derivatives). Students maintain their energy with the snacks that AP Strategies provides. The prep sessions in Dallas Independent School District draw 700 to 800 students. These are "mostly minority kids who are giving up a Saturday," Fleisher notes. "It just makes you feel a whole lot better about public schools when you see these kids doing this."[47]

4. Financial Incentives

A spearhead component of the O'Donnell Foundation/AP Strategies incentive programs—and one now widely used in various programs—is the financial incentives for students, teachers, and principals if students pass AP exams. Peter O'Donnell notes that the aim in giving financial rewards directly to students and teachers is to ensure that the recognition takes place where learning occurs: in the classroom through the teachers and by the students.[48]

The amount of money that goes to successful AP students, their teachers, and—at times—their principals and AP coordinators differs depending on the structure of the district's incentive program. Both the desires of the donor and the circumstances of the district dictate these amounts. Students commonly get $100 for passing an exam, although students in some districts receive $500 per exam passed. In other districts students gradually receive more money for each AP exam that they pass. They may, for example, earn $100 for the first exam they pass, $200 for the second, and $200 for each passed exam thereafter. In addition, the incentive program typically pays at least half, and in some districts all, of the student's AP examination fee (which is $52 for Texas students, since the state pays $30 of the $82 fee).[49]

Teacher incentives vary even more than student incentives. Before setting the incentive amounts for teachers in a district, AP Strategies staff interviews all AP and pre-AP teachers throughout the district to get the teachers' input concerning what incentive amounts would be effective. The resulting teacher incentives usually are threefold. First, AP teachers and pre-AP teachers receive a stipend, which typically ranges between $500 and $2,000, for teaching the courses. Second, teachers are rewarded generally between $100 and $500 for each of their students who pass the AP exam. Third, teachers often receive a bonus if they reach a preset goal concerning their students' AP exam performance, which commonly ranges from $500 to $2,000.[50]

Others—including principals, AP coordinators, and schools—may receive incentive rewards if students are successful on AP exams, depending upon the terms of each district's incentive program. Fleisher notes that one positive consequence when principals receive money based on student AP performance is that the principals pay extra attention to the AP program. They desire to receive the incentive, perhaps not as much for the money as for the pride of not failing to earn it.[51]

One critique that occasionally arises in connection with rewarding students and teachers monetarily for AP success is that we should not be paying students and teachers for what they should be accomplishing. Two responses answer these concerns. First, the money to students who are successful on AP exams is a form of mini-scholarship—just as students receive college scholarships as a result of high SAT scores. Second, the rewards for teachers and students represent extra rewards for extra work in a voluntary program.[52]

5. Professional Management

The professional management that Advanced Placement Strategies provides to AP Incentive Programs in districts across Texas is a central component of the programs' success. The roles that AP Strategies plays vary according to the needs of each district, but generally AP Strategies is involved in all aspects of a district's incentive program to some degree (except for the College Board workshops). Some tasks are always primary AP Strategies responsibilities: staff members are always involved in vertical team meetings as well as the training sessions that lead teachers conduct. AP Strategies also handles all paperwork concerning the donor's funding. Other common responsibilities touch all components of the incentive programs, ranging from coordinating and operating student prep sessions to providing classroom support for teachers to conducting training in the pre-AP curriculum guides. This coordination and management takes the weight off district personnel and makes the operation of the program manageable. Likewise, AP Strategies assists donors by not only helping establish the program in districts, but also by monitoring districts' use of funds.[53]

In addition to coordinating and managing the incentive programs, AP Strategies monitors progress in each district. AP Strategies sets goals for growth in the number of AP passing exams in a district or district school. The minimum goal is for the number to double in five years, meaning a 15 percent annual growth in the number of passing exams. Often, gains in the number of passing scores in incentive program districts greatly exceed those growth rate goals.[54]

Recent experiences in Wichita Falls Independent School District demonstrate the impact of AP Strategies' services on the success of incentive programs. Prior to the founding of AP Strategies in 2000, Wichita Falls ISD had an AP Incentive Program in place, which the district strove to manage on its own. After AP Strategies began managing the program during the 2001–2002 school year, the success of the Wichita Falls program increased dramatically, with a 46 percent increase in the number of AP passing scores in math, science, and English over two years.[55]

Individuals across the country who desire to establish AP Incentive Programs would be well-served by setting up an organization similar to

AP Strategies in each state to coordinate and boost the success of incentive programs. The structure of AP Strategies and the roles it plays are proven to work and replicable. Just as AP Strategies is tailored to serve Texas districts in the particular context of Texas laws and customs, so similar organizations in other states could serve the needs and requirements of citizens, teachers, and education agencies in that state. Without such an organization, those striving to manage incentive programs that incorporate the five essential components laid out in this chapter would soon find the job overwhelming. Indeed, Carolyn Bacon surmises that one reason that AP Incentive Programs have been slow to take off in various states is because those states have no organization similar to AP Strategies in place. Florida already recognizes this need and is considering establishing an entity to coordinate and manage AP Incentive Programs.[56]

Advanced Placement Incentive Programs that use these five central components are proven to work by hard data. So even though the scope of the challenge to prepare our high school students for college and workplace success seems daunting, the way to achieve the goal is clear: we must ensure that each student experiences a rigorous curriculum in high school. Evidence establishes that Advanced Placement Incentive Programs are an effective means to spur students' voluntary participation in such rigorous courses, particularly by students who have been traditionally underrepresented in challenging courses. AP Incentive Programs thus not only enhance the academic preparedness of all high school students who participate. Such incentive programs also provide a valuable key to helping us accomplish two vital goals in education: enhancing the academic opportunities and achievement of minority and economically disadvantaged students and closing the academic achievement gap between students of different races and socioeconomic strata.

Conclusion

WE ARE ENTERING a promising era in our efforts to improve our public schools. Frustrations still abound—and rightly so in many quarters—concerning the state of our education system. Many children are arriving at kindergarten lacking the necessary building blocks to be ready to learn. Far too commonly, frustrated students are dropping out of high school. Performance levels on national and international achievement tests are far from stellar, and low and declining scores by high school students are a particular concern. The achievement scores of minority and economically disadvantaged students continue to lag behind their white and more economically fortunate peers. And many students are leaving high school ill-prepared for college or the workplace.

Yet, thankfully, we are making progress. The standards and accountability movement that began in the 1980s and that has been maturing over the last decade has enabled us to make two major strides. First, there is now a commonly held recognition that *every* student can learn at high levels and that we should enable them to do so. This is a notable advance from former schools of thought that held that some students could handle demanding academic material while others could not. Second, this focus on enabling students to reach high achievement levels has led states across the country to specify what students should be expected to know in each grade. These state standards-based accountability systems are giving educators the freedom to determine how to enable students to master material, and are holding educators accountable for results. The federal No Child Left Behind Act of 2001—with its heartening aim of having all students be academically proficient—is providing the support as well as the impetus needed to make high academic standards and high academic achievement by every student across the country a reality.

Further, the valuable student performance data that these state accountability systems generate clearly show us that there are high-performing schools and districts across the country in even the most challenging of circumstances. Through studying such high performers, we now know how these schools and districts are spurring student achievement gains—and we know that the methods they are using are highly replicable. In short, the tools of student performance data and best practice studies discussed in previous chapters demonstrate that any school and any district, no matter what their circumstances, can provide students with an excellent education. But in order to do so, educators, parents, and others associated with the school system first must know specifically what to do to spur achievement.[1] Then, they must have the will to accomplish such a challenging task.

The materials in previous chapters address this first component by providing a "how-to" guide. Central among the lessons presented here is how vital the use of privacy-protected, student-linked longitudinal data is for accurately informing us of how our students are performing and how we can tailor instruction to meet their needs. Without such data, we simply cannot know if our students are learning and if we are instructing them effectively. By employing performance data that is presented in a usable, focused format (like that, for example, at www.just4kids.org), we can set clear goals and directly focus on the areas in which students need improvement.

Also essential is the use of proven, research-based educational practices and programs to educate our children. For too long and too often, educators have followed the latest, unproven trend in instructional practice—and the losers in this revolving door of ineffective programs have been our students. Through research-based best practice studies—such as those presented through the Just for the Kids' Best Practice Framework—we can learn about the precise practices that high-performing schools are employing to attain results with student populations similar to students at our own school. And we can then replicate those programs in our school (tailoring them to local influences and needs) with confidence that they are effective in raising student achievement.

The problems in our public education system are indeed vast and serious. However, programs that are proven to work can successfully address these problems—and are already enabling many students to experience a first-rate education. Hard data shows that children—particularly minority and economically disadvantaged children—who experience a quality preschool program that uses a language-rich, research-based curriculum like the Language Enrichment Activities Program (LEAP) are more prone to enter kindergarten ready to learn and progress through school on grade level. Further, although urban districts often experience higher dropout rates and lower student achievement than non-urban districts, the high-performing finalists for The Broad Prize for Urban Education demonstrate that academic excellence in urban districts is an attainable goal. As The Broad Prize process makes plain, the methods these finalists use to elicit such high performance are accessible and replicable. In addition, research shows us how to ensure that high school students are ready for college and the workplace: by having students take rigorous high school courses such as Advanced Placement courses. Data also shows us that Advanced Placement Incentive Programs increase high schoolers' interest and success in AP courses, particularly among minority and economically disadvantaged students.

Yet, even armed with these proven practices, we will never meet the goals of enabling all students to experience an excellent education and attain academic proficiency unless we have the will to attain these goals. Generating the collective political and social resolve to accomplish these vital aims is not a simple task. There are many competing agendas and conflicting priorities in education. Thus, to progress forward toward 100 percent academic proficiency, we must prioritize and remain focused on a few crucial objectives.

First, for all students to be able to read on grade level by the end of third grade. Studies show that students who are not fluent readers by the end of third grade likely will never catch up with their classmates. Hence, reading on grade level in third grade acts as a critical gatekeeper. Students who do not pass through the gate are tragically left behind, and all too commonly become frustrated and drop out of school. Fortunately, this objective has become a focal point of many efforts. The goal of President Bill Clinton's America Reads Challenge, established in 1996, was to enable every child to read independently and well by the end of third grade. President George W. Bush has stressed this aim both as governor of Texas and as president of the United States. Having all third graders read on grade level is also a central objective of the No Child Left Behind Act. Providing all children with high-quality reading instruction in their early elementary years is vital for us to reach this aim. However, there is a second, indispensable component: we must give all children—particularly economically disadvantaged children—the opportunity to experience a high-quality preschool program that incorporates a language-rich curriculum like LEAP. Only through providing such a quality preschool experience can we ensure that all children begin kindergarten and progress through later grades ready to read and ready to learn.[2]

Second, for all students to take and pass algebra in eighth grade. While reading ability acts as the crucial gatekeeper in the elementary school grades, exposure to algebra in the eighth grade serves as the principal gatekeeper for more advanced math and science studies in high school. Taking algebra in eighth grade provides a vital foundation for a progression of rigorous high school math and science courses—and taking such challenging high school courses is a decisive key to later success in college and the workplace, particularly for economically disadvantaged students. Fortunately, over the last decade, numerous states have begun requiring students to pass algebra to graduate from high school. As of August 2004, twenty-one states require algebra mastery of their students. And federal statistics show that the number of thirteen-year-olds taking algebra and pre-algebra has increased from 35 percent in 1986 to 56 percent in 1999. These developments are encouraging. Our goal now should be to use this momentum to ensure that all students benefit from taking and passing algebra in the eighth grade.[3]

Third, for every high school student to take at least one Advanced Placement course and pass the associated AP exam. As discussed in chapter 6, it is critical for us to do a better job of preparing our students for success beyond high school. One central key to achievement in higher education and the workplace—particularly among minority and economically disadvantaged students—is students' involvement in rigorous high school courses. Hence, to equip our students for later success, we must take two key but attainable steps. First, we must make Advanced Placement courses— among the most respected and accepted rigorous courses in the country— available to students in every high school. Second, we must encourage each student to take at least one AP course and pass the related AP exam.

Fourth, for educators and the larger community to work together to accomplish these goals. The most productive way for educators, parents, policymakers, and citizens in general to work toward accomplishing these tasks is through using two crucial tools: (1) employing privacy-protected, student-linked longitudinal data to inform and direct their efforts and (2) ensuring that students are benefiting from proven educational practices. Only through using such hard data and proven practices—such as that presented at www.just4kids.org—can all see clearly how students are performing, what student achievement goals are attainable in the near future, and what specific tools to use to reach those achievement goals.

Attaining these four objectives is central in our efforts to provide every child with an excellent education. If we set our sights any lower or on less crucial aims, we will be depriving our students of the benefits that a high-quality education provides throughout their life. In addition, we will be depriving our country of the full talents that America's youth can contribute. We have before us the exemplars and the tools to enable us to reach these four objectives—as well as the ultimate goal of 100 percent proficiency. Now, we just need to devote ourselves to the task.

Acknowledgments

One day in the summer of 1983, while working at my law firm desk, I received a telephone call from a client, Ross Perot, that changed my life for the next 21 years. Ross reported to me that he had been asked by the Governor of Texas to chair the Select Committee on Public Education that was to study the condition of public education in Texas and to make recommendations on how to improve the public education system in the state.

Ross asked me to take a leave of absence from my law firm for a year and to serve as chief of staff of that Committee. I did so, but after returning to my law practice, I was determined to do what I could as a lay person to continue to improve our public education system.

I think I became so passionate about the subject because of my life story. I was raised by my mother, a single parent who provided for my sister and me by working very hard in a ladies' dress shop selling clothes. Our family lived in a duplex in an area served by one of the best public school systems in the state, and as a result I received a wonderful public education that helped me establish a successful legal career.

However, when I began my work for the Committee in 1983 by traveling the state of Texas and studying the public education system, I found that literally millions of school children in our state were not receiving the same educational opportunity that I had received. I also quickly learned that the transition of the Texas economy from a natural resources-based economy to one able to compete globally in the information age meant that children who did not receive a first-rate public education opportunity would be consigned to low-paying jobs, a low standard of living, and likely a life of poverty.

As a result of my lack of experience in public education matters, I began my "education" by talking to scores of people, both in the education field and the legislative policy field. I learned a lot from many, many people. Some were public school teachers, principals, and superintendents, and many of them were members of the wonderful staff that I assembled to work for the Select Committee. As is often the case, it was actually these wonderful staff people who produced House Bill 72, which was the culmination of the work of our Committee, and they and a dedicated, selfless professional lobbying team led by my friend ever since, Rusty Kelley, helped persuade the Texas Legislature to adopt virtually all of our recommendations. These staff people included Camilla Bordie, Gwen Grigsby, Terry Heller, Margaret Spellings (who is now the domestic policy advisor for the president of the United States), and Melinda Terry.

Following my work in 1983 and 1984 with the Select Committee, I was determined to stay involved to monitor and help keep in place our recommendations that had been adopted as well as to push, at the state level, for ever rising education standards and continuous improvement of Texas public schools. In working with our state government to better our public schools, I became indebted to many state leaders, including, to name a few: Governors Mark White, Bill Clements, Ann Richards, George W. Bush, and Rick Perry; Lt. Governors Bill Hobby and David Dewhurst; House Speakers Gib Lewis and Pete Laney; and influential legislative leaders such as Senators Teel Bivins, Bill Ratliff, and Florence Shapiro, and Representatives Kent Grusendorf and Paul Sadler, all of whom have worked on a bipartisan basis to improve our public education system.

With other business leaders, I also helped to create an organization called the Texas Business and Education Coalition; and I subsequently learned a great deal from the participants in that coalition and their executive director, John Stevens.

In 1995, I felt that we had accomplished a great deal at the state policy level but with the increasing trend to site-based management of public schools and local control, we needed an organization that could help each independent local school improve its performance. This concept led to the creation of the nonprofit organization Just for the Kids, thanks to the support of then-Governor of Texas George W. Bush, now president of the United States, and then-State Education Commissioner Mike Moses, who recently retired as superintendent of the Dallas Independent School District. Then-Governor Bush was not only totally supportive of the concept of Just for the Kids, he also readily made available the state data that was the basis for the organization and spoke at two fundraising dinners that provided the funds to successfully launch Just for the Kids in Texas.

After becoming president of the United States, he helped us expand Just for the Kids to additional states across the country, which as of the writing of this book number 25 in total.

The dedicated staff of Just for the Kids originally led by Brad Duggan has always included first class professionals such as Dr. Chrys Dougherty, Dr. Jean Rutherford, Janet Spence, and Sandy Milkey. These talented individuals successfully implemented our original vision of presenting easy to understand academic achievement data that identified the top-performing schools in Texas by grade and by subject with every type of student population. The identification of these high-performing schools led us to study the "best practices" they were using at the district, school, and classroom levels to get top-flight results.

Our original board of directors, composed of friends and colleagues such as Jim Adams, Carolyn Bacon, Dennis Berman, Albert Black, Bob Buford, John Castle, Scott Caven, Bruce Gibson, Porky Haberman, Dealey Herndon, Sally Junkins, Jim Loose, Bernie Rapoport, Lionel Sosa, Don Williams, and Dr. Kneeland Youngblood, who had faith in the vision, provided the leadership to take us from a dream to a reality.

Later, in 2001, Ted Sanders, president of the Education Commission of the States, and Larry Faulkner, president of the University of Texas at Austin, helped us form the National Center for Educational Accountability, and provided the leadership to spread the Just for the Kids model to other states.

This success would not have happened without the leadership, dedication, and commitment of the following directors of the National Center for Educational Accountability:

Terry Kelley, Vice Chairman
Former CEO
Bank One Southern Region

John Anderson
Vice Chairman
New American Schools

Carolyn Bacon
Executive Director
O'Donnell Foundation

Dr. Barbara Byrd-Bennett
CEO
Cleveland Municipal School District

Lee Blitch
President
San Francisco Chamber of Commerce

The Hon. William Brock
Chairman
Bridges Learning Systems

Ken Duberstein
President
The Duberstein Group, Inc.

The Hon. James Edgar
Former Governor of Illinois

Charley Ellis
Managing Partner
Partners of '63

Tom Engibous
Chairman/CEO
Texas Instruments

Dr. Larry Faulkner
President
The University of Texas at Austin

Dr. John Hitt
President
University of Central Florida

Dr. G. Thomas Houlihan
Executive Director
Council of Chief State School Officers

The Hon. James Hunt
Former Governor of North Carolina

Roberts Jones
President
Education & Workforce Policy, LLC

Dr. Manuel Justiz
Dean, College of Education
The University of Texas at Austin

Kerry Killinger
President/Chair/CEO
Washington Mutual

Charles B. Reed
Chancellor
California State University System

Marilyn Reznick
VP Education Programs
AT&T Foundation

The Hon. Richard Riley
Former U.S. Secretary of Education

Ed Rust, Jr.
Chairman/CEO
State Farm Insurance Companies

Dr. Ted Sanders
President
Education Commission of the States

Dr. Sara Martinez Tucker
President and CEO
National Hispanic Scholarship Fund

Robin Willner
Director of Corporate Community Relations
IBM Corporation

Larry Yost
Chairman and CEO
ArvinMeritor, Inc.

The personal leadership and management skills of Vice Chairman Terry Kelley, a successful business leader, took us from a small, one-state operation to a multi-state, efficient operation with the largest database of academic achievement in the country. In 2004, Mike Hudson became our president and continues to spread our "message" and build relationships across the country.

I would be remiss if I did not also acknowledge the personal commitment of Tom Engibous, chairman of Texas Instruments, and the corporate support of Texas Instruments for public education reform, Just for the Kids, and the National Center for Educational Accountability. Not only have all these efforts benefited from the personal leadership of Tom Engibous and the prior chairman, Jerry Junkins, but the entire corporation and its corporate foundation have provided leadership in all aspects of public education reform in Texas and across the country for many decades.

In addition, as mentioned in the dedication to this book, every single effort I have worked on involving public education has been supported and encouraged by Peter and Edith O'Donnell. They have given generously of their time, talent, and treasure to ensure the success of Just for the Kids and the National Center for Educational Accountability.

For his superb art direction of the book's cover, I am grateful to Bob Wilson. In addition to being a good friend, he is one of the most creative people I have ever met.

My wife, Pam, who has been more than an equal partner in our marriage of forty-four years, and my children Ken, Ellen, and Susan have also been constant and invaluable supporters.

Last, but certainly not least, I want to clearly state that my co-author, Lee Thompson, was much more than a co-author. Lee was able to articulate better than I ever could the spirit and intent of what we are trying to achieve. Lee is a lawyer and Ph.D. in history by education and practice but was so dedicated to our mission that she decided to work full-time (well, at least until her beautiful daughter Elizabeth was born) with me to commit our philosophy to paper. I am indebted to her for her wonderful way of telling our story. Lee will be the first to tell you she received a lot of help as well.

TOM LUCE

When I had the good fortune to begin working with Tom Luce as a graduate student in 1998, little did I anticipate the rewarding journey that lay ahead. Tom has expanded the horizons for me and scores of others through two of his primary characteristics: his selfless devotion to ensuring that every child receives an excellent education and his clear vision—backed by hard evidence—as to how to accomplish this goal. He realizes, as do many who are devoted to education reform, that a paramount need in education right now is the provision of proven tools that will build the capacity of educators, parents, policymakers, and other citizens to provide children with a first-rate education. The goal of ensuring that all children are academically proficient is set, by virtue of the federal No Child Left Behind Act and various state laws. But how do we reach this goal?

Through work with the National Center for Educational Accountability and other organizations, we had before us a set of replicable tools that were proven to spur academic achievement in even the most challenging of school environments and in grades ranging from preschool through high school. What began as a series of writings spreading the news of these effective practices has culminated in this book: a work whose primary goal is to serve as a "toolbox" for educators, policymakers, parents, and others to use with confidence that the featured educational tools work.

This book has truly been a joint enterprise—not only between the co-authors but also among the many people who have contributed their knowledge and talent to the text. Gwen Grigsby, associate vice president for governmental relations at the University of Texas at Austin; Sandy Kress, partner of Akin, Gump, Strauss, Hauer & Feld; and John Stevens, executive director of the Texas Business and Education Coalition, each provided valuable input concerning the history of education reform in Texas and the country.

Individuals associated with various state affiliates of Just for the Kids—including Dr. Duane Baker, director of school information services at the Washington School Research Center, Dr. Linda Goudy, director of the Florida School Report, and Dr. Jeff Osowski, vice president of education policy at the New Jersey Chamber of Commerce—provided vital evidence of what is working in their states. Principal William Johnson, John Witherspoon Middle School, Princeton, New Jersey, and Dr. Dennis McDonald, principal of Demarest Middle School, Demarest, New Jersey, shared first-hand accounts of what their schools are doing to attain high student achievement.

Particular help with our text concerning The Broad Prize for Urban Education came from Becca Bracy, director of The Broad Foundation, and her Broad Foundation colleagues and Jim Lanich, executive director, and Ross Santy, deputy director of Just for the Kids-California. Thanks also go to Dan Katzir, managing director of The Broad Foundation.

Our discussion of what is working in early childhood education came together with the help of Bill Ball, consultant with the Texas Instruments Foundation; Nell Carvell, director of the Language Enrichment Activities Program and Head Start Initiatives, Southern Methodist University; Ralph Dosher of the Texas Instruments Foundation; Jim Fischer of the Texas Instruments Foundation; Henry Gandy, vice president, The Duberstein Group; Dr. Bill Harris of the Children's Research and Education Institute, Belmont, Massachusetts; Rob Massoneau, external affairs director, Head Start of Greater Dallas; Ann Minnis, former director, Texas Instruments Foundation; and Phil Ritter, senior vice president of public affairs, Texas Instruments. Appreciation also goes to Mike Rice, former president, Texas Instruments Foundation, and Wanda Smith, chief executive officer, Head Start of Greater Dallas.

Various members of the Foundation for Community Empowerment also provided vital help, including Cecilia Edwards, executive vice president and chief operating officer; Don Williams, chairman and founder; and Ellen Carter Williams, former education program manager.

Carolyn Bacon, executive director of the O'Donnell Foundation; Gregg Fleisher, president of AP Strategies, Inc.; and Peter O'Donnell, Jr., president of the O'Donnell Foundation, contributed their expertise to our text concerning the preparation of high school students for college and workplace success through Advanced Placement Incentive Programs. I am especially grateful to Carolyn Bacon, Edith O'Donnell, and Peter O'Donnell, Jr. for the privilege to work with them at the O'Donnell Foundation. They inspire me and many others through their generous, innovative, and effective philanthropy.

Various members of the talented staff at the National Center for Educational Accountability have rendered valuable help, including Susan Bonesteel, Sarah Collins, Dr. Chrys Dougherty, Aimee Guidera, Mike Hudson, Tom Lindsley, Dr. Jean Rutherford, and Susan Whisenant. Appreciation for help with graphics goes to National Center staff members Janey Chaplin and Patrece Reese. Kay Kimsey, Susan Luce, Janet Spence, and Carol Toberny provided indispensable support and input as we produced the book. The text benefited from the superior copyediting skills of Kathryne Morris.

The dedication of this book to my parents, Nancy Beth and Harry Roberts, is particularly apt. Throughout my life, they have shown me through word and example the value of a quality education and the richness of a life full of learning. I am grateful for these priceless gifts.

My brother and sister-in-law, Whit and Kristen Roberts, and my husband's parents, Peggy and Jere Thompson, have also provided much appreciated support.

One person who made especially notable contributions to this book is my husband, David Thompson. His incisive thoughts and technical expertise enhanced the quality and clarity of the text, while his unwavering encouragement and selflessness made it possible for Tom and me to proceed with the manuscript. For all these things, I am immensely thankful. Our 1 1/2-year-old daughter, Elizabeth, also contributed as only a toddler could, for watching her young mind develop makes very clear the promise that lies in all of our children.

LEE THOMPSON

Notes

Introduction

1   See, e.g., Public Education Network and Education Week, *2004 National Survey,* 4, 6; Marjorie Coeyman, "Twenty Years After 'A Nation at Risk,'" *Christian Science Monitor,* Apr. 22, 2003, http://www.csmonitor.com/2003/0422/p13s02-lepr.htm (accessed July 4, 2004); Howard Kurtz, "The Candidates' Lesson Plan: Education Becomes a Hot Theme in Campaign Ads," *Washington Post,* July 4, 1998, cited in Hacsi, *Children as Pawns,* 104, n. 1 ("A Harris poll found that more people were concerned about education than about any other issue.").

2   For discussion of the lack of substantial gains in student achievement after decades of reform, and yet the success of certain states and schools in substantially boosting student achievement, see chapter 1.

3   For a detailed investigation of this history, see chapter 1.

4   Kirkpatrick, "Nation Still at Risk"; Walberg, "Accountability Unplugged," 77.

5   See chapter 1 for a discussion of states that have reaped large gains in student achievement by instituting reforms based on these elements and the federal No Child Left Behind Act, which is based on these principles.

6   Luce, *Now or Never.*

7   The reform movement and results in Texas are discussed in chapter 1.

8   Statements of Michael Cohen and Marc Tucker, Partial Transcript of Panel, American Enterprise Institute for Public Policy Research, "A Nation at Risk: Twenty Years Later," Apr. 1, 2003, http://www.aei.org/events/eventID.260/transcript.asp (accessed July 4, 2004).

1. From *A Nation at Risk* to *No Child Left Behind:* Public Education Reform, 1983-2004

1　National Commission, *A Nation at Risk,* 1 (quoting Secretary Bell), 5.

2　Ibid., 8–9.

3　Marjorie Coeyman, "Twenty Years After 'A Nation at Risk,'" *Christian Science Monitor,* Apr. 22, 2003, http://www.csmonitor.com/2003/0422/p13s02-lepr.html (accessed July 26, 2004); Toch, *Name of Excellence,* 14–15.

4　Toch, *Name of Excellence,* 15–17.

5　Twentieth Century Fund, *Making the Grade,* 4, quoted in Toch, *Name of Excellence,* 40; Toch, *Name of Excellence,* 17.

6　Toch, *Name of Excellence,* 3.

7　Dr. Chris Pipho, an Education Commission of the States analyst in Denver, counted these mid-1980s education reform bodies until they reached 300, and then quit counting. Figure in Karel Holloway, "Decade of Education Reform Has Mixed Results, Experts Say," *Dallas Morning News,* July 25, 1993.

8　Toch, *Name of Excellence,* 36–38; Tyack and Cuban, *Tinkering,* 78.

9　Toch, *Name of Excellence,* 38; Luce, *Now or Never,* 138; John Stevens (executive director, Texas Business and Education Coalition), interview by Lee Thompson, tape recording, Austin, Texas, June 16, 2000.

10　Karel Holloway, "Decade," (listing figures calculated by Dr. Lawrence Picus, University of Southern California education finance analyst); Pete Du Pont, "Two Decades of Mediocrity: America's Public Schools, Still Risky After All These Years," *Opinion Journal, The Wall Street Journal,* May 5, 2003, http://www. opinionjournal.com/columnists/pdupont/?id=110003445 (accessed July 4, 2004); Kirkpatrick, "Nation Still at Risk"; Toch, *Name of Excellence,* 36–37.

11　Toch, *Name of Excellence,* 39, 239; Associated Press, "School Reforms Incomplete, Experts Say," *Dallas Morning News,* April 24, 1988.

12　Toch, *Name of Excellence,* 29–33, chap. 5; Tyack and Cuban, *Tinkering,* 79.

13　Moe, "Reform Blockers," 58.

14　Hanushek, "Lost Opportunity," 84.

15　Moe, "Reform Blockers," 59; Chester E. Finn, Jr., Partial Transcript of Panel, American Enterprise Institute for Public Policy Research, "A Nation at Risk: Twenty Years Later," Apr. 1, 2003 (hereafter Nation at Risk AEI Panel Transcript), http://www.aei.org/events/eventID.260/transcript.asp (accessed July 28, 2004). See also Marc Tucker, Nation at Risk AEI Panel Transcript ("the argument that people love to stage between those who have been for market solutions and those who have been for standards-based reform is an argument that many of us . . . who have actually been deeply involved in this think is a waste of breath.")

16   Joseph Garcia, "Reforms Get a C from Teachers," *Dallas Morning News*, May 22,
     1988 (quoting Boyer in connection with survey conducted by the Carnegie Foun-
     dation); *New York Times*, October 1, 1989, sec. 4, pp. 1, 22, quoted in Tyack and
     Cuban, *Tinkering*, 80–81; Karel Holloway, "What Does the Department of Educa-
     tion Do? Office Provides a National Focus on Schools and Aid to the Poorest Stu-
     dents," *Dallas Morning News*, July 18, 1995; John Stevens, written comments to
     authors, September-October 2000; Jerald, "State of the States."

17   See Walberg, "Accountability Unplugged," 77 ("School accountability was
     thought to require simultaneous centralization and decentralization: the central-
     ization of standards at the state level and the decentralization of operational
     responsibilities to the district or school level.").

18   American Federation of Teachers, *Making Standards Matter 2001*, 5, 25–27, 31, 34–35.

19   Ibid., 5, 29, 33–35.

20   Raymond and Hanushek, "High-Stakes Research," 53; "Quality Counts 2004,"
     State Data Tables: Standards and Accountability, 104, http://www.edweek.org/
     sreports/qc04/reports/standacct-t1.cfm (accessed July 26, 2004); Princeton Review,
     Testing the Testers 2003; Cross, Rebarber, and Torres, *Grading the Systems*, 2.

21   Skandera and Sousa, *School Figures*, 272 (citing an August 1999 survey by Peter D.
     Hart and an August 2000 survey by the Business Roundtable).

22   Only New York scored higher than Massachusetts, Texas, and North Carolina in
     the Princeton Review rankings, while Maryland and Massachusetts ranked high
     in the *Education Week* rankings. See Princeton Review, *Testing the Testers 2003*;
     Education Week, "Quality Counts 2003," 84. In *Education Week*'s 2004 rankings,
     the standards and accountability systems in Maryland and Massachusetts contin-
     ued to rank near the top, although Massachusetts's ranking had slipped slightly.
     Education Week, "Quality Counts 2004."

23   Achieve, Inc., *Three Paths*, 5–7; Massachusetts Department of Education, News
     Release, "2003 MCAS Result in All-Time High," Sept. 10, 2003,
     http://www.doe.mass.edu/news/news.asp?id=1605 (accessed July 3, 2004);
     National Center for Educational Accountability, "2003 4th Grade NAEP Reading
     Sorted by White, African American, and Hispanic Scale Scores" (2003) (internal
     reference document); National Center for Educational Accountability, "2003 4th
     Grade NAEP Mathematics Sorted by White, African American, and Hispanic Scale
     Scores," (2003) (internal reference document); National Center for Educational
     Accountability, "2003 4th Grade NAEP Writing Sorted by White, African Ameri-
     can, and Hispanic Students," (2004) (internal reference document) (the three pre-
     ceding NAEP documents, collectively, the NAEP Scaled Score Documents).

24   Achieve, Inc., "Three Paths," 5–7; Maryland State Department of Education,

News Release, "Maryland School Assessment Scores Improve Statewide, Release of 2004 Results Reveal Jumps in Math, Reading Achievement," June 15, 2004, http://www.marylandpublicschools.org/NR/exeres/A928C1E5-3014-4AF7-8E92-2D710CA415ED,frameless.htm?Year=2004&Month=6% (accessed July 3, 2004); NAEP Scaled Score Documents.

25   Grissmer and Flanagan, *Exploring*, summary preface. RAND researchers also issued an issue paper shortly before the 2000 presidential election that was critical of the differences between student gains on the Texas state test versus national tests. Klein et al., *What Do Test Scores*. Various nonpartisan critics have faulted this later 2000 RAND report for both its methods of analysis and conclusions. See "School Report Gets RAND-y Reception," *Stats*, Nov. 1, 2000, http://www.stats.org/record.jsp?type=news&ID=390 (accessed June 12, 2004).

26   Zulli and Cunningham, *State Report Card*, 2, 9; NAEP Scaled Score Documents; Todd Silberman, "Test Scores Leaping in N.C.," *Raleigh News & Observer*, June 18, 2003.

27   Texas Education Agency, Academic Excellence Indicator System (AEIS), "State AEIS Multi-Year Report, 1994–2002," http://www.tea.state.tx.us/perfreport/aeis/hist/state.html (accessed July 27, 2004); Clay Robinson, "State's Third-Graders Improve on New TAKS Tests," *Houston Chronicle*, Mar. 24, 2004; Joshua Benton, "Reading Students Make the Grade," *Dallas Morning News*, June 20, 2003; NAEP Scaled Score Documents.

28   Achieve, Inc., *Three Paths*, 5–12 (quote from p. 6). See also "Why Testing Can't Fail," *New York Times*, June 30, 2003 ("Evidence from several states shows that success rates on rigorous tests can be boosted dramatically when the state invests in education, helps troubled students—and holds the schools accountable for getting the best out of students in rich and poor neighborhoods alike.").

29   Achieve, Inc., *Three Paths*, 5–12; Grissmer and Flanagan, *Exploring Rapid Achievement Gains*, summary preface, i–v, 19–26.

30   However, a 2002 Phi Delta Kappa/Gallup Poll of the Public's Attitudes Towards the Public Schools indicates that over a majority of Americans favor an increased federal involvement in public schooling, and that they would not oppose the No Child Left Behind Act serving as the first step in increased federal influence in public school systems. Mason, "Can Federal Involvement."

31   Skandera and Sousa, *School Figures*, 193, 195; Hacsi, *Children as Pawns*, 175, 179.

32   Committee on Education and the Workforce, U.S. House of Representatives, "No Child Left Behind: Implementation Station," http://edworkforce.house.gov/issues/108th/education/nclb/nclb.htm (accessed June 27, 2004).

33   No Child Left Behind Act of 2001 (NCLB); U.S. Committee on Education and the Workforce, "Frequently Asked Questions About No Child Left Behind,"

updated April 1, 2004, 7, http://edworkforce.house.gov/issues/108th/
education/nclb/nclbfaq.pdf (accessed June 27, 2004); Hayes Mizell, "NCLB: Con-
spiracy, Compliance, or Creativity" (remarks, Maryland Council of Staff Devel-
opers, Columbia, Md., Apr. 25, 2003), http://www.middleweb.com/HMnclb.html
(accessed July 27, 2004); U.S. Department of Education, "Proven Methods:
Teacher Quality: Frequently Asked Questions," http://www.ed.gov/nclb/
methods/teachers/teachers-faq.html (accessed June 26, 2004). States must also
test students in reading and math at least once during grades 10 through 12. Also,
by the 2007–2008 school year, states must assess students' knowledge in science.
NCLB §1111(b)(3).

34 Sam Dillon, "States Are Relaxing Standards on Tests to Avoid Sanctions," *New
York Times* , May 22, 2003.

35 NCLB §1111(h)(1)–(2); Silberman, "Test Scores Leap."

36 NCLB §§1116(b), 1501(c), 1811, 2402, 2421, 1502, 6111(2)(H).

37 Liebman and Sabel, "Federal No Child Left Behind Act," 1708, 1749.

38 Chuck Haga, "Wisconsin Bucks No Child Left Behind," *Minneapolis Star Tribune*,
June 17, 2004, http://www.startribune.com/stories/1592/4832730.html (accessed
June 27, 2004); Michael Dobbs, "More States are Fighting 'No Child Left Behind'
Law," *Washington Post*, Feb. 19, 2004, http://www.washingtonpost.com/
wp-dyn/articles/A52720-2004Feb18.html (accessed June 27, 2004); Eric Kelder-
man, "Feds Quell States' Revolt on No Child Left Behind," *Stateline.org*, July 6,
2004, http://www.stateline.org/stateline/?pa=story&sa=showStoryInfo&id=383406
(accessed July 19, 2004).

39 Mathis, "Two Very"; Hoff, "Debate."

40 House Committee on Education and the Workforce, News, "New GAO Report
Shows Reform Opponents are Exaggerating State 'No Child Left Behind' Testing
Costs," May 8, 2003, http://edworkforce.house.gov/press/press108/05may/
nclbgaorpt050803.htm (accessed July 4, 2004); Associated Press, "New Tests for
Nation's Students to Cost $1.9B to $5.3B," *USA Today*, May 8, 2003, http://usato-
day.com/news/education/2003-05-08-testing_x.htm (accessed July 4, 2004). See
also Peyser and Costrell, "Exploring the Costs" ("Our analysis suggests that many
critics greatly exaggerate the shortfall of federal resources").

41 Hoff, "Debate" (quoting Augenblick).

42 Wiener and Carey, memo, 1, 2 (full report commissioned by Ohio legislature
located at same site address). See also comments of Finn, "Checker's Desk."

43 Mizell, "NCLB."

44 Rena Pederson, "The Public School Fix," interview with Tom Luce, *Dallas Morning News,* Mar. 14, 2004.

45 See Mizell, "NCLB."

46   Kirkpatrick, "Nation Still at Risk; Moe, "Reform Blockers," 56.

47   Haycock, Jerald, and Huang, "Closing the Gap," 3–4; Education Trust, *Education Watch*; Berkner, He, and Cataldi, *Descriptive Summary*, 24.

48   Greene and Forster, "Public High School"; Peterson, "Ticket," 43.

49   Joshua Benton, "TAKS Exposes the Grade Divide," *Dallas Morning News*, June 5, 2003, http://www.txsc.org/NewsArticles/TAKS%20exposes%20the%20grade%20divide.pdf (accessed July 28, 2004); Du Pont, "Two Decades"; Finn, "What Ails," 7; Grigg et al., *Nation's Report Card*; Diana Jean Schemo, "Reading Scores by Grade Show Widely Mixed Results," *New York Times*, June 20, 2003.

50   National Education Association, Inside Scoop, "Taking Risks," http://www.nea.org/neatoday/0304/scoop.html (accessed Apr. 21, 2003); Du Pont, "Two Decades" (quoting Chester Finn as Member of Koret Task Force); Hoxby, "What Has Changed," 106; Lynn Cheney, Nation at Risk AEI Panel Transcript; Moe, "Reform Blockers," 60. See also Terry M. Moe, "Teachers Unions Delay Education Reforms," *Detroit News*, June 10, 2003.

51   Luce, *Now or Never*, 8–11.

52   Hill, Guin, and Celio, "Minority Children," 112.

53   Indeed, some wonder if the press and public are captivated more by bad news than good. Marjorie Coeyman, "Can Johnny Read Yet?" *Christian Science Monitor*, June 24, 2003, http://www.csmonitor.com/2003/0624/p13s01-lepr.html (accessed July 28, 2004).

54   Hunt, "Unrecognized Progress," 24, 26; Marjorie Coeyman, "Mississippi Improves a Poor Report Card," *Christian Science Monitor*, June 3, 2003, http://www.csmonitor.com/2003/0603/p14s01-lepr.html (accessed July 28, 2004).

55   See comments of Michael Cohen, president of Achieve, Inc., Nation at Risk AEI Panel Transcript.

56   Council of the Great City Schools, *Beating the Odds IV*. For additional examples of how schools are spurring high student achievement among all racial groups, see Rosellini, "Getting Young Lives."

57   Pamela M. Prah, "States Get Leeway to Meet Education Law," *Stateline.org*, June 16, 2003, http://www.stateline.org/stateline/?pa=story&sa=showStory Info&id=310792 (accessed July 28, 2004); Olson, "All States.

2. Employing Performance Data: Its Empowering, Enabling Effect

1   A team of researchers, led by Dr. Chrys Dougherty, at the National Center for Educational Accountability formulated the approach to data laid out in this chapter, specifically the elements of high-quality state longitudinal data systems and how to most effectively employ the data in these systems. We are thankful for

their contribution of knowledge and talent to the material in this chapter.

2   See Reeves, foreword to *Leaving*, VIII–IX; Schmoker, *Results: The Key*.

3   See Jones and Mulvenon, *Leaving*.

4   Cathy Lassiter, Norfolk Public Schools, director of Leadership and Capacity Building, The Broad Prize for Urban Education, Site Visit Interview, 2003.

5   See Dougherty, "How States."

6   Drury and Doran, "Value"; Business Roundtable, "The Business Roundtable Releases Poll that Reveals Parents and Voters Support No Child Left Behind Reporting Requirements," press release, July 2, 2003, http://www.brt.org/Task-Forces/TaskForce/document.aspx?qs=6C95BF159F849514481138A74EA1851159169F EB56D3DB1 (accessed July 1, 2004) (Tucci quote).

7   Lassiter, interview; "Smart Data"; Massell, "District Role," 7; Drury and Doran, "Value," 2; Reeves, foreword to *Leaving*, VIII; Schmoker, *Results: The Key*, 33 (pointing to fear "of data's capacity to reveal strength and weakness, failure and success" as a reason why educators have avoided using data).

8   Jones and Mulvenon, *Leaving*, 12; Schmoker, *Results: The Key*, 35–36.

9   Pueblo, Colorado School District 60, *Pueblo 60: Celebration of Learning, Teaching, Leadership, and Support*, 2001, quoted in Jones and Mulvenon, *Leaving*, 16.

10   Dougherty, "How States," 2, 3–4 (discussing the various benefits mentioned here); Drury and Doran, "Value," 1; Dougherty, "More"; Achieve, Inc. and National Center for Educational Accountability, "All Tests"; Dougherty, "Education Data Manager's Guide."

11   Towne, "Scientific Evidence"; Steve Fleischman, James W. Kohlmoos, and Andrew J. Rotherham, "Forging the New Education Knowledge Infrastructure, From Research to Practice: Moving Beyond the Buzzwords," Joint Statement of Education Quality Institute, NEKIA, and Progressive Policy Institute, Jan. 2003, http://www.nekia.org/pdf/Ed_Week_Commentary.pdf (accessed July 19, 2004); Vinovskis, "Federal Role," 359; Shavelson and Towne, *Scientific Research*, 17, 23, 28.

12   Schmoker, *Results: The Key*, 31; Chall, *Academic*; Hacsi, *Children as Pawns*.

13   Feldman et al., "Developing"; Schmoker, *Results: The Key*, 3; Schmoker, *Results Fieldbook*, 3.

14   National Academies of Science, "Strategic Education Research Partnership," http://www7.nationalacademies.org/bcsse/Strategic_Education_Research_Partnership.html (accessed July 28, 2004); Abigail Bucuvalas, "Strategic Education Research Partnership: An Interview with Shattuck Professor Catherine Snow," *HGSE (Harvard Graduate School of Education) News*, [June 1, 2003,] http://www.gse.harvard.edu/news/features/snow06012003.html (accessed July 28, 2004); National Education Knowledge Industry Association, "About NEKIA," http://www.nekia.org/about-nekia.html (accessed July 28, 2004); Lauer, "Policymaker's Primer."

15   Business Roundtable, "Business Roundtable Releases Poll."

16   James Kohlmoos, NEKIA President, "The Emerging Era of Knowledge Utiliza-
     tion: The Impact of NCLB & the Education Sciences Reform Act on Our Field,"
     Jan. 2003, http://www.nekia.org/pdf/NEKIA_Commentary0103.pdf (accessed
     July 28, 2004).

17   No Child Left Behind Act of 2001 (NCLB); Education Sciences Reform Act of
     2002 (ESRA). For critiques of this recent federal emphasis on scientifically based
     research and its implementation, see Harvard Family Research Project, "Evalua-
     tion Exchange."

18   NCLB; Kohlmoos, "Emerging Era."

19   NCLB, §1111.

20   Dougherty, "States Must"; Rudner and Boston, "Data Warehousing"; Jones and
     Mulvenon, Leaving, 12.

21   ESRA §102(18)(b); Kohlmoos, "Emerging," 2.

22   NCLB §6111; ESRA §§208–209; Chrys Dougherty, "Longitudinal Student Data in
     the No Child Left Behind Act of 2001," National Center for Educational Account-
     ability, [July 2002,] http://www.nc4ea.org/files/ESEA_longitudinal_data_
     NCLBact.pdf (accessed July 28, 2004); Chrys Dougherty, "New Federal Education
     Research Legislation Promotes Longitudinal Student Data," n.d.,
     http://www.nc4ea.org/files/HR3801.pdf (accessed July 28, 2004).

23   Viadero, "Bill."

24   Barth et al., Dispelling the Myth, 9; Dispelling the Myth Online (DTM 2.0): The
     Power of Disaggregated Data, The Education Trust National Conference, Nov.
     6–8, 2003, http://www2.edtrust.org/NR/rdonlyres/216ACE26-3D35-4ABC-9154-
     2135BD840221/0/DispellingtheMythOnline2.ppt (accessed July 28, 2004). See also
     The Education Trust, Dispelling the Myth Online,
     http://www2.edtrust.org/edtrust/dtm/ (accessed July 2, 2004) (enabling the loca-
     tion of high-performing schools in almost every state that serves a high percent-
     age of minority and economically disadvantaged students).

25   Bay Area School Reform Collaborative, After the Test; Viadero, "Achievement-
     Gap."

26   Schmoker, Results Fieldbook, 1, 2; Schmoker, Results: The Key, 3 (quote).

27   Washington School Research Center, Continuing, 2, 3, 45; Washington School
     Research Center, Washington Best Practice Framework,
     http://www.just4kids.org/bestpractice/study_framework.cfm?study=washington
     (accessed July 2, 2004), and Washington Best Practice Framework: Practice: Reg-
     ularly Monitor Student Learning, Lind Elementary, Just for the Kids,
     http://www.just4kids.org/bestpractice/files/State/Washington/WA-Lind-
     Cls-Mon.pdf (accessed July 2, 2004).

28 Firestone, Schorr, and Mackey, *Curriculum and Culture,* see esp. pp. 2, 8.

29 Florida School Report, *Shining a Spotlight on School Success! Sharing Strategies that Work: Profiles of 20 High Performing Elementary Schools in Florida Based on the Florida School Report's Best Practices Study,* Mar. 2003; Florida School Report, *Shining a Spotlight on School Success: Profiles of [17] High Performing Middle and High Schools in Florida Based on the Florida School Report's Best Practices Study,* Nov. 2003.

30 Just for the Kids, Texas Best Practice Framework, http://www.just4kids.org/best-practice/study_framework.cfm?study=texas (accessed July 2, 2004); Just for the Kids, Texas Best Practice Study: Practice Definition/Evidence: Dowell Middle School, McKinney Independent School District, 2003 Case Study, http://www.just4kids.org/bestpractice/files/State/Texas/MS%20Dowell%20HP.pdf (accessed July 2, 2004).

31 See Towne, "Scientific Evidence"; Hoff, "States"; Feldman et al., "Developing"; Schmoker, *Results: The Key,* 3; Schmoker, *Results Fieldbook,* 3; Educational Research Service, "Making the Best Use of Assessment Data," *ERS On the Same Page Series,* 2001, http://www.ers.org/otsp/otsp5.htm (accessed July 29, 2004).

32 American Association of School Administrators, *Using data.*

33 Drury and Doran, "Value," 4.

34 Dougherty, *Nine Essential Elements.* For a discussion of importance of a student ID number in order to ascertain student achievement over time, see Drury and Doran, "Value," 2.

35 Hoff, "States"; National Center for Educational Accountability, "Data Survey Results: Minimum Requirements for a Student Achievement Information System," http://www.nc4ea.org/index.cfm?pg=surveyresults (accessed July 29, 2004).

36 Dougherty, "More than a Snapshot."

37 Shavelson and Towne, *Scientific Research,* 104 ("Simply collecting data is not in and of itself scientific. It is the rigorous organization and analysis of data to answer clearly specified questions that form the basis of scientific description, not the data themselves."); Massell, "State," 11; Togneri, *Beyond Islands,* 5.

38 See also Moore, "NCPA's Value-Added" (describing the National Center for Policy Analysis's Value-Added Report Card on Texas Schools); Carl Campanile, "Firm Will Create City Online-Up of Schools," *New York Post,* Online Edition, July 7, 2003, http://www.nypost.com/news/regionalnews/2590.htm (accessed July 7, 2003; article now archived); Standard & Poor's School Evaluation Services, http://www.ses.standardandpoors.com/about_ses.html (accessed July 29, 2004).

39 Rena Pederson, "The Public School Fix," interview with Tom Luce, *Dallas Morning News,* Mar. 14, 2004; Firestone, Schorr, and Mackey, *Curriculum and Culture,* 2.

40   See The School Information Partnership, www.schoolresults.org (accessed July 29, 2004); States News Service, "Reps. Boehner, Castle Hail Launch of No Child Left Behind Information Partnership Website," Jan. 29, 2004, http://www.states-news.com/ (accessed July 29, 2004; specific site address no longer valid).

41   Dougherty and Collins, "Use of the Just for the Kids Data." The study examined 2001 test scores and included 1997 and 1999 scores in the analysis to control for each school's prior rate of improvement.

42   Liebman and Sabel, "Federal No Child Left Behind Act," 1738.

43   Dougherty, *Nine Essential Elements.*

44   Just for the Kids, "High-Performing Schools: Data and Best Practices, Welcome to Consistently High-Performing Schools," http://www.just4kids.org/highperforming/index.cfm (accessed Sept. 16, 2004) and "Identification Criteria," http://www.just4kids.org/highperforming/identification_criteria.cfm?sub=criteria (accessed Sept. 16, 2004). Our thanks to Sarah Collins, director of School Effectiveness Analysis, at the National Center for Educational Accountability, for her knowledgeable contributions.

45   Just for the Kids, "High-Performing Schools: Data and Best Practices, Welcome to Consistently High-Performing Schools," http://www.just4kids.org/highperforming/index.cfm (accessed Sept. 16, 2004) and "Identification Criteria," http://www.just4kids.org/highperforming/identification_criteria.cfm?sub=criteria (accessed Sept. 16, 2004).

46   Dr. Dennis McDonald (principal, Demarest Middle School, N.J.), telephone interview by Lee Thompson, May 26, 2004.

47   Ibid.

3. Replicating Success: Pinpointing and Emulating High Performers in Education

1   A group of researchers, directed by Dr. Jean Rutherford, at the National Center for Educational Accountability developed the methodology concerning best practices communicated in this chapter, particularly the elements of an effective best practice study and the Best Practice Framework for communicating study findings. We are thankful to these individuals for their valuable contribution of time, effort, and talent to the creation of this effective approach.

2   National Research Council, *Improving,* 42–43.

3   U.S. Department of Education, "Identifying."

4   Carter, *No Excuses,* 24 (quoting Williams); Schmoker, *The Results Fieldbook,* 1–2; Togneri, *Beyond Islands,* 4, 5, 6; Corallo and McDonald, *What Works,* 3; Jones and Mulvenon, *Leaving,* 161.

5   Schmoker, *Results: The Key,* 65; Regional Educational Laboratories, 2003 Annual Report, "Evidence-based Education for All," http://www.relnetwork.org/2003ar/evidence.html (accessed July 29, 2004).

6   The father posed the question to one of the authors of Steve Fleischman, James W. Kohlmoos, and Andrew J. Rotherham, "Forging the New Education Knowledge Infrastructure, From Research to Practice: Moving Beyond the Buzzwords," Joint Statement of Education Quality Institute, NEKIA, and Progressive Policy Institute, Jan. 2003, http://www.nekia.org/pdf/Ed_Week_Commentary.pdf (accessed July 19, 2004).

7   National Research Council, *Improving,* 1, 11–13; Fleischman, Kohlmoos, and Rotherham, "Forging."

8   National Research Council, *Improving,* 13.

9   Ibid.

10 Schmoker, *Results: The Key,* 2, 66; Jones and Mulvenon, *Leaving,* 161; Shavelson and Towne, *Scientific Research,* 124; Slavin and Fashola, *Show Me*; Chall, *Academic Achievement*; Hacsi, *Children as Pawns*; Dr. Jean Rutherford (Director of Educational Initiatives, National Center for Educational Accountability), interview by Lee Thompson, July 22, 2002, tape recording, Austin, Tex.

11 Elmore, *Knowing.*

12 Shavelson and Towne, *Scientific Research,* 22; Fleischman, Kohlmoos, and Rotherham, "Forging"; Slavin, "Reader's Guide"; Corcoran, Fuhrman, and Belcher, "District Role."

13 No Child Left Behind Act of 2001 (NCLB); Education Sciences Reform Act of 2002 (ESRA); U.S. Department of Education, "Identifying," iii; Olson, "States Train."

14 Numerous recent education publications reflect this focus on proven educational practices. See Schmoker, *Results Fieldbook*; Schmoker, *Results: The Key*; Slavin and Fashola, *Show Me*; Chall, *Academic Achievement*; Feldman et al., "Developing"; Marzano, *What Works*; University of Pittsburgh Institute for Learning, *Principles of Learning,* http://www.lrdc.pitt.edu/netlearn/POL/pol-framepage.htm (accessed July 29, 2004); Lezotte, "Revolutionary"; Marzano, *What Works.*

15 What Works Clearinghouse, http://www.w-w-c.org (accessed July 29, 2004).

16 USDOE, "Teachers."

17 NGA Center for Best Practices, *Reaching.*

18 Regional Educational Laboratories, "2003 Annual Report: "Evidence-based Education for All," http://www.relnetwork.org/2003ar/evidence.html (accessed July 29, 2004) and "2003 Annual Report: Academic Success for All: Through Evidence-based Practice," http://www.relnetwork.org/2003ar/academic.html (accessed July 5, 2004).

19   Donovan and Pellegrino, *Learning*, 10–11. See also a discussion of SERP in chapter 2.

20   Public Schools of North Carolina, *Closing.*

21   Carter, *No Excuses.*

22   Cawelti, "Six Districts."

23   Marzano, *What Works*; Togneri, *Beyond Islands.*

24   Schafer et al., *Study.*

25   See Carter, *No Excuses*, 8.

26   Fleischman, Kohlmoos, and Rotherham, "Forging."

27   Donovan, Wigdor, and Snow, *Strategic*, 22.

28   Recent reports by the U.S. Department of Education and National Research Council have stressed the importance of a rigorous, high-quality research process, particularly randomized controlled trials and, to a lesser extent, well-structured comparison-group studies or case studies. Shavelson and Towne, *Scientific Research*, 105–8, 125; U.S. Department of Education, "Identifying," v.

29   See National Center for Educational Accountability (National Center), "Best Practices of High-Performing School Systems," http://www.just4kids.org/ bestpractice/index.cfm (accessed July 29, 2004); National Center, "Best Practices of High-Performing School Systems: About the Methodology," http://www.just4kids.org/bestpractice/research_methodology.cfm (accessed July 29, 2004); National Center, "Best Practices of High-Performing School Systems: The Themes," http://www.just4kids.org/bestpractice/theme_explanation .cfm?sub=framework (accessed July 29, 2004).

30   National Center, "High-Performing Schools: Data and Best Practices, Welcome to Consistently High-Performing Schools," http://www.just4kids.org/highper-forming/index.cfm (accessed July 29, 2004); National Center, "High-Performing Schools: Data and Best Practices, Identification Criteria," http://www.just4kids.org/highperforming/identification_criteria.cfm?sub=crite-ria (accessed July 29, 2004). See also discussion of using student performance data to locate consistently high-performing schools in chapter 2.

31   Slavin and Fashola, *Show Me*; William L. Bainbridge, "Education Research Should Be Nothing to Laugh At," *EducationNews.org*, June 9, 2003, http://www.educationnews.org/Educational-Research-Should-Be-Nothing-to-Laugh-At.htm (accessed July 29, 2004); Slavin, "Reader's Guide."

32   National Center, "Selecting."

33   Togneri, *Beyond Islands*, 1; Schafer et al., *Study*, Phase One, Conclusion (Part 7); Snipes, Doolittle, and Herlihy, *Foundations*, 8; Lezotte, "Revolutionary," 3; Fouts, *Decade*, 51.

34   Just for the Kids, "Best Practices of High-Performing School Systems: The

Framework," http://www.just4kids.org/bestpractice/framework.cfm?sub=frame-work (accessed July 29, 2004).

35 Just for the Kids, "Best Practices of High-Performing School Systems: The Themes," http://www.just4kids.org/bestpractice/theme_explanation.cfm?sub= framework (accessed July 29, 2004).

36 See Just for the Kids, "Best Practices of High-Performing School Systems: The School Levels," http://www.just4kids.org/bestpractice/schoollevel_explanation. cfm?sub=framework (accessed July 29, 2004).

37 Just for the Kids, "Best Practices of High-Performing School Systems: The Sup-ports," http://www.just4kids.org/bestpractice/support_explanation.cfm?sub= framework (accessed July 29, 2004).

38 Just for the Kids, "Best Practices of High-Performing School Systems: Self-Audits," http://www.just4kids.org/bestpractice/self_audit_framework.cfm?sub=tools (accessed July 29, 2004).

39 Rutherford, interview. See also George A. Clowes, "Outstanding High School Writing," *Heartland Institute,* Mar. 3, 2004, http://www.educationnews.org/out-standing-high-school-writing.htm (accessed July 29, 2004).

4. Overcoming the Gaps in State Data and Student Achievement: The Broad Prize for Urban Education

1 Sable and Young, *Characteristics*; Education Commission of the States, *Improv-ing,* iii.

2 Council of the Great City Schools, *Beating the Odds IV*; Education Commission of the States, *Improving*; Young, *Public,* 3–4, 6, 10, 14.

3 See the Education Trust's *Dispelling the Myth Online*, which enables users to identify high-minority and high-poverty schools in almost every state that attain high performance, at http://www2.edtrust.org/edtrust/dtm/ (accessed July 30, 2004); Council of the Great City Schools, *About the Council,* http://www.cgcs.org/about/index.html (accessed July 30, 2004); and *Beating the Odds IV* (the Council is composed of the largest sixty-three urban districts in the country; *Beating the Odds IV* included analysis of sixty-one of these districts).

4 National Center for Educational Accountability (National Center), *The Broad Prize Review and Selection Process,* 2003, http://www.just4kids.org/bestpractice/ files/Broad_2003SelProcess.pdf (accessed Mar. 9, 2004); National Center for Edu-cation Statistics, "2003 Trial Urban District Assessment: Mathematics," http://nces.ed.gov/nationsreportcard/mathematics/results2003/districtresults.asp (accessed July 15, 2004). As the Council of the Great City Schools rightly recog-

nizes, "The nation does not have an assessment system that allows our questions to be answered with certainty." *Beating the Odds IV*.

5   While Eli Broad supported former Vice president Al Gore for president in 2000, he has praised President George W. Bush's bipartisan efforts on education, and in particular the No Child Left Behind Act.

6   The Broad Foundation, *The Broad Prize for Urban Education: Overview*, http://www.broadfoundation.org/flagship/Prize-net.shtml (accessed Mar. 9, 2003). Coverage of the Broad Prize has recognized the award as the "top Prize" and the "biggest Prize" in public education. See "Long Beach District Wins Top Money Prize," CNN.com, Sept. 22, 2003, http://www.cnn.com/2003/EDUCA-TION/09/22/education.awards.ap (accessed Feb. 16, 2004); "Finalists for $1M in Scholarships Named," *New York Times on the Web*, Apr. 30, 2003, http://www.broadfoundation.org/med-articles/2003-0430nyt.shtml (accessed Mar. 10, 2004).

7   For a detailed overview of The Broad Prize process, see National Center, *Broad Prize Review*; The Broad Foundation, *The Broad Prize for Urban Education: 2003 Selection Process*, http://www.broadfoundation.org/flagship/selection-net.shtml (accessed Mar. 10, 2004); Just for the Kids, "Best Practices of High-Performing School Systems: About the Methodology," http://www.just4kids.org/bestprac-tice/research_methodology.cfm?sub=methodology (accessed July 15, 2004); Jim Lanich (Executive Director, Just for the Kids-California) and Ross Santy (Deputy Director, Just for the Kids-California), interview by Lee Thompson, July 1, 2002, tape recording, Dallas, Tex.

8   Compiling the list of nominees for The Broad Prize involved several steps. Researchers first compiled a list of every school district in the country that serves a "metropolitan statistical area" under the U.S. Census Bureau's definition. Then three different groups of districts on this list became nominees eligible for the Broad Prize: (1) all 25 districts that serve 100,000 or more students; (2) 62 districts with between 35,000 and 99,999 students that met three characteristics: (a) more than 40 percent of low-income students receiving free or reduced-price school lunch; (b) more than 40 percent of district students are of ethnic or racial minority groups; and (c) more than 40 percent of district schools serve an urban center or the census metropolitan statistical area code indicates that the district serves an urban center; and (3) 19 districts representing the largest K–12 school district from each state not yet represented among the nominees. This ensured representation by all states and the District of Columbia among the nominees. National Center, *Broad Prize Review*.

9   These five best practices reflect the five thematic areas and various best practices discussed in connection with the Best Practice Framework in chapter 3. As noted

in chapter 3, findings generated by the thorough Broad Prize process and numerous other studies enabled National Center researchers to pinpoint the five thematic best practice areas that are common to high-performing school systems across the country. These areas thus form a major component of the Best Practice Framework.

10   The Broad Foundation, *The Broad Prize for Urban Education: 2003 Finalists,* http://www.broadfoundation.org/flagship/2003-final-net.shtml (accessed Mar. 10, 2004).

11   Superintendent Laura Schwalm, Garden Grove Unified School District, Broad Site Visit Interview, 2003.

12   Boston Public Schools, *Citywide Learning Standards,* 16, 19.

13   Cathy Lassiter, Norfolk Public Schools, director of Leadership and Capacity Building, Broad Site Visit Interview, 2003.

14   Long Beach Unified School District, "Algebra Standards 2003," 9, http://www.lbusd.k12.ca.us/curriculum/Curriculum%20Services/Math/XCD/Sta ndardUnpackedAlgIdeas.pdf (accessed Mar. 2, 2004).

15   Kentucky Department of Education, "Core Content for Assessment," http://www.education.ky.gov/KDE/Instructional+Resources/Curriculum+Docu-ments+and+Resources/Core+Content+for+Assessment.htm (accessed Mar. 2, 2004); Jefferson County Public Schools (Ky.), "Core Content Guide, 11th United States History, Reconstruction to the Present: The Great Depression and the New Deal," http://fmpweb1.jefferson.k12.ky.us/corecontent/fmpro?-db=Topic.fp5&-lay=web&-format=topics.htm&UnitID=726&-sortfield=TopicNo&-find (accessed Mar. 2, 2004).

16   Norfolk Public Schools, "Principal Interview Questions," http://www.just4kids.org/bestpractice/files/National/Broad/DP2-1NPSaPrinIn-terview.Ques.pdf (accessed Mar. 3, 2004).

17   Boston Public Schools, "Leadership for Learning: Building a Career Ladder for Educators in Boston," Proposal Submitted to The Broad Foundation, November 2002, 2, http://www.just4kids.org/bestpractice/files/National/Broad/DP2-2BPSaBroadProposal.pdf (accessed Mar. 4, 2004); Boston Public Schools, "Principal Fellows Program Components," http://www.just4kids.org/bestprac-tice/files/National/Broad/DP2-2BPSbBosPrinFellows.pdf (accessed Mar. 3, 2004).

18   Norfolk Public Schools, "Norfolk Public Schools Principal Mentor Program," http://www.just4kids.org/bestpractice/files/National/Broad/DP2-2NPSaPrin-MentorProg.pdf (accessed Mar. 3, 2004).

19   Superintendent John Simpson, Norfolk Public Schools, Broad Site Visit Interview, 2003; Dorothy T. Harper to Middle and K-8 Principals, Long Beach Unified School District, memorandum regarding Professional Development Plan

2002–2003, Sept. 10, 2002, http://www.just4kids.org/bestpractice/files/
National/Broad/DP2-2LBUSDProfDevPlan.pdf (accessed Mar. 10, 2004).

20   Boston Public Schools, "Boston Teacher Residency Application,"
      http://www.just4kids.org/bestpractice/files/National/Broad/DP2-4BPSc-
      BosTeacherResLettertoApp.pdf (accessed Aug. 3, 2004); Boston Public Schools,
      "Boston Teacher Residency Fact Sheet,"
      http://www.just4kids.org/bestpractice/files/National/Broad/DP2-4BPSb-
      BosTeacherResFactSheet.pdf (accessed Aug. 3, 2004).

21   Christine Dominguez, assistant superintendent of Curriculum, Instruction, and
      Professional Development, Long Beach Unified School District, Broad Site Visit
      Interview, 2003.

22   See, for example, Lori Huggins, "Granholm Proposes Changes at Schools,"
      Detroit Free Press, Mar. 3, 2004,
      http://www.freep.com/news/education/ntrain3_20040303.htm (accessed Mar. 3,
      2004); Jimmy Kilpatrick, EducationNews Commentary and Reports, e-mail to
      EducationNews mailing list, Mar. 3, 2004.

23   Boston Public Schools, "Coaching in the Boston Public Schools," 2001,
      http://www.bpe.org/pubs/misc/BPS%20Coaching%20Model%206-01.pdf
      (accessed Mar. 4, 2004).

24   Pat Todd, executive director of Student Assignments, Health, Safety, and Gheens
      Professional Development Academy, Jefferson County Public Schools, Broad Site
      Visit Interview, 2003; Long Beach Unified School District, "Selection of Basic and
      Supplemental Textbooks and Instructional Materials,"
      http://www.just4kids.org/bestpractice/files/National/Broad/DP3-2LBUSDbSelec-
      tionofSupplementalTexts.pdf (accessed Mar. 5, 2004).

25   Lassiter, interview; Boston Public Schools, "Boston Plan for Excellence: Theory
      of Action Underlying Boston's Whole-School Improvement (WSI)," WSI
      Resource Binder SY 2002–2003,
      http://www.just4kids.org/bestpractice/files/National/Broad/DP3-3BPSWho-
      leSchoolImprovement.pdf (accessed Mar. 6, 2004).

26   Boston Public Schools, "Boston Plan"; Jane Jones, Director of K–12 Instruction,
      Garden Grove Unified School District, Broad Site Visit Interview, 2003.

27   Long Beach Unified School District, "Pacing Grade 3 (Math)," 3,
      http://www.lbusd.k12.ca.us/curriculum/Curriculum%20Services/Math/XCD/Gr3
      PacingChart.doc (accessed Mar. 6, 2004).

28   Dominguez, interview.

29   Superintendent Stephen Daeschner, Jefferson County Public Schools, Broad Site
      Visit Interview, 2003.

30 Maryellen Donahue, Boston Public Schools, director of Research, Assessment, and Evaluation, "Memorandum Regarding Statement of Capability of Boston to Track Students Longitudinally," June 25, 2003, http://www.just4kids.org/bestpractice/files/National/Broad/DP4-1BPSDataSystemsforStoringandDisaggregatingStudentData.pdf (accessed Mar. 6, 2004).

31 Boston Public Schools, 2004 President's Technology Grant Award Application, http://boston.k12.ma.us/bps/news/award_app.doc (accessed Mar. 6, 2004).

32 Long Beach Unified School District, Office of the Assistant Superintendent-High Schools, "Guidelines for a Focused Instructional Walkthrough," http://www.just4kids.org/bestpractice/files/National/Broad/DP4-1LBUS-DeGuidelinesforAFocusedInstrucWalkthrough.pdf (accessed Mar. 6, 2004); Description of Boston Public Schools Best Practice, 2003 Broad Prize for Urban Education, Best Practice Framework, http://www.just4kids.org/bestpractice/practice_definition.cfm?detailid=10 (accessed Mar. 10, 2004).

33 Boston Public Schools, "Whole School Improvement Plan, Boston Public Schools, Spring 2003," http://www.just4kids.org/bestpractice/files/National/Broad/DP4-4BPSaWholeSchoolImprovementPlan-BPS.pdf (accessed Aug. 3, 2004).

34 Superintendent Chris Steinhauser, Long Beach Unified School District, Broad Site Visit Interview, 2003; Norfolk Public Schools, *Teacher of the Year Rubric and Awards Banquet Invitation*, 2003, http://www.just4kids.org/bestpractice/files/National/Broad/DP5-1NPSeTeacheroftheYearAwardsProgram.pdf (accessed Aug. 3, 2004); Boston Public Schools, *Performance Incentives for Principal*, http://www.just4kids.org/bestpractice/files/National/Broad/DP5-1BPSaPerformanceIncentivesforPrincipals.pdf (accessed Aug. 3, 2004).

35 Todd, interview.

36 Boston Public Schools, *Boston Public Schools Accountability System*, 7.

37 Steinhauser, interview; Lassiter, interview; Norfolk Public Schools, "Memorandum, Standards of Learning Remediation," Sept. 6, 2002, http://www.just4kids.org/bestpractice/files/National/Broad/DP5-2NPSdStandardsofLearningRemediationPlan.pdf (accessed Aug. 3, 2004).

38 Dominguez, interview.

39 Lassiter, interview; Superintendent Thomas Payzant, Boston Public Schools, Broad Site Visit Interview, 2003; Terry Shook, Bolsa Grande High School Science Teacher, Garden Grove Unified School District, Broad Site Visit Interview, 2003; Sherri Franklin, Director of K–6 Instruction, Garden Grove Unified School District, Broad Site Visit Interview, 2003.

5. Ensuring School Readiness: Making Significant Gains in Early Childhood Education

1   National Center for Education Statistics, *Condition of Education 2003,* iii, 30; James T. Campbell, "We Lose if 'Preparation Gap' Not Closed," *Houston Chronicle,* Aug. 17, 2003, http://www.chron.com/cs/CDA/ssistory.mpl/editorial/2050205 (accessed Mar. 17, 2004); Boyer, *Ready to Learn,* 6–8; Coley, *Uneven Start,* 6–7; Lee and Burkam, *Inequality*; Stipek, "Head Start," 52; Whitehurst, "Much Too Late," 18 (discussing findings by University of Michigan psychologist Harold Stevenson of a strong correlation between a child's ability to name letters upon entering kindergarten and that child's performance on a reading-comprehension standardized test in tenth grade and research by Harvard University professor of education Connie Juel concluding that 88 percent of children who were poor readers at the end of first grade remained poor readers at the end of fourth grade).

2   Cohen, "Monetary Value," 26.

3   Campbell, "We Lose"; Boyer, *Ready,* 7. In 2003, only a bare majority (52%) of students in Maryland—the only state that formally assesses school readiness—were "fully ready" for kindergarten. Mike Bowler, "52% of Kindergarteners in Md. Judged 'Fully Ready'," *Baltimore Sun,* Mar. 26, 2003.

4   Lee and Burkam, *Inequality.* Likewise, the 2003 Maryland study also found that white and economically better off students were more likely to be ready for kindergarten, with an 18 percentage point gap between the readiness of children from middle-income families versus low-income families and an 18 percentage point gap also between white and African American children's readiness. Bowler, "52% of Kindergartners."

5   Stipek, "Head Start," 52.

6   No Child Left Behind Act of 2001.

7   Hanushek and Jorgenson, *Improving,* 12; Winters, *Teachers,* under "National Education Goals," http://www.ed.gov/G2K/teachers/negs.html (accessed July 30, 2004); Hoff, "2000 Looming."

8   Hart and Risley, "Early Catastrophe"; National Center for Education Statistics, *Condition of Education 2003,* ix–x. See also Associated Press, "Study: Preschool Children Better Prepared for Kindergarten than Peers without Preschool," *Boston Globe,* Mar. 28, 2004, http://www.boston.com/news/education/k_12/articles/2004/03/28/study_preschool_children_better_prepared_for_kindergarten_than_peers_without_preschool/ (accessed July 30, 2004) (discussing study showing preschoolers' preparation advantage over those who do not attend preschool); Kober, *It Takes More,* 23.

9   Barnett, "Early Childhood"; Barnett and Hustedt, "Preschool"; Reynolds et al., "Long-term Effects," 2345.

10   Stipek, "Head Start," 52.

11   Barnett et al., *State of Preschool*; Hyson, "Putting"; Shonkoff and Phillips, *Neurons to Neighborhoods*, 1–2, 5; Jonathan C. Rockoff, "Early Start to Close Learning Gap," *Baltimore Sun*, June 9, 2003, http://www.sunspot.net/news/education/bal-te-md.red09june09,0,3456308.story?coll=bal-local-headlines (accessed June 9, 2003); Rolnick and Grunewald, "Early Childhood"; Whitehurst, "Much Too Late."

12   Barnett and Hustedt, "Preschool"; Barnett, "Early Childhood"; National Institute for Early Education Research, "State Preschool Budgets Cut in Wake of Unprecedented Budget Crises, July 21, 2003, http://nieer.org/mediacenter/index.php?PressID=32 (accessed July 30, 2004); Schweinhart, "How"; Chicago Longitudinal Study, *Newsletter*; Reynolds et al., "Long-term Effects."

13   Hyson, "Putting"; Shonkoff and Phillips, *Neurons to Neighborhoods*, 11; Whitehurst, "Much Too Late"; Dickinson, "Shifting Images"; Bowman, Donovan, and Burns, *Eager to Learn*, 40–41; Stipek, "Head Start," 43. For an example of the debate between those who stress preschoolers' social-emotional development and those stressing academic development, see Elkind, "Much Too Early," and Whitehurst, "Much Too Late."

14   Espinosa, "High Quality Preschool," 2; Joe Nathan, "Early Childhood Education Must Meet Some Standards to Be Valuable," *St. Paul* (Minn.) *Pioneer Press*, Mar. 8, 2004, http://www.twincities.com/mld/twincities/news/columnists/joe_nathan/8105715.htm (accessed July 30, 2004); Bowman, Donovan, and Burns, *Eager to Learn*, 307–8; FPG-UNC Smart Start Evaluation Team, *Smart Start*; Hyson, "Putting"; Barnett, "Early Childhood Education"; Shonkoff and Phillips, *Neurons to Neighborhoods*.

15   Whitehurst, "Much Too Late"; Dickinson, "Shifting Images."

16   Shonkoff and Phillips, *Neurons to Neighborhoods*, 9; Barnett et al., *State of Preschool*, 4; Hacsi, *Children as Pawns*, 208; Bowman, Donovan, and Burns, *Eager to Learn*, 308.

17   Francine Kiefer, "Under Bush, 'Head Start' Focuses on Early Literacy," *Christian Science Monitor*, Apr. 4, 2002, http://www.csmonitor.com/2002/0404/p02s01-uspo.htm (accessed June 16, 2003); Diana Jean Schemo, "House G.O.P. Delays Vote on Remaking Head Start," *New York Times*, July 18, 2003, http://nytimes.com/2003/07/18/politics/18HEAD.html (accessed July 18, 2003); Hacsi, *Children as Pawns*, 27–28; U.S. Department of Health and Human Services, *Head Start FACES 2000*, 8–31 (discussing results of FACES 2000 and preliminary results of a study of Head Start centers in New York State: J. E. Fishel et al., *Enhancing Emergent Literacy Skills in Head Start: First Year Curriculum Evaluation Results*, Presented at the Biennial Meeting of the Society for Research in Child Development, Tampa, Fl., 2003). Some early childhood scholars and Head

Start workers fear that an increased academic focus will weaken Head Start's comprehensive health, nutrition, and other services. As Deborah Stipek notes, "These concerns are understandable, but there is no reason why attention to young children's intellectual skills needs to come at the cost of health care and opportunities to develop socially and emotionally." "Head Start," 52.

18   Schumacher, "Long and Winding"; Kiefer, "Under Bush"; The White House: President George W. Bush, Head Start Policy Book, http://www.whitehouse.gov/infocus/earlychildhood/hspolicybook/summary.htm l (accessed July 30, 2004).

19   Hyson, "Putting"; Barnett et al., *State of Preschool,* 36–37.

20   Barnett et al., *State of Preschool,* 4–5, 35, 41, 43, 45.

21   Ann Minnis (former director, Texas Instruments Foundation), interview by Lee Thompson, Aug. 1, 2002, tape recording, Dallas, Tex.; Texas Instruments Foundation, "TI and Education: Model Preschool," http://www.ti.com/corp/docs/company/citizen/foundation/leapsbounds/preschool.shtml (accessed July 30, 2004); Texas Instruments Foundation, "History and Research Summary: Margaret H. Cone Head Start Center," n.d.

22   Minnis, interview; Language Enrichment Activities Program (LEAP), "Cone Center Overview," http://www.leapsandbounds.org/overview.htm (accessed July 30, 2004). The Batelle Developmental Inventory assesses children ages birth to 8 in five areas: Cognitive, Personal-Social, Motor, Adaptive, and Communication. U.S. Department of Health and Human Services, Administration for Children and Families, "Child Development Instruments: Batelle Developmental Inventory," http://www.acf.hhs.gov/programs/core/ongoing_research/ehs/resources_measuring/res_meas_cdie.html (accessed July 30, 2004).

23   Nell Carvell (Director of the Language Enrichment Activities Program and Head Start Initiatives, Southern Methodist University), interview by Lee Thompson, Aug. 13, 2002, tape recording, Dallas, Tex.; Leap into a Brighter Future, *Learning,* 5, 7; Vail, "Ready."

24   LEAP, *Cone Center Overview*; Leap into a Brighter Future, *Learning,* 5–6.

25   See [Texas Instruments Foundation,] "Reading Performance Comparisons, Julia C. Frazier Elementary School," [2002–2001, 2001–2002], n.d.; [Texas Instruments Foundation], "Third-Grade Performance of the Julia C. Frazier Elementary School," [2001–2002], n.d. On a new, more difficult state assessment in 2003, students at Frazier did not perform as well in reading as in past years (with around 72 percent of students passing the test) but they continued to score well in math (with 96 percent passing). See Just for the Kids, 2003 Data: Julia C. Frazier Elementary, http://www.just4kids.org/jftk/ (accessed May 14, 2004).

26   Dougherty, *Improving,* 7; First Lady Laura W. Bush, [Education Initiative Booklet

Release,] http://www.whitehouse.gov/firstlady/news-speeches/releases/read-booklet.html (accessed July 30, 2004).

27   See, for example, John Mooney, "Preschoolers Make Modest Gains," New Jersey *Star Ledger,* Mar. 26, 2004, http://www.nj.com/news/ledger/jersey/index.ssf?/base/news-0/ 1080285098118231.xml (accessed Apr. 6, 2004).

28   Bowman, Donovan, and Burns, *Eager to Learn,* 310, 314.

29   Nell Carvell, e-mail to Lee Thompson, attachment concerning early childhood education and LEAP, Apr. 6, 2004; Language Enrichment Activities Program, *Learning,* Curriculum Guide; Head Start of Greater Dallas, Education: Curriculum, LEAP, http://www.hsgd.org/leap.htm (accessed July 30, 2004). The type of activities used in LEAP are thus similar to those the National Research Council found to be effective, research-based strategies for teaching children to read. Burns, Griffin, and Snow, eds., *Starting Out Right*; Stipek, "Head Start," 43 (describing NRC findings).

30   Language Enrichment Activities Program, *Learning,* Curriculum Guide.

31   Ibid.

32   Trust for Early Education, "Trust"; Scherer, "Perspectives"; Barnett and Hustedt, "Preschool"; Kiefer, "Under Bush."

33   Hyson, "Putting"; Bowman, Donovan, and Burns, *Eager to Learn,* 311; Barnett et al., *State of Preschool,* 4; National Head Start Association, "National"; Trust for Early Education, "Trust."

34   Schumacher, "Long and Winding."

35   Carvell, interview; SMU Center for Teacher Education, "Breaking Down Language Barriers: Pre-School Teacher Education," http://www.smu.edu/teacher_education/reading/prekteacher.asp (accessed July 30, 2004); LEAP for Dallas Kids, U.S. Department of Education Grant Application, Mar. 2004, 12.

36   Dallas Kids, "Dallas Kids Fact Sheet." PDAs will be funded by a grant to the Foundation for Community Empowerment from the Bass Foundation. Texas CCMS coordinates federal and state child care subsidies for economically disadvantaged families. CCMS determines if families are eligible for subsidies and pays participating child care providers directly. Welfare Information Network, "Promising Practices: Child Care Management Services (CCMS)," http://www.financeprojectinfo.org/WIN/promising/childcaremanagementservices.htm (accessed July 30, 2004).

37   Nell Carvell, report/comments to Lee Thompson, June 2004.

38   Julius B. Richmond and Judith Palfrey, "Keeping Head Start Strong and Successful," *Boston Globe,* July 19, 2003; Barnett et al., *State of Preschool,* 4.

39   Kris Axtman, "In Fast-Growing Texas, Businesses Aid Schools," *Christian Science Monitor,* Mar. 18, 2004, http://www.csmonitor.com/2004/0318/p02s01-usec.html (accessed July 30, 2004); Preschool for All, www.preschoolforall.org (accessed July 30, 2004); Education Development Center, "EDC Releases Study on Early Education Partnerships," Mar. 2003, http://main.edc.org/newsroom/features/partnerships.asp (accessed July 30, 2004); Schilder, Kiron, and Elliott, *Early Care.*

40   Dallas Kids, "Dallas Kids Fact Sheet."

41   Ibid. Tom Luce, co-author of this work, is a member of the board of directors of the Foundation for Community Empowerment.

42   Cecilia Edwards (executive vice-president and chief operating officer, Foundation for Community Empowerment), e-mail to Lee Thompson, July 28, 2004 (citing 2000 Census data, Texas A&M population projections, and Dallas Kids analysis as the sources for population figures for economically disadvantaged children in Dallas County and the area served by DISD); Dallas Kids, "Dallas Kids Fact Sheet"; Foundation for Community Empowerment, "Early Childhood Reading Initiative Reaches 11,000 Children," http://www.fce-dallas.org/pg_child.cfm (Apr. 12, 2004); Dallas Early Childhood Reading Initiative, Quarterly Meeting, Sept. 17, 2003, 2.

43   In addition, Texas Instruments Foundation researchers Ralph Dosher and Jim Fischer, in collaboration with DISD researchers Darshana Weerasinghe and Robert Mendro, have studied what factors contribute most to enabling economically disadvantaged children to read on grade level by the third grade. They analyzed eleven years of DISD data, from 1991–1992 through 2001–2002, and followed the academic progress of over 40,000 economically disadvantaged, African American students—a group that represented around 75 percent of DISD students in grades kindergarten through third grade during the studied years. Their analysis revealed that (1) a cognitively focused preschool program that uses a curriculum like LEAP, (2) few student transfers between schools, and (3) high-quality teaching were significant factors in enabling children from low-income circumstances to read on grade level by the third grade. See Dosher, Fischer, Weerasinghe, and Mendro, "Improving Third Grade Reading."

44   Minnis, interview; Carvell, interview.

45   Dickinson, "Shifting Images," 30. See also, for example, the National Research Council's recommendation that state and federal agencies work to develop assessment tools to accompany quality preschool curricula. Bowman, Donovan, and Burns, *Eager to Learn.*

46   Hyson, "Putting"; Bowman, Donovan, and Burns, *Eager to Learn,* 321; Jacobson, "Debate"; Stipek, "Head Start," 43.

47   Bill D. Ball, Jr., "Test Descriptions," [Feb. 18, 2003].

48   Bill D. Ball, Jr., e-mail to Lee Thompson, Feb. 19, 2003.

6. Inspiring and Rewarding Excellence in High Schools: Advanced Placement Incentive Programs

1   American Diploma Project, *Ready or Not*; Adelman, *Principal Indicators,* iv, 20–21.

2   Education Trust, "New Core Curriculum," 13–16; Education Trust, "Unfinished Business."

3   Adelman, *Answers in the Tool Box*; Carnevale and Desrochers, *Standards,* 53–56.

4   Olson, "Quantity," 14; Adelman, *Answers in the Tool Box,* Executive Summary, http://www.ed.gov/pubs/Toolbox/Exec.html (accessed July 31, 2004), and Part V. Conclusion: The Tool Box Story, http://www.ed.gov/pubs/Toolbox/Part5.html (accessed July 31, 2004); Adelman, Short Web-Based Version of *Answers in the Tool Box.*

5   Carnevale and Desrochers, *Standards,* 54–56; American Diploma Project, *Ready or Not,* 106.

6   Perkins et al., *High School Transcript Study,* 2-2, 2-6.

7   Olson, "Quantity," 14–15.

8   Ibid.; Commission on the Future of the Advanced Placement Program, *Access,* v; Gollub et al., *Learning and Understanding,* 65, 198–99; National Education Goals Panel, "Advancing AP," 2 (quoting Caperton). The equity of access issue came to a head in a 1999 suit filed by civil rights organizations on behalf of minority students against the University of California for giving extra weight to AP courses in college admission decisions on the grounds that many schools that serve minority populations do not offer AP courses. The suit has since settled. Burdman, "New"; Burdman, "Civil Rights."

9   Commission on the Future of the Advanced Placement Program, *Access,* v; CollegeBoard.com for Students, "AP: Subjects," http://www.collegeboard.com/student/testing/ap/subjects.html (accessed July 31, 2004); National Education Goals Panel, "Advancing AP," 1; Susan C. Thompson, "Students with Eye on College Say Aye to AP Courses," *St. Louis Post-Dispatch,* Apr. 10, 2004, http://www.stltoday.com/ (accessed May 22, 2004).

10   Commission on the Future of the Advanced Placement Program, *Access,* 1, 2; National Education Goals Panel, "Advancing AP," 1; Jay Mathews, "Arlington School Pushing AP Courses," *Washington Post,* Feb. 17, 2004, http://www.washingtonpost.com/wp-dyn/articles/A46511-2004Feb16.html (accessed May 22, 2004); Mathews, "100 Best"; Associated Press, "Academic Arms Race: Are Advanced Placement Courses Growing Too Fast?" http://www.cnn.com/2004/EDUCATION/08/22/advanced.placement.ap/index.html (accessed Sept. 13, 2004).

11   Commission on the Future of the Advanced Placement Program, *Access,* 1; Lichten, "Whither"; Carolyn Bacon (executive director, The O'Donnell Foundation), interview by Lee Thompson, Aug. 30, 2002, tape recording, Dallas, Tex.; Burdman, "New"; Advanced Placement Strategies, Inc. (APS), "Advanced Placement"; Gregg Fleisher (president, Advanced Placement Strategies, Inc.), interview by Lee Thompson, Sept. 9, 2002, tape recording, Dallas, Tex.; Thompson, "Students" (quoting Porter).

12   Mathews, "100 Best"; Jay Mathews, "AP Courses Not for Everyone, Educator Says," *Washington Post,* Aug. 5, 2003, http://www.washingtonpost.com/wp-dyn/articles/A20023-2003Aug5.html (accessed Aug. 5, 2003); Linda K. Wertheimer, "College-Level Work to Keep Paying Off: TI Foundation to Fund School Program," *Dallas Morning News,* July 21, 2000; Perkins et al., *High School Transcript Study*, ix.

13   Mellor et al., "Impact"; Bacon, "Advanced Placement," 25.

14   Hoff, "Scholars"; Lichten, "Whither"; Thompson, "Students"; Mathews, "100 Best"; Mathews, "AP Courses"; Education Trust, "Ticket to Nowhere," 30–31; "High Schools Skip Over Basics to Rush to College Classes," *USA Today,* Feb. 27, 2004, http://www.usatoday.com/news/opinion/editorials/2004-02-26-our-view_x.htm (accessed Aug. 1, 2004). Indeed, in what some claim is an elitist reaction to the greater accessibility of AP programs by all students, some affluent schools have dropped their AP programs in recent years. Thompson, "Students"; Mathews, "100 Best."

15   Mathews, "100 Best"; U.S. Department of Education, *Achieving Diversity.*

16   Bacon, interview, 2002; Peter O'Donnell (president, The O'Donnell Foundation), interview by Lee Thompson, Nov. 19, 2003, tape recording, Dallas, Tex. Both of the present authors are associated with the O'Donnell Foundation: Tom Luce serves as a trustee and Lee Thompson as deputy director.

17   APS, "Advanced Placement," 18.

18   Bacon, interview, 2002; APS, "Advanced Placement," 19; Carolyn Bacon (executive director, The O'Donnell Foundation), interview by Lee Thompson, Nov. 19, 2003, tape recording, Dallas, Tex.

19   Bacon, interview, 2002.

20   Wertheimer, "College-Level"; U.S. Department of Education, "Prepare Academically and Financially for College: Who's Doing It?," n.d., http://www.ed.gov/pubs/PFIE/collwho.html (accessed Aug. 1, 2004); Hudgins, "Kick Start"; APS, "Advanced Placement," 19.

21   Hudgins, "Kick Start"; APS, "Advanced Placement," 19.

22   Bacon, interview, 2002; Bacon, interview, 2003; APS, "Advanced Placement"; Hudgins, "Kick Start"; Fleisher, interview, 2002.

23 APS, "Advanced Placement," 51–53.

24 O'Donnell Foundation, *AP Arts*; O'Donnell, interview; Bacon, interview, 2002.

25 Commission on the Future of the Advanced Placement Program, *Access,* 3; Bacon, interview, 2003; U.S. Department of Education, "Achieving Diversity."

26 Texas Advanced Placement Incentive Program; Texas Center for AP/IB Initiatives, Funding, http://txapib.tamu.edu/ (accessed Aug. 1, 2004); National Education Goals Panel, "Advancing AP," 3; Bacon, "Advanced Placement," 8–10.

27 U.S. Department of Education, "Achieving Diversity."

28 Bacon, interview, 2003; Bacon, interview, 2002; U.S. Department of Education, "Achieving Diversity"; National Education Goals Panel, "Advancing AP," 3.

29 Thompson, "Students"; Kenning, "Grant to Bolster Advanced Classes," *Louisville (Kentucky) Courier-Journal,* May 4, 2004, http://www.courier-journal.com/local-news/2004/05/04ky/B1-grant0504-4448.html (accessed Aug. 1, 2004); U.S. Department of Education, "Achieving Diversity"; Office of Management and Budget, *Budget: Department of Education,* http://www.whitehouse.gov/omb/budget/fy2005/education.html (accessed Aug. 1, 2004).

30 Bacon, interview, 2003.

31 Fleisher, interview, 2002; O'Donnell, interview.

32 Gollub et al., *Learning and Understanding,* 79–80; Thompson, "Students"; Fleisher, interview, 2002; Hudgins, "Kick Start" (quoting Rickels).

33 Fleisher, interview, 2003; Fleisher, interview, 2002; Hudgins, "Kick Start."

34 Fleisher, interview, 2002; Bacon, interview, 2002.

35 Fleisher, interview, 2003; Bacon, interview, 2002.

36 Fleisher, interview, 2002.

37 Gollub et al., *Learning and Understanding,* 79–80; Fleisher, interview, 2002.

38 APS Client Information Sheet, 2003.

39 U.S. Department of Education, "Achieving Diversity," (quoting Secretary Paige); College Board, *Access,* 8; Burdman, "Students"; Charles A. Dana Center, "Advanced Placement Equity Initiative, Building Capacity: Vertical Teaming in Mathematics and Science," University of Texas at Austin, 2002, http://www.utdanacenter.org/ap/math/bldcap.html (accessed Aug. 1, 2004).

40 APS, "Advanced Placement," 14; Fleisher, interview, 2002.

41 APS, "Advanced Placement," 16–17; Bacon, interview, 2002; O'Donnell, interview, 2002; Fleisher, interview, 2003; Bacon, interview, 2003; O'Donnell Foundation, "Building a Strong Teacher Corps in English and Math in Texas Middle Schools and High Schools," June 24, 2003, 2.

42 See, for example, Advanced Placement Strategies, Inc., *Connecting.* See also the skills progression highlighted in the *Laying the Foundation* science curriculum guides, including Advanced Placement Strategies, Inc., *Resource and Strategies.*

43   Fleisher, interview, 2002; Fleisher, interview, 2003.

44   Fleisher, interview, 2002; Fleisher, interview, 2003.

45   Fleisher, interview, 2002.

46   Ibid.; Bacon, interview, 2003.

47   Fleisher, interview, 2002.

48   O'Donnell, interview, 2003.

49   Fleisher, interview, 2002.

50   Ibid.; APS Client Information Sheet, 2003.

51   Fleisher, interview, 2002.

52   Hudgins, "Kick Start"; Fleisher, interview, 2002; Bacon, interview, 2002; Bacon, interview, 2003.

53   Fleisher, interview, 2002.

54   Ibid.

55   Bacon, interview, 2002; APS, "Advanced Placement," 54.

56   O'Donnell, interview; Bacon, interview, 2003.

Conclusion

1   Elmore, *Knowing*.

2   Lloyd, "Prediction"; Slavin, Karweit, and Wasik, "Preventing"; U.S. Department of Education (USDOE), "Read Write Now!: Simple Things You Can Do, How to Start An After School, Weekend, or Summer Literacy Program," Dec. 1997, (archived information), http://www.ed.gov/pubs/SimpleThings/intro.html (accessed Aug. 1, 2004); President George W. Bush, The White House, "Fact Sheet: No Child Left Behind is Making a Difference for America's Children," May 11, 2004, http://www.whitehouse.gov/news/releases/2004/05/20040511-2.html (accessed Aug. 1, 2004); No Child Left Behind Act of 2001, sec. 1201.

3   USDOE, *Mathematics;* National Center for Education Statistics, "Do Gatekeeper Courses"; USDOE, *Seven Priorities*; Gregg Toppo, "Algebra's for Everyone Now—Expectations Are Rising," *USA Today,* Aug. 12, 2004.

Bibliography

Achieve, Inc. Washington, D.C.: Achieve, Inc., 2002.

Achieve, Inc. and National Center for Educational Accountability. *All Tests Are Not Equal: Why States Need to Give High-Quality Tests.* [July 2003]. http://www.nc4ea.org/files/statement%20of%20principles%20final.pdf (accessed July 28, 2004).

Adelman, Clifford. *Answers in the Tool Box: Academic Intensity, Attendance Patterns, and Bachelor's Degree Attainment.* Washington, D.C.: U.S. Department of Education, 1999. http://www.ed.gov/pubs/Toolbox/index.html (accessed July 31, 2004).

———. *Principal Indicators of Student Academic Histories in Postsecondary Education, 1972-2000.* Washington, D.C.: U.S. Department of Education, Institute of Education Sciences, 2004. http://www.ed.gov/rschstat/research/pubs/prinindicat/prinindicat.pdf (accessed July 31, 2004).

———. Short Web-Based Version of *Answers in the Tool Box: Academic Intensity, Attendance Patterns, and Bachelor's Degree Attainment.* Washington, D.C.: U.S. Department of Education, 1999. http://www.ed.gov/pubs/Toolbox/toolbox.html (accessed July 31, 2004).

Advanced Placement Strategies, Inc. "Advanced Placement Incentive Programs: Improving Education, Changing Lives." Presentation for San Antonio Independent School District Meeting, Mar. 26, 2003, updated Aug. 8, 2003.

———. *Connecting the Middle School Grades to Advanced Placement Mathematics: A Resource and Strategy Guide.* Laying the Foundation series. Dallas: Advanced Placement Strategies, Inc., 2004.

———. *A Resource and Strategies Guide for Middle Grades Life and Earth Science,* Laying the Foundation series. Dallas: Advanced Placement Strategies, Inc., 2004.

American Association of School Administrators. *Using Data to Improve Schools: What's Working.* Arlington, Va.: American Association of School Administrators, n.d. http://www.aasa.org/cas/UsingDataToImproveSchools.pdf (accessed July 29, 2004).

American Diploma Project. *Ready or Not: Creating a High School Diploma that Counts.* Washington, D.C.: The American Diploma Project, [Feb. 2004].

http://www.achieve.org/dstore.nsf/Lookup/ADPreport/$file/ADPreport.pdf (accessed July 31, 2004).

American Federation of Teachers. *Making Standards Matter 2001: A Fifty-State Report on Efforts to Implement a Standards-Based System.* 2001. http://www.aft.org/ (accessed July 4, 2004).

Bacon, Carolyn. "Advanced Placement Incentive Programs: Improving Education, Changing Lives." Presentation to Texas Senate Education Committee, April 2004.

Barnett, W. Steven. "Early Childhood Education." In *School Reform Proposals: The Research Evidence,* edited by Alex Molnar, 1-26. Greenwich, Conn.: Information Age Publishing, 2002.

Barnett, W. Steven, and Jason T. Hustedt. "Preschool: The Most Important Grade." *Educational Leadership* 60, no. 7 (Apr. 2003): 54-57. http://www.ascd.org/publications/ed_lead/200304/barnett.html (accessed July 30, 2004).

Barnett, W. Steven, Kenneth B. Robin, Jason T. Hustedt, and Karen L. Schulman. *The State of Preschool: 2003 State Preschool Yearbook.* New Brunswick, N.J.: National Institute for Early Education Research, 2003. http://nieer.org/yearbook/pdf/yearbook.pdf (accessed July 30, 2004).

Barth, Patte, Kati Haycock, Hilda Jackson, Karen Mora, Pablo Ruiz, Stephanie Robinson, Amy Wilkins, eds. *Dispelling the Myth: High Poverty Schools Exceeding Expectations.* Washington, D.C.: Education Trust, 1999.

Bay Area School Reform Collaborative. *After the Test: Using Data to Close the Achievement Gap.* Dec. 2003.

Berkner, Lutz, Shirley He, and Emily Forrest Cataldi. *Descriptive Summary of 1995-96 Beginning Postsecondary Students: Six Years Later.* NCES 2003-151. Washington, D.C.: U.S. Department of Education, National Center for Education Statistics, 2003.

Boston Public Schools. *Boston Public Schools Accountability System SY2000-2001.* Jan. 2001. http://www.just4kids.org/bestpractice/files/National/Broad/DP5-2BPSa2000-01AccountabilitySystem.pdf (accessed Aug. 3, 2004).

———. *Citywide Learning Standards, Grade Level Summary: English Language Arts, History and Social Studies, Mathematics, Science, and Technology.* Sept. 2002. http://boston.k12.ma.us/teach/standards/Grade6.doc (accessed Aug. 3, 2004).

Bowman, Barbara T., M. Suzanne Donovan, and M. Susan Burns, eds. *Eager to Learn: Educating Our Preschoolers.* Washington, D.C.: National Academy Press, 2000.

Boyer, Ernest L. *Ready to Learn: A Mandate for the Nation.* Princeton, N.J.: Carnegie Foundation for the Advancement of Teaching, 1991.

Burdman, Pamela. "Civil Rights Groups, Berkeley Settle Lawsuit Over Admissions Policy." *Black Issues in Higher Education,* July 31, 2003. http://www.findarticles.com/cf_dls/m0DXK/12_20/106422258/p1/article.jhtml (accessed July 31, 2004).

———. "The New Advanced Placement Push: Emphasis on the Popular College-Level Courses Increases." *National CrossTalk.* Summer 2000. http://www.highereducation.org/crosstalk/ct0700/news0700-placement.shtml (accessed July 31, 2004).

Burns, M. Susan, Peg Griffin, and Catherine E. Snow, eds. *Starting Out Right: A Guide to Promoting Children's Reading Success.* Washington, D.C.: National Academy Press, 1999.

Carnevale, Anthony P., and Donna M. Desrochers. *Standards for What? The Economic Roots of K-16 Reform.* ETS Leadership 2003 Series. Princeton, N.J.: Educational Testing Service, 2003. http://www.ets.org/research/dload/standards_for_what.pdf (accessed July 31, 2004).

Carter, Samuel Casey. *No Excuses: Lessons from 21 High-Performing, High-Poverty Schools.* Washington, D.C.: The Heritage Foundation, 2000.

Cawelti, Gordon. "Six Districts, One Goal of Excellence." *Journal of Staff Development* 22, no. 4 (Fall 2001): 30-35. http://www.nsdc.org/library/publications/jsd/cawelti224.pdf (accessed July 29, 2004).

Chall, Jeanne S. *The Academic Achievement Challenge: What Really Works in the Classroom?* New York: Guilford Press, 2000.

Chicago Longitudinal Study. "What Is the Chicago Longitudinal Study?" *Newsletter of the Chicago Longitudinal Study,* no. 2, June 2002. http://www.waisman.wisc.edu/cls/NEWSLETTER2.PDF (accessed July 30, 2004).

Cohen, Mark. "The Monetary Value of Saving a High Risk Youth." *Journal of Quantitative Criminology* 14, no. 1 (1998): 5-33.

Coley, Richard J. *An Uneven Start: Indicators of Inequality in School Readiness.* Princeton, N.J.: Educational Testing Service, 2002. http://www.ets.org/research/pic/Unevenstrat.pdf (accessed July 30, 2004).

Commission on the Future of the Advanced Placement Program. *Access to Excellence: A Report of the Commission on the Future of the Advanced Placement Program.* New York: College Entrance Examination Board, 2001. http://apcentral.collegeboard.com/repository/ap01.pdf.ac_7907.pdf (accessed July 31, 2004).

Corallo, Christopher, and Deborah H. McDonald. *What Works with Low-Performing Schools: A Review of Research.* Charleston, W.Va.: AEL, 2002.

Corcoran, Tom, Susan H. Fuhrman, and Catherine L. Belcher. "The District Role in Instructional Improvement." *Phi Delta Kappan* 83, no. 1 (Sept. 2001): 78-84.

Council of the Great City Schools. *Beating the Odds IV: A City-by-City Analysis of Student Performance and Achievement Gaps on State Assessments,* Executive Summary. Mar. 2004. http://www.cgcs.org/reports/beat_the_oddsIV.html (accessed July 15, 2004).

Cross, Richard W., Theodor Rebarber, and Justin Torres, eds. *Grading the Systems: The Guide to State Standards, Tests, and Accountability Policies.* Washington, D.C.: Thomas B. Fordham Foundation and AccountabilityWorks, 2004. http://www.edexcellence.net/doc/GradingtheSystems.pdf (accessed July 27, 2004).

Dallas Kids. "Dallas Kids Fact Sheet." June 2004.

Dickinson, David K. "Shifting Images of Developmentally Appropriate Practice as Seen Through Different Lenses." *Educational Researcher* 31, no. 1 (Jan.-Feb. 2002): 26-32. http://www.aera.net/pubs/er/pdf/vol31_01/AERA310105.pdf (accessed July 30, 2004).

Donovan, M. S., A. K. Wigdor, and C. E. Snow. *Strategic Education Research Partnership.* Washington, D.C.: National Academies Press, 2003.

Donovan, M. Suzanne, and James W. Pellegrino, eds. *Learning and Instruction: A SERP Research Agenda.* Washington, D.C.: National Academies Press, 2004.

Dosher, Ralph, Jim Fischer, Darshana Weerasinghe, and Robert Mendro. *Improving Third Grade Reading.* [Dallas: Texas Instruments and Dallas Independent School District,] 2004.

Dougherty, Chrys. "How States Can Use Information Technology to Support School Improvement Under NCLB." White Paper, U.S. Department of Education Secretary's No Child Left Behind Leadership Summits: Empowering Accountability and Assessment Using Technology, Mar. 2004. http://www.nclbtechsummits.org/summit1/ChrysDoughertyWhitePaper.pdf (accessed July 1, 2004).

———. "More than a Snapshot." *Education Week* 20, no. 33 (May 2, 2001): 39, 42. http://www.edweek.org/ew/ewstory.cfm?slug=33dougherty.h20 (accessed July 19, 2004).

———. "States Must Improve Data for Adequate Yearly Progress." *Education Assessment Insider* 1, no. 5 (2002): 6-7.

———. "The Education Data Manager's Guide to the Value of Longitudinal Student Data." Education Commission of the States Issue Brief, Sept. 2002. http://www.nc4ea.org/files/data_managers_guide.pdf (accessed July 28, 2004).

———. *Nine Essential Elements of Statewide Data-Collection Systems.* Austin: National Center for Educational Accountability, [2003]. http://www.nc4ea.org/files/9%20elements%20Brochure.pdf (accessed July 29, 2004).

———, ed. *Improving Early Literacy: A Handbook for Prekindergarten Educators.* Austin: LBJ School of Public Affairs, 1999.

Dougherty, Chrys, and Sarah Collins. *Use of the Just for the Kids Data by Texas Elementary Schools,* NCEA Research Report #1, Austin, Tex.: National Center for Educational Accountability, Jan. 2002. http://www.nc4ea.org/files/implementation%20study%201-30-02.pdf (accessed July 29, 2004).

Drury, Darrel, and Harold Doran. "The Value of Value-Added Analysis." *Policy Research Brief* 3, no. 1 (Jan. 2003): 1-4. http://www.nsba.org/site/docs/12000/11966.pdf (accessed July 28, 2004).

Education Commission of the States. *Improving Academic Achievement in Urban Districts: What State Policymakers Can Do.* Denver: Education Commission of the States, 2003. http://www.ecs.org/html/educationIssues/Urban/urbanpdf/Urbanbook.pdf (accessed July 30, 2004).

Education Sciences Reform Act of 2002. Pub. L. No. 107-279, 116 Stat. 1941 (2002).

Education Trust. *Education Watch: Achievement Gap Summary Tables.* Spring 2004. http://www2.edtrust.org/edtrust/summaries2004/2004AchievementGapandSummaryTables.PDF (accessed July 28, 2004).

———. "A New Core Curriculum for All," *Thinking K-16* 7, no. 1 (Winter 2003). http://www2.edtrust.org/NR/rdonlyres/26923A64-4266-444B-99ED-2A6D5F14061F/0/k16_winter2003.pdf (accessed July 31, 2004).

———. "Ticket to Nowhere: The Gap Between Leaving High School and Entering College and High-Performance Jobs." *Thinking K-16* 3, no. 2 (Fall 1999), 1-31. http://www2.edtrust.org/NR/rdonlyres/1196FBF0-FB01-4B75-B363-B1D525869F29/0/k16_fall99.pdf (accessed Aug. 1, 2004).

———. "The Unfinished Business of Brown v. Board of Education," Press Release, May 13, 2003. http://www2.edtrust.org/EdTrust/Press+Room/brown+board.htm (accessed July 31, 2004).

Education Week. "Quality Counts 2004: Count Me In: Special Education in an Era of Standards," *Education Week* 23, no. 17 (2004). http://www.edweek.org/sreports/qc04 (accessed July 26, 2004).

———. "Quality Counts 2003: Standards and Accountability." *Education Week* 22, no. 17 (2003). http://www.edweek.org/sreports/qc03/reports/standacct-t1.cfm (accessed July 4, 2004).

Elkind, David. "Much Too Early," Forum, Young Einsteins. *Education Next,* Summer 2001, 9-15. http://www.educationnext.org/20012/8a.pdf (accessed July 30, 2004).

Elmore, Richard F. *Knowing the Right Thing to Do: School Improvement and Performance-Based Accountability.* Washington, D.C.: NGA Center for Best Practices, 2003. http://www.nga.org/cda/files/0803KNOWING.PDF (accessed July 29, 2004).

Espinosa, Linda M. "High Quality Preschool: Why We Need It and What It Looks Like." *Preschool Policy Matters,* no. 1 (Nov. 2002). http://nieer.org/resources/policybriefs/1.pdf (accessed July 30, 2004).

Feldman, Jay, Gail Lucey, Sarah Goodrich, and Dana Frazee. "Developing an Inquiry-Minded District." *Educational Leadership* 60, no. 5 (Feb. 2003). http://www.ascd.org/publications/ed_lead/200302/feldman.html (accessed July 28, 2004).

Finn, Chester E., Jr. "From Checker's Desk: Is NCLB an Unfunded Mandate?" *The Education Gadfly* 4, no. 6 (Feb. 12, 2004). http://www.edexcellence.net/foundation/gadfly/index.cfm (accessed Feb. 15, 2004).

———. *What Ails U.S. High Schools? How Should They Be Reformed? Is There a Federal Role?* Apr. 2002. http://www.ed.gov/about/offices/list/ovae/pi/hs/finn.doc (accessed July 28, 2004).

Firestone, William A., Roberta Y. Schorr, and Philip E. Mackey. *Curriculum and Culture: Findings from New Jersey's Illustrative Best Practices Study. Just for the Kids-New Jersey.* May 2004. http://www.just4kids.org/bestpractice/files/state/New%20Jersey/New_Jersey_JFTK_Final_Report_05-10-04.pdf (accessed July 2, 2004).

Florida School Report. *Shining a Spotlight on School Success: Profiles of [17] High Performing Middle and High Schools in Florida Based on the Florida School Report's Best Practices Study.* Nov. 2003.

———. *Shining a Spotlight on School Success! Sharing Strategies that Work: Profiles of 20 High Performing Elementary Schools in Florida Based on the Florida School Report's Best Practices Study.* Mar. 2003.

Fouts, Jeffrey T. *A Decade of Reform: A Summary of Research Findings on Classroom, School, and District Effectiveness in Washington State.* Research Report No. 3. Lynnwood, Wa.: Washington School Research Center, 2003. http://www.spu.edu/orgs/research/ADecadeofReformOctober192003v5.pdf (accessed July 29, 2004).

FPG-UNC Smart Start Evaluation Team. *Smart Start and Preschool Child Care Quality in NC: Change Over Time and Relation to Children's Readiness.* Chapel Hill, N.C.: FPG Child Development Institute, 2003. http://www.fpg.unc.edu/smartstart/reports/Child_Care_Quality_2003.pdf (accessed July 30, 2004).

Gollub, Jerry P., Meryl W. Bertenthal, Jay B. Labov, and Philip C. Curtis, eds. *Learning and Understanding: Improving Advanced Study of Mathematics and Science in U.S. High Schools.* Washington, D.C.: National Academy Press, 2002. http://www.nap.edu/books/0309074401/html/ (accessed July 31, 2004).

Greene, Jay P., and Greg Forster. "Public High School Graduation and College Readiness Rates in the United States." Manhattan Institute for Policy Research, Education

Working Paper No. 3, Sept. 2003. http://www.manhattan-institute.org/html/ewp_03.htm#14 (accessed July 28, 2004).

Grigg, Wendy S., Mary C. Daane, Ying Jin, and Jay R. Campbell. *The Nation's Report Card: Reading 2002.* NCES 2003-521. Washington, D.C.: U.S. Department of Education, National Center for Education Statistics, 2003. http://nces.ed.gov/nationsreportcard/pdf/main2002/2003521a.pdf (accessed Sept. 17, 2004).

Grissmer, David, and Ann Flanagan. *Exploring Rapid Achievement Gains in North Carolina and Texas.* National Education Goals Panel, Nov. 1998. http://www.negp.gov/reports/grissmer.pdf (accessed July 3, 2004).

Hacsi, Timothy A. *Children as Pawns: The Politics of Educational Reform.* Cambridge: Harvard University Press, 2002.

Hanushek, Eric A. "Lost Opportunity." *Education Next,* Spring 2003, 84-87.

Hanushek, Eric A., and Dale W. Jorgenson, eds. *Improving America's Schools: The Role of Incentives.* Washington, D.C.: National Academy Press, 1996. http://www.nap.edu/books/0309054362/html/index.html (accessed July 30, 2004).

Hart, Betty, and Todd R. Risley. "The Early Catastrophe: The 30 Million Word Gap by Age 3." *American Educator,* Spring 2003. http://www.aft.org/american_educator/spring 2003/catastrophe.html (accessed July 30, 2004).

Harvard Family Research Project, "The Evaluation Exchange Special Report on Scientifically Based Research." *Evaluation Exchange* 9, no. 2 (Summer 2003). http://www.gse.harvard.edu/hfrp/eval/issue22/special.html (accessed July 28, 2004).

Haycock, Kati, Craig Jerald, and Sandra Huang. "Closing the Gap: Done in a Decade." *Thinking K-16* 5, no. 2 (Spring 2001): 3-22. http://www2.edtrust.org/NR/rdonlyres/85EB1387-A6B7-4AF4-BEB7-DF389772ECD2/0/k16_spring01.pdf (accessed July 28, 2004).

Hill, Paul T., Kacey Guin, and Mary Beth Celio. "Minority Children at Risk." In *Our Schools & Our Future . . . Are We Still At Risk?,* edited by Paul E. Peterson, 111-39. Palo Alto: Hoover Institution Press, 2003.

Hoff, David J. "Debate Grows on True Costs of School Law." *Education Week* 23, no. 21 (Feb. 4, 2004): 1, 22. http://www.edweek.org/ew/ewstory.cfm?slug=21NCLBCost.h23 (accessed July 27, 2004).

———. "Scholars Critique Advanced Classes in Math, Science." *Education Week* 21, no. 23 (Feb. 20, 2002): 1, 12. http://www.edweek.org/ew/newstory.cfm?slug=23nrc.h21 (accessed Aug. 1, 2004).

———. "States Need Updates for Managing Data, Analysis Concludes." *Education Week* 23, no. 8 (Oct. 22, 2003): 1, 20. http://www.edweek.org/ew/ewstory.cfm?slug=08data.h23 (accessed July 29, 2004).

———. "With 2000 Looming, Chances of Meeting National Goals Iffy." *Education Week* 18, no. 18 (Jan. 13, 1999): 1, 28-30. http://www.edweek.org/ew/vol-18/18goals.h18 (accessed July 30, 2004).

Hoxby, Caroline. "What Has Changed and What Has Not." In *Our Schools and Our Future . . . Are We Still at Risk?,* edited by Paul E. Peterson, 73-110. Palo Alto: Hoover Institution Press, 2003.

Hudgins, Karen. "A Kick Start for College: Advanced Placement Program Proves It Pays to Study Hard." *Fiscal Notes,* May 2003.

http://www.window.state.tx.us/comptrol/fnotes/fn0305/kick.html (accessed Aug. 1, 2004).

Hunt, James B., Jr. "Unrecognized Progress." *Education Next*, Spring 2003, 24-27.

Hyson, Marilou. "Putting Early Academics in Their Place." *Educational Leadership* 60, no. 7 (April 2003): 20-23.

Jacobson, Linda. "Debate Continues Over Head Start Assessment." *Education Week* 23, no. 26 (Mar.10, 2004): 10. http://www.edweek.org/ew/ewstory.cfm?slug=26Head-start.h23 (accessed Apr. 13, 2004).

Jerald, Craig D. "The State of the States—Quality Counts 2000: Who Should Teach?" *Education Week* 19, no. 18 (2000): 62-65. http://edweek.com/sreports/qc00/tem-plates/article.cfm?slug=sosintro.htm (accessed July 4, 2004).

Jones, Marsha, and Sean Mulvenon. *Leaving No Child Behind: How Data Driven Decision-Making Can Help Schools Meet the Challenge.* Phoenix: All Star Publishing, 2003.

Kirkpatrick, David W. "A Nation Still at Risk." *The Heartland Institute: School Reform News*, Apr. 1, 2003. http://www.heartland.org/Article.cfm?artId=11776 (accessed July 4, 2004).

Klein, Stephen P., Laura S. Hamilton, Daniel F. McCaffrey, and Brian M. Stecher. *What Do Test Scores in Texas Tell Us?* Issue Paper. RAND Education, 2000. http://www.rand.org/publications/IP/IP202/ (accessed July 4, 2004).

Kober, Nancy. *It Takes More Than Testing: Closing the Achievement Gap.* Washington, D.C.: Center on Education Policy, 2001. http://www.ctredpol.org/improvingpublic-schools/closingachievementgap.pdf (accessed July 30, 2004).

Kongshem, Lars. "Smart Data: Mining the School District Data Warehouse." *www.electronic-school.com*, Sept. 1999. http://www.electronic-school.com/199909/0999fl.html (accessed Aug. 3, 2004).

Language Enrichment Activities Program. *Learning by Leaps and Bounds*, Curriculum Guide. Vol. 2. [Dallas, Tex.: Language Enrichment Activities Program, 2003.]

Lauer, Patricia A. *A Policymaker's Primer on Education Research: How to Understand, Evaluate and Use It.* Mid-continent Research for Education and Learning and the Education Commission of the States. Feb. 2004. http://www.ecs.org/html/educa-tionIssues/Research/primer/foreword.asp (accessed July 28, 2004).

Leap into a Brighter Future. *Learning by Leaps and Bounds: Margaret H. Cone, A Model Head Start Center.* Head Start's Third National Research Conference, Washington, D.C., June 22, 1996. http://www.ti.com/corp/docs/company/citizen/foundation/leaps-bounds/leap.pdf (accessed July 30, 2004).

Lee, Valerie E. and David T. Burkam. *Inequality at the Starting Gate: Social Background Differences in Achievement as Children Begin School,* Executive Summary. Washington, D.C.: Economic Policy Institute, 2002. http://www.epinet.org/content.cfm/books_starting_gate (accessed July 30, 2004).

[Lezotte, Lawrence W.] *Revolutionary and Evolutionary: The Effective Schools Movement.* Okemos, Mich.: Effective School Products, Inc., 2001. http://www.effectiveschools.com/downloads/Revolutionary.pdf (accessed July 29, 2004).

Lichten, William. "Whither Advanced Placement?" *Education Policy Analysis Archives* 8, no. 29 (June 24, 2000). http://epaa.asu.edu/epaa/v8n29.html (accessed July 31, 2004).

Liebman, James S., and Charles F. Sabel. "The Federal No Child Left Behind Act and the

Post-Desegregation Civil Rights Agenda." *North Carolina Law Review* 81, no. 4 (May 2003): 1703-49.

Lloyd, Dee N. "Prediction of School Failure from Third-Grade Data." *Educational and Psychological Measurement* 38 (1978): 1193-1200.

Luce, Tom, with Chris Tucker. *Now or Never: How We Can Save Our Public Schools.* Dallas: Taylor Publishing, 1995.

Marzano, Robert J. *What Works in Schools: Translating Research into Action.* Alexandria, Va.: Association for Supervision and Curriculum Development, 2003.

Mason, Heather. "Can Federal Involvement Help Struggling Schools?" Phi Delta Kappa/Gallup Poll of the Public's Attitudes Toward the Public Schools, Education & Youth. Sept. 10, 2002.

Massell, Diane. "The District Role in Building Capacity: Four Strategies." *CPRE Policy Briefs,* RB-32 (Sept. 2000): 1-7. http://www.cpre.org/Publications/rb32.pdf (accessed July 19, 2004).

———. "State Strategies for Building Local Capacity: Addressing the Needs of Standards-Based Reform." *CPRE Policy Briefs,* RB-25 (July 1998): 1-15. http://www.cpre.org/Publications/rb25.pdf (accessed Aug. 3, 2004).

Mathews, Jay. "The 100 Best High Schools in America." *Newsweek,* May 26, 2003. http://www.washingtonpost.com/ac2/wp-dyn?pagename=article&node=&contentId=A44211-2003May27&notFound=true (accessed July 31, 2004).

Mathis, William J. "Two Very Different Questions." *Education Week,* 23, no. 32 (Apr. 21, 2004): 33, 48. http://www.edweek.org/ew/ewstory.cfm?slug=32mathis.h23 (accessed June 27, 2004).

Mellor, Lynn, Chrys Dougherty, Ya-Ping Hsieh, and Shuling Jian. *Impact of Increasing Participation and Success in Advanced Placement (AP) Programs.* National Center for Educational Accountability Research Report #3. Rev. Sept. 19, 2003.

Moe, Terry M. "Reform Blockers." *Education Next,* Spring 2003, 56-61.

Moore, Matt. "NCPA's Value-Added Report Card on Texas Schools: A Model for Meaningful Assessments." *NCPA Brief Analysis,* no. 446 (July 9, 2003). http://www.ncpa.org/pub/ba/ba446/ba446.pdf (accessed July 29, 2004).

National Center for Education Statistics. *The Condition of Education 2003.* Washington, D.C.: U.S. Department of Education, 2003.

———. "Do Gatekeeper Courses Expand Education Options?" *Statistics in Brief,* Feb. 1999. http://nces.ed.gov/pubs99/1999303.pdf (accessed Aug. 1, 2004).

National Commission on Excellence in Education. *A Nation at Risk: The Imperative for Educational Reform.* Washington, D.C.: National Commission on Excellence in Education, 1983.

National Education Goals Panel. "Advancing AP." *The NEGP Monthly* 2, no. 17 (May 2000): 1-8.

National Head Start Association. "National Head Start Association Statement on New Study Detailing Major Shortcomings of State Pre-K Programs." Press Statement, Feb. 20, 2004. http://www.educationnews.org/national-head-start-association.htm (accessed July 30, 2004).

National Research Council. *Improving Student Learning: A Strategic Plan for Education Research and Its Utilization.* Washington, D.C.: National Academy Press, 1999.

NGA Center for Best Practices. *Reaching New Heights: Turning Around Low Performing*

Schools—a Guide for Governors. Washington, D.C.: National Governors Association, 2003. http://www.nga.org/cda/files/0803REACHING.pdf (accessed July 29, 2004).

No Child Left Behind Act of 2001. Pub. L. No. 107-110, 115 Stat. 1425 (2002).

O'Donnell Foundation. *AP Arts: 2002-2003 O'Donnell Foundation Advanced Placement Incentive Program for Art History, Studio Art, and Music Theory.* [2003.]

Office of Management and Budget. Executive Office of the President. *Budget of the United States Government, Fiscal Year 2005.* http://www.whitehouse.gov/omb/budget/fy2005/budget.html (accessed Aug. 1, 2004).

Olson, Lynn. "All States Get Federal Nod on Key Plans." *Education Week* 22, no. 41 (June 18, 2003): 1, 20, 21. http://www.edweek.org/ew/ewstory.cfm?slug=41account.h22 (accessed July 28, 2004).

———. "Quantity of Coursework Rises Since 1983, But Gaps in Coursetaking by Students' Race, Income Remain." *Education Week* 22, no. 32 (Apr. 23, 2003): 1, 14-17. http://www.edweek.org/ew/ewstory.cfm?slug=32courses.h22 (accessed July 31, 2004).

———. "States Train Sights on School Districts for Interventions." *Education Week* 23, no. 20 (Jan. 28, 2004): 1, 21. http://www.edweek.org/ew/ewstory.cfm?slug=20Districts.h23 (accessed July 29, 2004).

Perkins, Robert, Brian Kleiner, Stephen Roey, and Janis Brown. *The High School Transcript Study: A Decade of Change in Curricula and Achievement, 1990-2000.* NCES 2004-455. Washington, D.C.: U.S. Department of Education, Institute of Education Sciences, 2004. http://nces.ed.gov/pubs2004/2004455.pdf (accessed July 31, 2004).

Peterson, Paul E. "Ticket to Nowhere." *Education Next,* Spring 2003, 39-46.

Peyser, James, and Robert Costrell. "Exploring the Costs of Accountability." *Education Next,* Spring 2004, 22-29.

Princeton Review. *Testing the Testers 2003: An Annual Ranking of State Accountability Systems Executive Summary.* 2003. http://www.princetonreview.com/footer/testingTesters.asp (accessed June 27, 2004).

Public Education Network and Education Week. *2004 National Survey of Public Opinion: Learn, Vote, Act; The Public's Responsibility for Public Education.* 2004. http://www.publiceducation.org/pdf/national_poll/2004_Learn_Vote_Act.pdf (accessed July 4, 2004).

Public Schools of North Carolina. *Closing the Achievement Gap: Views from Nine Schools.* Raleigh, N.C.: Public Schools of North Carolina, 2000. http://www.ncpublicschools.org/schoolimprovement/closingthegap/reports/downloads/nineschools.pdf (accessed July 29, 2004).

Raymond, Margaret E., and Eric A. Hanushek. "High-Stakes Research." *Education Next,* Summer 2003, 48-55.

Reeves, Douglas B. Foreword to *Leaving No Child Behind: How Data Driven Decision-Making Can Help Schools Meet the Challenge,* by Marsha Jones and Sean Mulvenon, VII–IX. Phoenix: All Star Publishing, 2003.

Reynolds, Arthur J., Judy A. Temple, Dylan L. Robertson, and Emily A. Mann. "Long-term Effects of an Early Childhood Intervention on Educational Achievement and Juvenile Arrest: A 15-Year Follow-up of Low-Income Children in Public Schools." *Journal of the American Medical Association* 285, no. 18 (May 9, 2001): 2339-46.

Rolnick, Art, and Rob Grunewald. "Early Childhood Development: Economic Development with a High Public Return." *FedGazette,* Mar. 2003.

http://minneapolisfed.org/pubs/fedgaz/03-03/earlychild.cfm (accessed July 30, 2004).

Rosellini, Lynn. "Getting Young Lives in Line." *U.S. News and World Report,* Mar. 22, 2004. http://www.usnews.com/usnews/issue/040322/usnews/22work.kipp.htm (accessed July 28, 2004, archived article).

Rudner, Lawrence M., and Carol Boston. "Data Warehousing: Beyond Disaggregation." *Educational Leadership* 60, no. 5 (2003): 62-65.

Sable, Jennifer, and Beth Aronstamm Young. *Characteristics of the 100 Largest Public Elementary and Secondary Districts in the United States: 2001-2002.* NCES 2003-353. Washington, D.C.: U.S. Department of Education, National Center for Education Statistics, 2003. http://nces.ed.gov/pubs2003/2003353.pdf (accessed July 30, 2004).

Schafer, William D., Francine H. Hultgren, Willis D. Hawley, Andrew L. Abrams, Carole C. Seubert, and Susan Mazzoni. *Study of Higher-Success and Lower-Success Elementary Schools.* Maryland State Department of Education, n.d. http://www.mdk12.org/process/benchmark/improve/study/index.html (accessed July 29, 2004).

Scherer, Marge. "Perspectives/Not Too Early to Learn." *Educational Leadership* 60, no. 7 (April 2003): 5. http://www.ascd.org/publications/ed_lead/200304/scherer.html (accessed July 30, 2004).

Schilder, Diane, Ellen Kiron, and Kimberly Elliott. *Early Care and Education Partnerships: State Actions and Local Lessons.* Newton, Mass.: Education Development Center, 2003. http://ccf.edc.org/ecare_edupartner.pdf (accessed July 30, 2004).

Schmoker, Mike. *Results: The Key to Continuous School Improvement.* Alexandria, Va.: Association for Supervision and Curriculum Development, 1996.

———. *The Results Fieldbook: Practical Strategies from Dramatically Improved Schools.* Alexandria, Va.: Association for Supervision and Curriculum Development, 2001.

Schumacher, Rachel. "The Long and Winding Road: Head Start Reauthorization So Far." Presentation, Johnson and Johnson Head Start Management Fellows Conference, UCLA Anderson School of Management, Los Angeles, Calif., Jan. 15, 2004. http://www.clasp.org/DMS/Documents/1075493169.82/HS_reauth_Jan04.pdf (accessed July 30, 2004).

Schweinhart, Lawrence J. *How the High/Scope Perry Preschool Study Grew: A Researcher's Tale.* Research Bulletin, no. 32. Phi Delta Kappa Center for Evaluation, Development, and Research, June 2002. http://www.highscope.org/Research/PerryProject.tale.htm (accessed July 30, 2004).

Shavelson, Richard J., and Lisa Towne, eds. *Scientific Research in Education.* Washington, D.C.: National Academy Press, 2003.

Shonkoff, Jack P., and Deborah A. Phillips, eds. *From Neurons to Neighborhoods: The Science of Early Childhood Development.* Washington, D.C.: National Academy Press, 2000.

Skandera, Hanna, and Richard Sousa. *School Figures: The Data Behind the Debate.* Stanford: Hoover Institution Press, 2003.

Slavin, Robert E. "A Reader's Guide to Scientifically Based Research." *Educational Leadership* 40, no. 3 (Feb. 2003): 12-16.

Slavin, Robert E., and Olatokunbo S. Fashola. *Show Me the Evidence! Proven and Promising Programs for America's Schools.* Thousand Oaks, Calif.: Corwin Press, 1998.

Slavin, Robert E., Nancy L. Karweit, and Barbara A. Wasik. "Preventing Early School

Failure: What Works?" *Educational Leadership* 50, no. 4 (Dec. 1992/Jan. 1993): 10-18. http://www.ascd.org/publications/ed_lead/199212/slavin.html (accessed Aug. 1, 2004).

Snipes, Jason, Fred Doolittle, and Corinne Herlihy. *Foundations for Success: Case Studies of How Urban School Systems Improve Student Achievement,* Executive Summary. New York: MDRC of the Council of the Great City Schools, 2002. http://www.mdrc.org/publications/47/execsum.html (accessed July 29, 2004).

Stipek, Deborah. "Head Start: Can't We Have Our Cake and Eat It Too?" *Education Week* 23, no. 34 (May 5, 2004): 43, 52.

Texas Advanced Placement Incentive Program. 19 Tex. Admin. Code, §74.29 (2004).

Toch, Thomas. *In the Name of Excellence: The Struggle to Reform the Nation's Schools, Why It's Failing, and What Should Be Done.* New York: Oxford University Press, 1991.

Togneri, Wendy. *Beyond Islands of Excellence: What Districts Can Do to Improve Instruction and Achievement in All Schools—A Leadership Brief.* Learning First Alliance, Mar. 2003. http://www.learningfirst.org/lfa-web/rp?pa=doc&docId=63 (accessed July 29, 2004): 43, 52.

Towne, Lisa. "Scientific Evidence and Inference in Educational Policy and Practice: Defining and Implementing 'Scientifically Based Research.'" Paper presented at the Educational Testing Service Invitational Conference: Measurement and Research Issues in a New Accountability Era, New York, N.Y., Oct. 3-4, 2003.

Trust for Early Education. "Trust for Early Education ED Amy Wilkins Labels Bush Budget Head Start Proposal Inadequate on Quality Improvement," Press Release, Feb. 3, 2003. http://www.trustforearlyed.org/release.aspx?idCat=0&strCat=&strSearch=&id=6 (accessed July 30, 2004).

Twentieth Century Fund Task Force on Federal Elementary and Secondary Education. *Making the Grade.* New York: The Twentieth Century Fund, 1983.

Tyack, David, and Larry Cuban. *Tinkering Toward Utopia: A Century of Public School Reform.* Cambridge: Harvard University Press, 1995.

U.S. Department of Education. *The Seven Priorities of the U.S. Department of Education: Priority Two: Mastering Challenging Mathematics, Including the Foundations of Algebra and Geometry, by the End of Eighth Grade 11."* July 1997. http://www.ed.gov/updates/7priorities/part4.html (accessed Aug. 1, 2004).

———. "Identifying and Implementing Educational Practices Supported by Rigorous Evidence: A User Friendly Guide." Dec. 2003. http://www.ed.gov/rschstat/research/pubs/rigorousevid/rigorousevid.pdf (accessed July 13, 2004).

———. "Teachers to Listen, Learn, Share Practices to Improve Student Achievement," Press Release, Apr. 21, 2004. http://www.ed.gov/news/pressre-leases/2004/04/04212004.html (accessed July 29, 2004).

———. *Mathematics Equals Opportunity.* White Paper Prepared for U.S. Secretary of Education Richard W. Riley, Oct. 27, 1997. http://www.ed.gov/pubs/math/index.html (accessed Aug. 1, 2004).

———. Office for Civil Rights. *Achieving Diversity: Race-Neutral Alternatives in American Education.* Jessup, Md.: U.S. Department of Education, 2004. http://www.ed.gov/about/offices/list/ocr/edlite-raceneutralreport2.html (accessed Aug. 1, 2004).

U.S. Department of Health and Human Services. Administration for Children and Families. *Head Start FACES 2000: A Whole-Child Perspective on Program Performance.* May 2003. http://www.paheadstart.org/FACES4thprogressreport.pdf (accessed July 30, 2004).

Vail, Kathleen. "Ready To Learn." *American School Board Journal* 190, no. 11 (Nov. 2003), http://www.asbj.com/2003/11/1103coverstory.html (accessed July 30, 2004).

Viadero, Debra. "Achievement-Gap Study Emphasizes Better Use of Data." *Education Week* 23, no. 19 (Jan. 21, 2004): 9. http://www.edweek.com/ew/ewstory.cfm?slug=19Gap.h23 (July 29, 2004).

———. "Bill Would Like Research, Classroom Practice," *Education Week* 23, no. 30 (Apr. 7, 2004): 25. http://www.edweek.org/ew/ewstory.cfm?slug=30Knowledge.h23 (accessed July 2, 2004).

Vinovskis, Maris A. "The Federal Role in Educational Research and Development." *Brookings Papers on Education Policy: 2000*, edited by Diane Ravitch, 359-79. Washington, D.C.: Brookings Institution Press, 2000.

Walberg, Herbert J. "Accountability Unplugged." *Education Next,* Spring 2003, 76-79.

Washington School Research Center. *Continuing to Bridge the Opportunity Gap: Taking a Closer Look at 10 High Performing Elementary Schools in Washington State.* Research Report #4, August 2003.

Whitehurst, Grover J. "Much Too Late." Forum, Young Einsteins. *Education Next,* Summer 2001, 9, 16-19. http://educationnext.org/20012/8b.pdf (accessed July 30, 2004).

Wiener, Ross, and Kevin Carey. Memo to Mitchell Chester, Assistant Superintendent for Policy Development, Ohio Department of Education. Jan. 16, 2004. At p. 130 of electronic document, http://www.ode.state.oh.us/legislator/COST_OF_NCLB/COST%20OF%20IMPLE-MENTING%20NCLB-012104.pdf (accessed July 28, 2004).

Winters, Kirk. *Teachers and GOALS 2000: Leading the Journey Toward High Standards for All Students.* http://www.ed.gov/G2K/teachers/index.html (accessed July 30, 2004).

Young, Beth Aronstamm. *Public High School Dropouts and Completers from the Common Core of Data: School Year 2000-01: Statistical Analysis Report.* NCES 2004-310. Washington, D.C.: U.S. Department of Education, National Center for Education Statistics, 2003. http://nces.ed.gov/pubs2004/2004310.pdf (accessed July 15, 2004).

Zulli, Rebecca A., and Elizabeth Kolb Cunningham. *State Report Card: 2003 Progress Report.* First in America Series. Chapel Hill: North Carolina Education Research Council, Jan. 2004. http://erc.northcarolina.edu/docs/fia/2003%20Final%20Progress%20Report.pdf (accessed July 27, 2004).

Index